CREATIVE DRAMA IN THE INTERMEDIATE GRADES

CREATIVE DRAMA IN THE INTERMEDIATE GRADES
A Handbook for Teachers

NELLIE McCASLIN
New York University

PLAYERS PRESS, Inc.

Studio City, California

Creative Drama in the Intermediate Grades: A Handbook for Teachers

Copyright © 1987 by Longman.

Reprinted under special agreement with the Publisher.

Players Press, Inc.
P. O. Box 1132
Studio City, CA 91614

Library of Congress Cataloging-in-Publication Data

McCaslin, Nellie
    Creative drama in the intermediate grades: a handbook for teachers / Nellie McCaslin.
        p.   cm.
    Includes bibliographical references (p.).
    ISBN 0-88734-605-7
    1. Drama in education.   I. Title.
PN3171.M4   1989   89-63228
371.3'32--dc20   CIP

CONTENTS

ACTIVITIES

EXPRESSIVE USE OF THE BODY AND VOICE

BODY: This section develops body awareness and spatial perception.

VOICE: This section develops expressive use of the voice through sound and dialogue.

CREATIVE DRAMA

DRAMATIZING LITERARY SELECTIONS AND ORIGINAL STORIES

AESTHETIC GROWTH THROUGH APPRECIATION OF THEATRICAL EVENTS

VIEW THEATRICAL EVENTS EMPHASIZING:

PLAYER-AUDIENCE RELATIONSHIP   CHAPTER 13
ETIQUETTE   CHAPTER 13
PRE- AND POST-PERFORMANCE ACTIVITIES   CHAPTER 13, APPENDIX
RECOGNITION OF SIMILARITIES AND DIFFERENCES BETWEEN RADIO, TV, FILM, AND
    THEATRE   CHAPTERS 6, 13

PARTICIPATE IN GROUP PLANNING FOR STORY DRAMATIZATION INCORPORATING:

FOREWORD

I must confess to a facetious quality in me that at times is discomforting to my students. How often they defend a curricular practice with the observation, "Children love it." The devil's advocate in me rises to the surface as I respond, "Children love dessert. Does that justify a menu of cakes and puddings?"

Professor McCaslin carefully reminds us that dramatic activities in the classroom are not the frills added on to the diet but an essential and integral component of a curriculum that responds to children's healthy development. The wealth of recent research in language acquisition cannot be ignored. Programs that promote oral language development in young children are based on a quest for literacy; meaningful use of symbol systems in reading and writing are viewed as an extension of a rich environment in which a wide variety of oral communication opportunities exists for young children. Nellie McCaslin begins there and takes us into a world in which we can safely say, "Children love it but, even more importantly, they need it."

I cannot forget Eddie and Ezra, who were about 10 or 11 at the time. One day they appeared in my classroom, the excited authors of a pair of "operettas," complete with librettos and musical scores both sophisticated and childlike. There was no way in which these musical extravaganzas could be ignored. They had to be *performed* and so they were—a number of times—with the polish demanded by the composers. Professor McCaslin tells us that a carefully rehearsed finished product has its place but that day-to-day dramatic activities are the substance of a sound curriculum. To that end she suggests many possibilities, in rich illustrations aimed at realizing the important threads in education— to help children verbalize as well as recall, to encourage children to clarify *their* perceptions as well as those of others, and to promote children's working together to develop group living.

The ideas McCaslin presents help put to rest one of education's biggest myths—that the more valued the experience, the more money we must invest. A classroom can be turned into unending settings for a world of drama, she tells us; the investment must be one of commitment and creativity.

I remember, too, a group of 7- and 8-year-olds for whom "Rapunzel" was a cherished commodity. I never ceased to be amazed at how, at a moment's notice, a new interpretation of the story emerged, always with new dialogue, makeshift props, and new performers. What did not change was the children's joy and their ever-deepening feeling of belonging to a group. I treasure most a parent's saying, "The biggest thing I notice in Jimmy this year is that he doesn't say 'I' as much. When he talks about school, he always says 'we.'" McCaslin highlights this as an important goal for drama in the classroom.

Nellie McCaslin's book has both a timely and a timeless quality. As individual states mandate drama in the classroom, it serves as an immediate resource for teachers. But at the same time, it speaks to universals, reminding us of the need for the classroom to be a world of childhood.

The theme of my college yearbook returns to me—"Children's Faces Looking Up, Holding Wonder Like a Cup." Nellie McCaslin presents us with many ways in which we can fill the cup.

Robert Clausen
Professor of Education
New York University

PREFACE

Surely the arts need no justification for inclusion in the curriculum; they have been an important part of human life from prehistoric times. We first communicated through the arts: we embellished our tools with designs; we expressed our deepest emotions and worshiped our gods through the dance; we created and passed on our myths and legends before we had a written language with which to preserve them; we wore costumes, jewelry, and face paint for our celebrations. The young have learned, been entertained, and, in time, expressed themselves through the visual and performing arts.

During the greatest periods of history, the arts have flourished. It seems odd, therefore, that today, in an affluent, democratic society, we must find a rationale for including them in our educational system. In the 1977 Rockefeller Report, *Coming to Our Senses*, the majority of Americans expressed their belief in the arts as an important component of a liberal education. It is up to us to see that this professed belief is implemented, for to deny the arts is to rob our children of some of life's most enriching and humanizing experiences. It is heartening to know that despite budget cuts and a "back-to-basics" movement, the theatre arts, as well as music and the visual arts, are being mandated into the curricula of a number of states, not just as means to other more utilitarian goals but as ends in their own right.

Creative Drama in the Intermediate Grades and its companion, *Creative Drama in the Primary Grades*, are based on a philosophy of education that regards child drama as a subject in its own right and as an important component of the curriculum. While drama is unquestionably an effective tool for teaching, the thrust of these two books is the involvement in a process that enriches the participant on many levels, the primary one being the aesthetic experience. Unlike my other creative-drama texts, which were designed for use in the college classroom, these handbooks are written specifically for teachers of grades 4, 5, and 6 and for grades 1, 2, and 3.

Although there is no philosophic difference between *Creative Drama in the Classroom* and these two new books, the former is primarily theoretical, whereas the latter are, by intent, practical. Although some of the material in the first handbook can be used equally well with children in the upper grades, the reverse is not always true. Many of the stories, poems, and activities suggested for older children are too long or complex for boys and girls just starting school. The goals and procedures, however, are identical; it is only the materials and expectations that differ.

Through my own teaching, I long ago discovered that most classroom teachers, no matter how experienced, feel insecure when it comes to the theatre arts. They have had little, if any, drama in their own professional preparation. What experience they have had generally has been acting in high-school and college plays, where performance and production were paramount. Enjoyable and valuable as this activity undoubtedly was, participation in formal theatre for adults is in no way preparation for work in creative drama with children. The familiar practice of "putting on a play for assembly" conjures up visions of hours of rehearsal, wooden performances by bored or self-conscious actors, vast auditoriums that strain young voices, and valuable time lost from studies. The picture has changed, however, as a result of the pioneering efforts of Winifred Ward at Northwestern University and her successors, who not only first practiced a new approach to this art form with children, but also gave us our first books on the subject. They clarified the concepts of drama and theatre by defining *drama* as that which a child does or creates and *theatre* as that which a child views as a spectator. Both have value, but the goals and experiences differ. An ideal drama/ theatre program provides a time and a place for each, but for the younger child, creative drama should take priority. Understanding the difference between drama and theatre and relieved of the necessity of putting on a play, teachers today can relax and enjoy the experience with their classes. For, indeed, children love to try on the roles of others, to enact favorite stories and create plays of their own, to move, and to mime. The teacher who is able to guide these activities and encourage the creative energy that children bring into the classroom will find not only that the classroom is a livelier place, but also that learning is enhanced and social relationships are strengthened.

Most teachers are aware of the interests, tastes, and backgrounds of their pupils. What they seek is guidance in the planning of lessons and the adaptation of material that is appropriate not only for creative drama and language arts classes, but also for all classes across the curriculum. With these needs in mind, these two handbooks were written. The contents include a rationale for the inclusion of drama in the curriculum, suggestions for pantomime and improvisation, a discussion of simple play structure, and a few basic steps to follow if or when a class shares its work with an audience. I recognize that a class occasionally wants to show its work or put on a play. When it does, new problems are posed. Suggestions for solving those problems are not intended to encourage the practice, but to help make the transition from process to presentation. I must add that very little creative drama ever reaches the performance level, especially in the first and second grades, frequently in the fourth to sixth. When it does, it should be recognized as growth and therefore supported, not with elaborate costumes and settings but with respect for the ideas and honest work of the group. The teacher provides the showmanship at this point in order that new goals may be realized and the young participants may find satisfaction in their efforts. Showmanship, incidentally, does not mean learning special techniques, but, helping the group present itself as well as possible.

Because puppets provide an opportunity for an extension of creative drama, a chapter on puppet construction and handling is included. Very young children can make simple puppets, and they enjoy using them, especially under circumstances and in situations where large body movement is not possible. As for the shy youngster, hiding behind the puppet is an excellent first step toward communication with others. Mask making is also a popular activity, hence the inclusion of a section on the construction of masks. The combining of puppets, masks, and human actors, regarded as innovative in adult theatre, is a natural solution to staging problems for a child, whose approach to drama often includes incorporating all three without hesitation or apology.

Many teachers and principals have expressed a concern regarding audience behavior when a touring company performs for assembly or when a class goes on a field trip to a local community or college theatre. Therefore, a chapter on preparing children for the experience, the role of the audience, and suggestions for follow-up activities is included. Appreciation of any art is difficult to measure, if indeed it can be measured at all, but there are things the teacher can do to introduce children to a program or play so as to make it an enjoyable and meaningful experience. For some children, this may be the first live theatre they have ever seen, and we want it to be memorable—entertaining and worthy of their attention. Because most children enjoy live performance, the preparation, including observing a few ground rules, is relatively easy. Assuming that the children can see and hear well and are physically comfortable, discipline should not be a problem.

Activities are suggested throughout the text, not as ends in themselves but as springboards to later, more extensive projects. Stories, verse, and suggestions for dramatization are included as illustrations of what can be used and how; with a point of view and a creative approach, the leader will find other materials relevant to his or her own and the group's interests.

Finally, for teachers who are interested in further reading on the subject, I have included an annotated bibliography. books on creative drama, children's theatre, choral speech, rhythms and movement, and literature for use in the elementary grades have been selected with the classroom teacher in mind. The growing number of states that are mandating drama in the curriculum to be taught along with music and art requires guidance based on a philosophy of aesthetic education with some practical suggestions and sample materials: ideas for pantomime and improvisations; appropriate stories, poetry, rhythms, and movement; and the steps to take in planning and conducting such activities. Once teachers have used creative drama with their classes, they will discover a wealth of ideas of their own.

The arrangement of chapters suggests a good way of using this book. Throughout, theory is demonstrated by activities. The chapters begin with simple basic exercises and move on to more complex ones. By following this outline, students build on a foundation of what they have done and learned. Chapter 14, "Putting It All Together," offers a few examples of ways that specific objectives can be reached through activities followed by class discussion.

For assistance in the preparation of this manuscript, I want to thank the teachers and principals who gave so generously of their time and thought and whose suggestions have guided me. I hope that my efforts on their behalf may prove as valuable to them as their help has been to me.

Nellie McCaslin

HOW TO USE THIS BOOK

This book is for teachers—for teachers who have some or no experience in creative drama, for teachers who plan to teach creative drama in the future, for teachers who want to or who are required to introduce and integrate creative drama into their elementary curricula.

Creative Drama in the Intermediate Grades really contains two courses of instruction—a methodology for teachers and curriculum material for students. Based on the theory that one learns best by doing, the book is designed so that the teacher with no experience can immediately begin teaching creative drama in the elementary grades. It is paced developmentally from simple to complex. As the teacher acquires skills for teaching creative drama, the students acquire creative drama skills. Thus, in the early lessons, a teacher needs only minimal information and skill in order to teach because these lessons comprise the least sophisticated components of creative drama. As the teacher practices and masters teaching skills, so the students learn increasingly sophisticated creative drama skills.

The book contains all the methodology, all the content, all the lesson components necessary to teaching several sequences of creative drama in the three intermediate grades. There are two basic components—text and activities. The text explains methods and theories of teaching creative drama. The numbered activities, which follow the text in each chapter and are printed in a different type style, comprise the practical core of the book. They detail the specifics of what goes on in the creative drama class. In the early chapters, each activity is a self-contained "recipe" for a creative drama event and includes:

1. The educational objective for the activity.

2. A step-by-step guide on how to conduct the activity.
3. Complete subject matter of the event—for example, if the activity is to be a game, full instructions for the game are provided. If the subject is a story, even a well-known story, the full story is provided. (A teacher does not have to rely on memory or refer to other sources to conduct any activity.)
4. Follow-up questions and discussion topics.

As the book progresses and teachers become more sophisticated, less detail is provided in the activities. At all stages, however, the teacher can enter the classroom with the confidence that unless special equipment such as costumes, music, or props is desired, the book contains all the components necessary to conduct the activity he or she has planned for the day's lesson.

So the ideal way to use the book is sequentially. As the teacher reads the book he or she selects the activities for presentation in the classroom.

However, not all teachers have the leisure for such careful reading and selection. For these teachers the following ways of using the book might be preferable.

ESSENTIAL ELEMENTS

The list of activities that follows the Contents is organized by essential elements and therefore can be used to develop a sequence of lessons containing all the elements. Within each category, the activities are listed in order of complexity—from simple to complex. Individual lesson plans can be based on the activities in a single category or activities selected from a number of different categories.

As states recommend or mandate the inclusion of creative drama in the curriculum, teachers are called on to demonstrate that a comprehensive sequence of creative drama is presented in class. The state of Texas has mandated the teaching of creative drama. In order to clarify the requirement, a taxonomy of essential elements was developed. The essential elements of the activities list in this book are derived from that taxonomy. In Table 1, the Texas classification system is correlated with the treatment of the elements in this book. For a teacher who wants to take the approach of teaching essential elements, it is recommended that he or she read the relevant chapters listed in Table 1 before presenting the activities in class.

TABLE 1. *Correlation of Essential Elements and Contents of the Text*

Essential Elements	*Creative Drama in the Intermediate Grades*
1. Expressive use of the body and voice	Chapters 2, 3, 4, 5, 11
1.1 Develop body awareness and spatial perception using	Chapter 3
Rhythmic movement	Chapter 2: Activity 2.3
	Chapter 3: Activities 3.1, 3.2
	Chapter 11: Activity 11.1
Imitative movement	Chapter 3: Activities 3.3, 3.4, 3.5
	Chapter 4: Activities 4.9, 4.10
Sensory awareness	Chapter 4: Activities 4.2, 4.3, 4.4, 4.5
Pantomime	Chapters 4 and 5
1.2 Express concepts using interpretive movement	Chapter 3: Activities 3.2, 3.3, 3.4, 3.5
1.3 Create original dialogue	Chapters 5, 6, 7, 9, 14
1.4 Recall sensory and emotional experiences and utilize sensory and emotional recall in characterizations	Chapter 4: Activities 4.8, 4.9, 4.12 Chapter 5: Activities 5.1, 5.2, 5.3, 5.4
2. Creative drama	Chapters 5, 6, 7, 8, 9, 10
2.1 Dramatize literary selections and original stories using	
Shadow play	Chapter 9
Pantomime	Chapter 4: Activities 4.6, 4.7, 4.8, 4.9, 4.12 Chapter 8: Activities 8.3, 8.5, 8.6 Chapter 11: Activity 11.1
Imitative dialogue	Chapter 6: p. 80; Activity 6.7 Chapter 7: Activities 7.1, 7.2, 7.3, 7.4, 7.5 Chapter 10 Chapter 12: Activity 12.1
Characterization	Chapters 5, 6, 7
Puppetry	Chapter 9
Situation role playing	Chapter 5: Activity 5.8 Chapter 14: Activities 14.1, 14.2
3. Aesthetic growth through appreciation of theatrical events	Chapter 13
3.1 View theatrical events emphasizing	
Player-audience relationship	Chapter 13
Audience etiquette	Chapter 13
Recognition of similarities and differences between TV, film, and live theatre	Chapters 6, 13

TABLE 1.   (*Continued*)

Essential Elements	Creative Drama in the Intermediate Grades
3.2 Participate in group planning for story dramatization incorporating	Chapters 6, 12
Analysis of character behavior	Chapters 6, 7, 12
Recognition of dramatic conflicts	Chapters 6, 7, 12 Chapter 14: Activities 14.1, 14.2
Prediction of plot resolutions	Chapters 6, 7, 14
Suggestions for alternative courses of action	Chapters 6, 7, 14

SCOPE AND SEQUENCE

With the exception of the few activities that are identified as more appropriate for one grade level, most activities can be used effectively with all three intermediate grades. If teachers wish to prepare sequences designed specifically for one grade or for all three grades, they can use the scope and sequence chart in Table 2 as a guide.

The following sample sequences for grades four, five, and six can be taught sequentially as a class progresses from one grade to the next. Likewise, a school that wants to adopt this program and to establish three different grade sequences could assign the sequences concurrently. All three sequences include all the essential elements. For each element there are a number of suggested activities. Teachers may select one or more activities for an element. Several activities pertain to more than one element. When performing these activities, students may focus on one or more of the applicable elements.

Grade Four

You will note that many of the selections are listed under more than one category. Likewise, a number of activities are suggested for more than one grade level. This is because there are values to be found in them as players mature. The older the child, the more he or she is able to do and the richer and more detailed the results will be.

This section develops body awareness and spatial perception.

Rhythmic movement
Use of the Body (several sessions)   3.1
Rhythms (30 minutes)   p. 35

TABLE 2. *Scope and Sequence for Intermediate Grades*

Theatre Arts Curriculum			
A theatre arts program in the intermediate grades should include the following elements	*The student shall be provided opportunities to:*		
Theatre Arts	*Grade IV*	*Grade V*	*Grade VI*

Expressive use of the body and voice	Express concepts through
	  Interpretive
	    movement
	  Original dialogue
	
	Recall sensory and emotional experiences
		Express concepts through
		  Interpretive
		    movement
		  Original dialogue
		
		Utilize sensory and emotional recall in characterizations
			Express concepts using
			  Interpretive
			    movement
			  Circus skills
			  Original dialogue
			
			Utilize sensory and emotional recall in characterizations

Creative drama	Dramatize literature using
	  Improvisation
	  Characterization
	  Puppetry
	  Mask making
		Dramatize original stories using
		  Improvisation
		  Characterization
		  Puppets and masks
			Dramatize literature and original stories using
			  Improvisation
			  Characterization
			  Puppetry
			  Playwriting
			  Situation role playing

Aesthetic growth through appreciation of theatrical events	Attend theatrical events to see and understand differences and similarities among live theatre, film, and television
	
	Work on story dramatization involving
	  Analysis of character
	  Recognition of
	    conflicts
	  Plot and conflict
	    resolution
		Attend theatrical events emphasizing
		  Evaluation and
		    aesthetic judgments
		  Audience etiquette
		
		Work on story dramatization involving
		  Analysis of characters
		  Recognition of
		    conflicts
		  Plot and conflict
		    resolution
			Attend theatrical events noting
			  Player-audience
			    relationship
			  Audience etiquette
			
			Work on group planning for story dramatization incorporating
			  Analysis of characters
			  Recognition of
			    conflicts
			  Plot and conflict
			    resolution

This section develops expressive use of the voice.

This section develops creative drama skills.

* Most of the stories in this book can be enacted in puppetry or shadow play.

Improvisation—because the following activities contain so many ideas, it would be better to spread them over a period of time rather than to use them all at once.

This section deals with aesthetic growth through appreciation of theatrical events.

* Most of the stories in this book can be enacted in puppetry or shadow play.

Grade Five

This section develops body awareness and spatial perception.

* Most of the stories in this book can be enacted in puppetry or shadow play.

This section deals with aesthetic growth through the appreciation of theatrical events.

Grade Six

This section develops body awareness and spatial perception.

This section develops expressive use of the voice.

This section develops creative drama skills.

This section deals with aesthetic growth through appreciation of theatrical events.

* Most of the stories in this book can be enacted in puppetry or shadow play.

CREATIVE DRAMA IN THE INTERMEDIATE GRADES

1
CREATIVE DRAMA
AND ITS PLACE
IN THE CLASSROOM

Of all the arts, drama is the most inclusive, for it involves the participant mentally, emotionally, physically, verbally, and socially. As players, children work cooperatively on projects; as spectators, they are engaged in the lives and adventures of others. Discipline is an important aspect of the theatre arts, but it is a discipline readily accepted in much the same way that members of an athletic team are willing to suspend their personal wishes and interests for the sake of group goals.

Children in the middle grades are lively, energetic, and curious. They like to explore new things, and they enjoy fantasy and fairy tales. They can be expected to have better physical and verbal skills than first and second graders. They have a longer attention span and have developed a sense of organization in their handling of material. Occasionally, children of this age want to share their drama with others. When this happens, and the play is carried so far as to include scenery and costumes, the visual arts are added. Music, dance, and circus skills frequently are elements of children's theatre. Although these are rarely a part of creative drama, the adult actor in children's theatre finds them important skills to master.

As for the child audience, there is the opportunity to become absorbed in a story and the problems of a character with whom it can identify. A good experience in the theatre may be the beginning of appreciation that leads to lifelong pleasure.

1

The child who is given an opportunity to participate in creative drama in a comfortable and nonpressured classroom and to see plays of high quality has advantages that extend into all areas of life. With such an abundance of riches, it is easy to understand the widespread belief that drama and theatre constitute an elaborate art form, difficult to implement and expensive to maintain. Actually, nothing is further from the truth. Creative drama needs no special equipment, no studio, and no stage; time, space, and an enthusiastic, well-prepared leader are the only requirements. As for theatre, most actors can perform anywhere, provided the play does not depend on special effects or sophisticated staging. Professional touring companies are prepared to perform in all-purpose rooms and cafeterias. A stage may enhance the production, to be sure, but it is seldom a necessity. There are aesthetic values to be found in beautiful visual effects, but they are not necessary to the majority of plays designed for young audiences. Sincerity, sensitivity, and intelligent planning are the most important components of an effective performance. In many communities, the local university or civic theatre offers plays to which classes are bused during school hours at little or

Children build a magic wall. (Courtesy of Milton Polsky; photograph by Ann Rayshel)

no cost to the children. Many of these productions are excellent, sensitively played, and tastefully staged. In recent years, an educational component has become an important service offered by producers. Workshops for children following a performance, special workshops for teachers, and an effort to relate plays to the curriculum enrich the experience.

In summary, the theatre arts are the least difficult of the arts to implement, with the greatest potential for learning. They have a place in our schools on all levels because they constitute a subject in its own right, to be treated seriously, not added as a frill or an enhancement if the budget permits. Moreover, in the best arts programs, students learn the basic skills through the process of creative drama, for the commonly held objectives of education are remarkably similar to the objectives of creative drama. Let us compare them.

EDUCATIONAL OBJECTIVES

One of the most frequently stated aims of education is the maximal growth of the child both as an individual and as a member of society. In order to achieve this aim, certain educational objectives have been set up. Although these objectives vary somewhat, there is general agreement that knowledge and appreciation of and skills in the arts are essential. The modern curriculum tries to ensure that each child will:

1. *Develop basic skills in which reading, writing, arithmetic, science, social studies, and the arts are stressed*
2. *Develop and maintain good physical and mental health*
3. *Grow in ability to think*
4. *Clarify values and verbalize beliefs and hopes*
5. *Develop an understanding of beauty, using many media, including words, color, sound, and movement*
6. *Grow creatively and thus experience one's own creative powers*[1]

Although other objectives are mentioned, these six are most frequently listed in the development of educational programs designed for today's world and the complex problems that life offers.

The most enthusiastic proponent of creative drama would not go so far as to claim that its inclusion in the curriculum will ensure the meeting of these objectives. But many objectives of modern education and creative drama are unquestionably shared. Among them are:

[1] Robert S. Fleming, *Curriculum for Today's Boys and Girls* (Columbus, Ohio: Charles E. Merrill, 1963), p. 10.

1. Creativity and aesthetic development
2. The ability to think critically
3. Social growth and the ability to work cooperatively with others
4. Improved communication skills
5. The development of moral and spiritual values
6. Knowledge of self

Before we discuss creative drama in greater detail, some definitions are in order. The terms *dramatic play, creative drama, playmaking, role playing, children's theatre,* and *participation theatre* often are used interchangeably, although they have quite different meanings. The following definition will clarify the meanings as they are used in this text.

DEFINITIONS

DRAMATIC PLAY

Dramatic play is the free play of the very young child, in which she explores her universe, imitating the actions and character traits of those around her. It is her earliest expression in dramatic form, but must not be confused with drama or interpreted as performance. Dramatic play is fragmentary, existing only for the moment. It may last for a few minutes or go on for some time. It even may be played repeatedly, if the child's interest is sufficiently strong; but when this occurs, the repetition is in no sense a rehearsal. It is, rather, the repetition of a creative experience for the pure joy of doing it. It has no beginning and no end and no development in the dramatic sense.

CREATIVE DRAMA AND PLAYMAKING

The terms *creative drama* and *playmaking* may be used interchangeably, since they refer to informal drama that is created by the participants. As the word *playmaking* implies, this activity goes beyond dramatic play in scope and intent. It may make use of a story with a beginning, a middle, and an end. It may also explore, develop, and express ideas and feelings through dramatic enactment. It is, however, always improvised. Dialogue is created by the players, whether the content is taken from a well-known story or an original plot. Lines are not written down or memorized. With each playing, the story becomes more detailed and better organized, but it remains extemporaneous and is at no time designed for an audience. Participants are guided by a leader rather than a director, and the leader's goal is the optimal growth and development of the players.

The replaying of scenes is therefore different from the rehearsal of a formal play, in that each member of the group is given an opportunity to play various parts. No matter how many times a story is played, it is done for the purpose of deepening understanding and strengthening the performers, rather than for that of perfecting a product. Scenery and costumes have no place in creative drama, although an occasional property or article of clothing may be permitted to stimulate the imagination. When these are used, they should not be considered costuming. Most groups do not feel the need of properties of any kind and are generally freer without them.

CHILDREN'S THEATRE

The phrase *children's theatre* refers to formal productions for child audiences, whether acted by amateurs or professionals, children or adults, or a combination of both. It is directed rather than guided; dialogue is memorized; and scenery and costumes usually play an important part. Since it is audience centered, it is essentially different from creative drama. The child in the audience is the spectator, and the benefits derived are aesthetic.

What do children gain from attending good children's theatre? They gain much. First of all, there is the thrill of watching a well-loved story come alive on a stage. Then, there is the opportunity for a strong, vicarious experience as the children identify with characters who are brave, steadfast, noble, loyal, and beautiful. Emotions are released as the audience shares the adventures and excitement of the play. And, finally, the children learn to appreciate the art of the theatre if the production is tasteful and well executed.

We are speaking now of the child in the audience, not the child in the play. While there is much that is creative and of value for the performer, it is generally agreed that participation in creative drama is more beneficial than are public performances for children up to the age of 10 or 11. Occasionally, there is an expressed desire "to put on a play," and when this comes from the children themselves, it probably is wise to grant the request. There are times when sharing is a joy and a positive experience, but it is to be hoped that formal play production will be infrequent. Certainly, if it is done, the production should be simple and all precautions should be taken to guard against the competition and tension that so often characterize formal presentation.

Some leaders in the field of child drama believe that any performance in front of an audience is harmful because it automatically interferes with the child's own free expression. I agree up to a point. But the theatre is, after all, a performing art; when the audience is composed of understanding and sympathetic persons, such as parents or members of a younger class, performance may be the first step toward communicating a joyful experience. Without question, however, very young children should not perform publicly. Those in the middle and upper grades will not be harmed if their desire and the right occasion indicate that the advantages outweigh the disadvantages. A performance is a disciplined and carefully organized endeavor, involving a variety of skills that children of elementary-school age do not and should not be expected to possess.

ROLE PLAYING

The term *role playing* is used most often in connection with therapy or education. It refers to the assuming of a role for the particular value it may have to the participant, rather than for the development of an art. Although all art may be considered to have certain curative powers, it is not the primary purpose of either creative drama or theatre to provide therapy or solve social and emotional problems. Role playing is what the young child does in dramatic play, it is true, but it is also a tool used by psychologists and play therapists.

THEATRE-IN-EDUCATION

Theatre-in-Education (TIE) is a British concept that differs from traditional children's theatre in its use of curricular material or social problems as themes. Performed by professional companies of actor-teachers, it presents thought-provoking content to young audiences for educational purposes rather than for entertainment. Obviously, it must entertain in order to hold the spectators' attention, but the primary aim is to challenge the spectators and push them to further thinking and feeling about the issue. John O'Toole describes it as follows:

TIE (Theatre-in-Education) was conceived as an attempt to bring the techniques of the theatre into the classroom, in the service of specific educational objectives . . . its aim was more than to be entertaining and thought-provoking, or to encourage the habit of theatre-going. . . . First, the material is usually tailor-made to the needs of the children and the strength of the team. Second, the children are asked to participate; endowed with roles, they learn skills, make decisions, and solve problems, so the programs' structures have to be flexible. . . . Third, teams are usually aware of the importance of the teaching context, and try to prepare suggestions for follow-up work, or to hold preliminary workshops for classroom teachers. . . .[2]

VALUES IN CREATIVE PLAYING

Television has made us a nation of spectators. Children view television from infancy, and surveys reveal that they spend more hours in front of the screen each week than they spend in school. The current craze for video games has intensified this situation; therefore, it is more important than ever that we make opportunities available for children to experience participation in the arts. Creative drama is an ideal form for this participation, with its inclusion of the physical, mental, emotional, and social abilities of the participant.

There is general agreement among teachers of creative drama that important values can be gained from creative playing. Depending on the age of the children, the situation, and the orientation of the leader, these values may be ranked in varying order. It is the contention of the author, however, that in spite of these differences, certain values exist in some measure for all, regardless of age, circumstances, or previous experience. To be sure, the activities must be planned with the group in mind, and the emphasis placed on the needs and interests of those involved. The 5- or 6-year-old needs and enjoys the freedom of large movement and much physical activity, but this should not deny a similar opportunity to older boys and girls.

The 10- or 11-year-old enjoys the challenge of characterization and often creates with remarkable insight and understanding. Young children also can create on their level, although they cannot be expected to compete with older children. In other words, it is not a question of assigning different values to various age levels; it is a matter of accepting basic values that exist on all levels, varying more in degree than in kind. Specifically, these values may be listed as follows.

An Opportunity to Develop the Imagination

Imagination is the beginning. In order to work creatively, it is necessary, first of all, to push beyond the boundaries of the here and now, to project oneself into another situation or into the life of another person. Few activities have greater potential for developing the imagination than does playmaking. Little children move easily into a world of make-be-

---

[2] John O'Toole, *Theatre-in-Education* (London: Hodder and Stoughton, 1976), p. vii.

Creative-drama class at Kendall Demonstration Elementary School for the Deaf at Gallaudet College, Washington, D.C. (Courtesy of Victoria Brown)

lieve; but as they grow older, this amazing human capacity often is ignored or even discouraged. The development of the imagination to the point where the student responds spontaneously may take time, but it is the first step toward satisfying participation.

The sensitive teacher will not demand too much in the beginning but will accept with enthusiasm the first attempts of beginners to use their imaginations to solve a problem. Once players have had the fun of seeing, hearing, feeling, touching, tasting, or smelling something that is not there, they will find that their capacity to imagine grows quickly. Holding the image until they can do something about it is the next step, but the image must come first. Through drama, the imagination can be stimulated and strengthened, to the student's everlasting pleasure and profit. We learn through experience. Unless we want a child to experience everything—which is, of course, impossible—we are obliged to give up the idea except by way of books and theatre. Through participation in drama and vicariously through attendance at plays, teachers can provide realistic experiences in acceptable and exciting ways.

An Opportunity for Independent Thinking

A particular value of creative playing is the opportunity it offers for independent thinking. Although the drama, both informal and formal, is a group art, it is composed of the contributions of each participant, and every contribution is important. As the group plans together, members are encouraged to express their own ideas and thereby contribute to the whole. The leader recognizes the part that each child plays and the value that planning has. If the group is not too large, there will be many opportunities for creative thinking before the activity is exhausted. Thinking is involved in such questions as: Who are the characters? What are they like? What part do they play? Why do they behave as they do? What scenes are important? Why? How can we suggest this action or that place?

The evaluation that follows the creative playing is as important as the planning; indeed, it is preparation for a replaying. Children of all ages are remarkably perceptive, and their critical comments indicate the extent of their involvement. A well-planned session in creative drama provides exercises in critical thinking as well as an opportunity for creativity.

Freedom for the Group to Develop Its Own Ideas

It has just been stated that through creative drama, an individual has a chance to develop and grow. This is also true of the group, in which ideas are explored, evaluated, changed, and used. As the members of a group of any age work together under sensitive and skilled leadership, they learn to accept, appreciate, and stimulate one another. Every teacher has experienced a group in which the dynamics were such that all members seemed to produce more because of their association. This is not to say that creative drama is a magic formula for successful teamwork, but it unquestionably offers a rare opportunity for sharing ideas and solving problems together. The formal play, whatever problems it may pose, cannot offer a group the same challenge. The written script imposes a structure in which improvisation has no place. There are values in putting on a play for an audience, to be sure, but the major emphasis is on the product, not on the participants.

Incidentally, the strength that is acquired through planning and playing together is a valuable asset when, at some later date, the group decides to give a formal play. Far from limiting the players, improvisation strengthens techniques and builds self-confidence.

AN OPPORTUNITY FOR COOPERATION

When a group builds something together, its members are learning a valuable lesson in cooperation. Social differences are forgotten in the business of sharing ideas and improvising scenes. Teachers who guide children in creative drama cite numerous examples of social acceptance based on respect for a job well done and the bond that develops from the fun of playing together.

AN OPPORTUNITY TO BUILD SOCIAL AWARENESS

Putting oneself in the shoes of another is a way of developing awareness and human understanding. By the time players have decided who characters are, why they behave as they do, and how they relate to others, they have come to know a great deal about them. Even young players gain insights that help in their understanding of people and, therefore, of living. Both literature and original stories provide players with this opportunity to study human nature.

In one class of 10 year olds, the teacher began the session by asking the children to think of someone they had seen on their way to school or perhaps someone they often saw who had attracted their attention. It was suggested that the person should have interested them enough to be a character in a play. Immediately, every hand went up, and a variety of persons were described. After a period of telling what the people looked like, where they were, and what they were doing, the teacher asked the class to select three who would be good subjects for original stories. The class was then divided into three groups, six or seven in a group, and given an opportunity to make up a story centered around the person of their choice.

The first group decided on the character whom Peter suggested—an old man whom Peter described as sitting on the steps of his apartment building. The children decided that the old man might have been a school janitor who, in his retirement, spent the morning watching the children go to school. Having reached this decision, the children took no time at all to develop a plot in which the old man's memory of having saved a child's life became a sudden reality: a boy had run across the street after his ball, and the old man, in an automatic reaction, had rescued him from being hit by a car. The story, with its throwback scene imposed on the present, was dramatic and exciting both to the players and to the rest of the class; more significant than that, however, was the warm and sympathetic portrayal of the old man. Two adults who were in the room that day have spoken many times of the scene. If the memory remained with the observers, is it not likely that the children who created the play must have grown in the process?

A HEALTHY RELEASE OF EMOTION

Much has been said and written about the thinking, both creative and critical, that characterizes creative drama. Another value is of equal importance: the opportunity to feel and release emotion. As children grow up, the chance for emotional release is too often restricted to responding to television shows and movies. While there is value in being a spectator, the deeper involvement of active participation is lacking.

Control of emotion does not mean suppression of emotion. It means the healthy release of strong feelings through appropriate and acceptable channels. At some time or another, all persons feel anger, fear, anxiety, jealousy, resentment, and negativism. Through the playing of a part in which these emotions are expressed, the player may release them and so relieve tension: "By permitting the child to play freely in a setting of security and acceptance, we enable him to deal satisfactorily and healthfully with his most urgent problems."[3]

BETTER HABITS OF SPEECH

To many teachers, a primary value of creative drama is the opportunity it affords for oral communication. There is a built-in motivation for the player who wishes to be heard and understood. Volume, tempo, pitch, and diction are involved in a natural way; no other form of speech exercise captures the child to the same degree or offers so good a reason for working on speech as does creative drama. The little girl who can barely be heard in a classroom recitation will be reminded by her fellow players to speak up so the lines will not be lost. And the boy with the strident tone will also be told when his voice is too loud for the character he is playing. Being, in turn, a giant, a prince, an old man, an animal, or a comic character in a modern story offers further opportunities for developing variation of tone and expression.

Not only articulation, but also vocabulary is served through this form of oral expression. Conceptual thinking and the cognitive aspect of language are encouraged when words are put to practical use. For the disadvantaged child or the child with a foreign-language background, vocabulary can be built and distinctions in word meanings made clear

[3] Ruth Hartley, Lawrence Frank, and Robert Goldenson, *Understanding Children's Play* (New York: Columbia University Press, 1984), p. 16.

through participation in creative drama. Even abstract learning comes more readily when words are acted or shown.

AN EXPERIENCE WITH GOOD LITERATURE

The story that is played makes a lasting impression. Therefore, the opportunity to become well acquainted with good literature, through dramatizing it, is a major value of creative drama. The teacher soon discovers that the stories that hold interest longest are those of the best literary quality. Both folk tales and modern tales provide fine opportunities for acting. Bruno Bettelheim has given powerful arguments for the folk and fairy tale, a genre that in recent years has been questioned as to its relevance for the modern child.[4] In addition to the narrative interest of these tales, there are important psychological reasons why they continue to have value and why they should be used—although, of course, not to the exclusion of contemporary literature. A program that includes a variety of material helps to build appreciation and set a standard for original writing. Television shows and comic books attract temporary interest, but compared with a story that has stood the test of time, these rarely sustain attention. Believable characters, a well-constructed plot, and a worthwhile theme make for good drama. What better way of discovering and learning to appreciate literature?

AN INTRODUCTION TO THE THEATRE ARTS

Art is said to represent the human being's interpretation of life, expressed in a way that can be universally recognized and understood. Creative drama is primarily participant centered and offers the young player his or her first taste of the magic and make-believe of the theatre. In the imagination, a chair becomes a throne; a stick, a wand or a cane; a change in lighting, a difference in time; and a character, a human being in whom to believe and with whom to identify. Listening, watching, and becoming involved are required of the theatre audience. Children who are introduced to the theatre through playing are going to look for more than superficial entertainment when they attend a performance.

RECREATION

Implicit in everything that has been said so far, yet different and of value in itself, is the opportunity for recreation, or "re-creation," that drama affords. In certain settings—such as camps, community centers,

---

[4] Bruno Bettelheim, *The Uses of Enchantment* (New York: Knopf, 1976).

after-school-activity programs, and neighborhood clubs—the highest priority of drama may be recreation. Drama is fun. It exists for the pleasure of the players, and it expresses free choice. It may also, in time, lead to serious work or a lifelong avocation.

VALUES FOR THE SPECIAL CHILD

Creative drama offers an opportunity for children with learning or physical disabilities to participate in a performing art. Because of its flexibility, drama can be a joyful and freeing adventure for groups of all ages. Special needs can be served by adjusting emphases and activities. Often, the experience of participation in drama by special children stimulates interest in other subjects and, in so doing, strengthens skills and awakens latent abilities.

VALUES FOR THE TEACHER

What do teachers get from creative drama? Probably the most important thing is a perspective on every child in the class. A child's participating in drama reveals his or her imagination, skill in problem solving, and ability to work with others.

What if an exercise fails? Don't be discouraged. No activity is foolproof, and no idea stimulates every class equally well. But we learn as the children do, by doing. Be prepared; then take the risk. The worst thing that can happen is that *one* lesson did not go as you had hoped. You will discover more from your "flops" than from your successes.

While I do not suggest that special study of creative drama is unnecessary to its practice, I believe that the average classroom teacher, because of preparation and experience, is better equipped to teach it than he or she may realize. The reason? Drama does not require mastery of the kinds of technical skills that are required for the teaching of music, dance, or the visual arts. Drama does, however, demand sensitivity to and a knowledge of children; the goals and principles of education and a knowledge of child psychology—these the classroom teacher already possesses. If we enjoy the theatre, and most of us do, then sharing this interest with children should be a pleasure. Skill comes with experience. Experience, combined with study under well-prepared leaders, leads to an ease and ability that marks the professional.

PROBLEMS IN CREATIVE PLAYING

Sooner or later, the teacher of creative drama is bound to encounter problems of one sort or another. They may be the simple ones of time and space: periods that are too short to accomplish curriculum goals; space that is inadequate for movement; classes that are too large. These problems usually can be solved, although the solutions are not always easy. Other problems confronting the teacher, even under ideal conditions, are the individual behavioral problems that he or she finds in the group.

SELF-CONSCIOUSNESS

Self-consciousness is the greatest obstacle to creativity. Self-consciousness or fear takes many forms. The shy child and the show-off are examples of the two forms in which self-consciousness is most often encountered. The insensitive child is also a problem, for he or she usually lacks friends and so finds it difficult to work cooperatively in a group. And, finally, there is the disabled child, whose physical, mental, or emotional needs pose special problems for the leader.

Teachers must keep in mind that children are exposing themselves more in drama than in any other art or activity, for they are their instruments. Therefore, the handling of a behavior problem implies awareness of the cause. If the problem is severe, it should be handled by a therapist and not by the classroom teacher; in many cases, an intelligent, sympathetic effort to build self-respect and bring fun into the lives of the players can go a long way toward solving problems. When therapy is required, however, a good working relationship between the therapist and the teacher is advantageous to both.

TIMIDITY

The timid child is the most common problem of all, but one that creative drama can help. Such children are usually quiet in class, preferring to sit in the back of the room and let others do the talking. Their fear of making a mistake, or even of being noticed, causes them to withdraw, even though they may want to participate. Children who never volunteer need special encouragement. The teacher who gives them an opportunity to show what they can do may be taking the first step in helping them build a better self-image. Warm praise for whatever contribution they make invariably leads to a second effort.

As an example, there was 8-year-old Patty, who was referred to a Saturday-morning play group because of her extreme shyness. At first, she took part only when the whole group was moving, and then, I suspected, because it would have been more conspicuous to remain seated than to get up with the others. After several weeks, she did a pantomime of a child finding a kitten. Her pleasure and tenderness as she fondled its soft body drew spontaneous admiration from the other children in the class. This was the breakthrough. From that day, Patty's eagerness to enter into the activities was apparent. Her voice was almost inaudible at first, but it grew stronger in proportion to her growing self-confidence. This was no sudden miracle; indeed, it took three years for a transformation to take place. Patty's feelings of inadequacy had been so deepseated that many successes were necessary to convince her that she had something to offer that her peers would accept. Whether or when she would have found her way anyhow, no one can say. Creative drama as a technique was deliberately used, and the change during the three years she attended the class was striking.

Exhibitionism

The show-offs are just as much in need of help as the shy children, but rarely elicit sympathetic attention. Their problem is also one of uneasiness, and in trying to prove their importance, they do all the wrong things. Their behavior ranges from monopolizing class discussion to interfering with the work of others. They may deliberately use a wrong word for the sake of a laugh or play the clown so as to give their peers something to laugh at. Because they are so focused on the effect they are having, they have difficulty concentrating on what they are supposed to be doing.

I remember John, a nervous little fellow of 7, with facial mannerisms and a habit of interrupting. John was accepted by the others for a while because he amused them. Nevertheless, he was unable to remain involved in a role for more than a few minutes. Then he would look around the room to see how he was affecting the other children. In John's case, there was no sudden incident that accounted for the change that took place. Rather, it was a matter of working patiently with him, taking every opportunity to praise his honest expression and helping him find satisfaction in getting attention legitimately. By the end of the year, John was able to work cooperatively with the group much of the time and to forgo the need to show off. His problem was still not entirely solved, but he had learned something of the give-and-take of working with others and the pleasure that comes from honest work.

Sometimes the teacher may be forced to ask a disruptive child to return to his or her seat—not as punishment, but as the consequence of unacceptable behavior. Creative drama demands, above all, teamwork and respect for others. The player who cannot work with the team must withdraw until he or she is willing and able to accept the ground rules.

ISOLATION

The isolate, or loner, is often a child who cannot relate to the group. He or she may work hard and have good ideas and the ability to present them, but always in isolation. This may, of course, be an indication of superior talent and high motivation. Independence is a desired goal, but when withdrawal is the result of inability to relate to others, it is a serious problem. Through movement and group activities, the isolate may be drawn into the group naturally; together, the group members experience interdependence and the importance of working together as well as independently. The teacher should persist, explaining that drama is a *group* art and needs the contributions of every participant. If nothing works, the school psychologist should be consulted; the problem would appear to be deep-seated and, therefore, serious.

INSENSITIVITY

The insensitive child is similar to, but different from, the show-off because he or she usually is rejected by the others and does not understand why. Insensitive children tend to ridicule the ideas of others and criticize their efforts, often harshly. Playing a variety of roles may help them gain insights into and develop an awareness of the feelings of others. This takes time, but patient attention to the problem in human relations may eventually help insensitive children to listen and accept suggestions from their peers.

Because of their insensitivity, such children can be dealt with quite directly by calling attention to the fact that they are harsh and that others are hurt or angered by their criticism. Insensitive persons do not realize this and have to have it pointed out to them. They may be very intelligent children, but they have a blind spot in dealing with others; teachers do not do them a service by ignoring it.

DISTRACTION

Every teacher has known the easily distracted child—the one whose concentration is broken at any unexpected sight or sound. Work to strengthen concentration is the best approach to the problem. But success may take a long time, and the teacher may have to find satisfaction in the slightest improvement—a longer attention span and the child's ability to remain focused beyond the point where he or she used to be thrown off. Again, if the problem persists, professional help for the child should be sought, for it may be a symptom of something serious.

Physical Disabilities

Children with special handicaps need special attention. They need sympathy, understanding, and encouragement. The teacher is not equipped to practice therapy, but he or she must know what to expect of disabled children and try to adapt the activities to their capabilities. Such children often are in therapy, and if the teacher can work with the therapist, she or he will be able to receive helpful suggestions about the proper approach.

Stuttering, a harelip, any condition that interferes with locomotion, or a hearing loss presents problems that must be faced within the context of a class, yet most classroom teachers have had little or no experience with them.

The first thing to remember is that all persons gain in self-respect when their ideas are accepted. The child with a problem has a special need for acceptance, and the teacher must try to find the best way in which to meet it. Creative drama provides an ideal opportunity to help the timid child overcome inhibitions; to provide the show-off with a better way of getting attention; to guide the insensitive child to some awareness of the feelings of others; to help the disabled child find an avenue of expression. In each case imagination is the first step in discovering ways to see beyond the problem and create a solution. It takes imagination both on the child's part and on the teacher's, and the task is not easy.

Today's children are subjected to pressures and demands that, if not greater than in the past, are certainly new and different. Not only inner-city children, but also affluent, suburban children reflect these changes in values and mores. The pressures and demands often result in unpredictable behavior, causing problems for teachers and creating difficulties when freedom is encouraged. Creative-drama teachers are particularly vulnerable to these problems, for they deal with the emotional and social, as well as the intellectual, aspects of child development.

Although freedom is essential to creativity, it often is necessary to impose restraints in the beginning, or at least until the children become comfortable with the group, the leader, and the activity. It is important that teachers be sensitive to unusual behavior and try to handle it with understanding and firmness. While they cannot accept certain antisocial behavior in a child, it is important for the child to know what is being rejected. In other words, teachers do not reject the child but do reject behavior that interferes with the freedom of others to express their ideas and feelings.

EVALUATING CHILDREN'S RESPONSES

A question that always comes up is how to evaluate children's responses. This is difficult to answer, for progress varies from one child to the next. The teacher has different expectations for each child, and what may be extraordinary growth for one is scarcely an adequate performance for another. With that in mind, the teacher should ask:

1. Have the individuals in the class become a group, willing and able to work together? Is there easy give-and-take?
2. Is each child an integral part of the group, sharing ideas without fear of failure or need to impress?
3. Is the work sincere?
4. Has physical movement become more free and more expressive?
5. Have verbal skills—speech, voice and diction, vocabulary, and oral expression—improved?
6. Depending on the focus, have other goals—use of resource materials, integration of learning, and involvement in subject—been met?
7. Does the group exhibit vitality—eagerness to begin and reluctance to stop at the end of the period?
8. Does the noise level reflect industry and enthusiasm?

It is easier in many ways to evaluate the work of the older child than that of the younger because of the older child's better handling of materials. The younger child lacks the experience, vocabulary, and verbal skills that can be assumed in a child in the middle and upper grades. Evaluation of students of any age is difficult, particularly in the arts, where progress is so closely related to where the child is and how far he or she has come.

SUMMARY

Creative drama may be regarded as a way of learning, a means of self-expression, a therapeutic technique, a social activity, or an art form. Children are helped to assume responsibility, accept group decisions, work cooperatively, develop new interests, and seek new information.

Drama is the most highly socialized, as well as the most completely personal, art form we have.

It is often observed that few persons perform on their highest level. This is true of the beginning player, child or adult, who because of shyness or actual fear needs encouragement and acceptance. The sensitive leader recognizes this and tries to create an atmosphere of mutual trust. In the acceptance of every child and what he or she has to offer, the leader has taken the first big step toward building the child's self-confidence. Freedom will follow; learning will occur; and an ordinary classroom will become a place in which exciting things can happen.

2

IMAGINATION:
THE STARTING POINT

We must feed the imagination, trust the curiosity of children and youth; we adults must provide space, time and situations in which they can experiment with an "as if" world before they settle down to a real world.

MARGARET MEAD

The *fact* of imagination has long been known, but it is only recently that the *value* of imagination has been recognized. Today, not only artists, but also businesspeople, scientists, military leaders, and educators describe imagination as the magic force that goes beyond the mastery of facts and techniques in the search for new ideas. The child brings this magic force into the classroom, but it is up to the teacher to encourage its use. For imagination leads to creation, and the creative child is the one who can transform the *ordinary* into the *extraordinary* and unique.

CREATIVITY

Creativity may be defined in a number of ways. It may be thought of in terms of process or product, depending on whether we are concerned with the way in which a problem is solved or the solution to a problem. If creativity is interpreted as process, it is considered as a new way of seeing, a different point of view, an original idea, or a new relationship between ideas. Inventiveness and adaptation are often included in the thinking of those who believe creativity to be a way of working.

If, however, creativity is defined in terms of product, it is best illustrated by works of art (poems, stories, paintings, music, dance), scientific inventions, and new arrangements or designs. There has been great interest in the study and measurement of creativity in recent years, and a considerable body of data has appeared. One assumption accepted by psychologists is that creativity is not a special gift possessed by a fortunate few, but a human capacity possessed to some degree by everyone.

According to some authorities, the beginning of creative thinking may be found early in the life of the infant, in its manipulative and exploratory activities. In its awareness of human facial expressions, gestures, and sounds, the baby is first observer and then investigator. It is but a short step from here to experimentation, at which point the child becomes creator. The words *observer, investigator, creator* are of particular interest to the teacher of creative drama. One leader held a discussion on the subject of creativity and imagination with a group of fourth-grade

Children improvise with imagination. (Courtesy of Coleman A. Jennings, University of Texas at Austin; photograph by Alan Smith)

children in a creative-drama class. Their dialogue went something like this:

TEACHER: What does creativity mean to you?

PATRICIA: I think it means to make.

DENISE: No, not to make. To make up.

TEACHER: Can you explain the difference?

KENNY: Well, if a man made a pair of shoes, he'd be creating.

TEACHER: Do you all agree with Kenny?

DENISE: No, I think only the first pair of shoes would be created. If the man made a lot of others like them, they'd just be made—not made up.

TEACHER: Then everything that's made is not created?

DENISE: (*sticking to her original point*) Only the things that aren't copied.

TEACHER: How do you feel about copying?

PATRICIA: You don't get any fun out of copying.

CATHY: I think it's all right to copy some things.

TEACHER: What kind of things, Cathy?

CATHY: Well, like good manners. And words. You wouldn't know what to do lots of times if you didn't have something to copy.

TEACHER: Then you don't think copying is always a bad thing to do? (*general agreement that it is not*)

DENISE: Just the same, you shouldn't use somebody else's mind. You want a thing to be just yours.

ALAN: You have to know what to copy and what not to. Sometimes it's hard to know which is which.

TEACHER: How would you explain imagination? Dean?

DEAN: You think of something that isn't there.

TEACHER: Would anyone like to add to that?

BILLY: Yes, it isn't that it isn't there. It's more like you make yourself believe.

PATRICIA: You see, outside of you it isn't real. Inside your head, it's there.

TEACHER: Do you enjoy using your imagination?

JOHN: Oh, yes. Because you can make anything happen.

PATRICIA: Sometimes they're silly things. What we do isn't always good.

TEACHER: What do you mean, "not good"?

PATRICIA: I mean, some children have better ideas than others.

TEACHER: But you still want a chance to try them all out?

DENISE: Oh, yes. It's better for an idea to be yours than good.

BILLY: I think your imagination means being creative. It means making up something that wasn't ever there before.

The discussion went on like this for some time, but it was obvious that the terms *creativity* and *imagination* held real meaning for the children. Their observations—that it is important to have ideas and the freedom to try them out—are basic to good work in creative drama.

BEGINNING EXERCISES FOR IMAGINATION

The first day the class meets, the teacher will do well to begin with the simplest exercises in which imagination is involved. Regardless of age level, the participants must be given an opportunity to go beyond the here and now, but they cannot and should not be expected to handle a story or create an improvisation. It is wise to begin with the entire class, if space permits, rather than with individuals. This removes all thoughts of audience, thereby diminishing fear and self-consciousness.

How the leader begins will be determined by the age, experience, and number of children in the group, as well as by the size of the playing space. If the group is fortunate in meeting in a very large room, physical movement is an excellent opening exercise. Music or even a drumbeat will help to focus the attention. One simple and effective way of beginning is to have the group walk to the beat of the drum. As the group becomes more comfortable and relaxed, the beat can be changed: rapid, double time, slow, and so on. The participants, in listening for the change in beat, forget themselves and usually are able to use their entire bodies. Galloping, skipping, and hopping are fun for younger children and are good exercise for those much older. From purely physical movement, the teacher may move on to games of imagination (Activities 2.1 and 2.2).

CONCENTRATION

If imagination is the beginning, concentration—the capacity to hold an idea long enough to do something about it—must come next. This is where young or inexperienced players often have difficulty. A game is often the best way to start.

MAKING A MACHINE

There are many variations on the game Making a Machine, which has great appeal for older children and is a good warm-up at any time. To begin, the leader may start a regular drumbeat and ask one person to go into the center of the room and begin a movement. When the movement has been stabilized, a second person comes forward with another movement that relates to the first. This continues until as many as a dozen players become parts of a machine, each one contributing a movement that is coordinated with the rest. The effect can be interesting and dynamic when all players are working together.

This exercise may be made more interesting by adding sounds. Each player makes a noise appropriate to the movement. When all parts of the machine are moving rhythmically, the sounds enhance the effect. This exercise requires imagination, inventiveness, concentration, cooperation, and the ability to sustain both sound and movement until the mechanical quality is established. The machine can run indefinitely, or it can break down—either stopping or falling apart.

The group may also start with a particular machine in mind (threshing machine, wrecking equipment, ice-cream maker, sewing machine, computer), or a machine may develop from an activity. As a group gains experience, the results will become more precise. Incidentally, this technique can be incorporated effectively into an improvisation, and it often is far more interesting than the use of conventional props. Activities 2.3 and 2.4 carry this exercise further.

SUMMARY

Imagination is the spark that sets off the creative impulse. *Concentration* (the capacity to hold an idea long enough to do something about it) and *organization* (the arrangement of the parts) are necessary to a satisfying self-expression. *Communication* (the bridge to others) comes last and is less the concern of the creative-drama class than of the formal play. It exists, however, as a desirable goal.

In all creative work, there are obstacles that must be recognized and dealt with. Wise teachers learn first to identify the problems and then look for solutions, remembering that they are neither therapists nor theatre directors but educators, guiding players through the medium of informal drama. Brian Way has defined the role of the teacher: "Schools do not exist to develop actors but to develop people, and one of the major factors in developing people is that of preserving and enriching to its fullest the human capacity to give full and undivided attention to any matter at hand at any given moment."[1]

---

[1] Brian Way, *Development Through Drama* (New York: Humanities Press, 1967), p. 15.

ACTIVITY 2.1

IMAGINING GAMES

Objective: To spark the imagination and strengthen concentration

Suggestions for the Teacher

Clear the room for maximum space. Then, depending on the size of the class, have the children form a circle or divide the group in half. Toss an imaginary ball to the players. It is a good idea to play along with them in order to direct attention to the size, shape, and weight of the ball. The catcher tosses the ball to another player, who catches it and tosses it to another. This continues until everyone in the circle has had a turn. At this point, ask that the ball be thrown back to you. You successively change it to another kind of ball:

1. A basketball
2. A tennis ball
3. A beach ball
4. A golf ball

Ask each person to bounce in place the ball that he or she likes best.

Questions for the Observers

1. Which ball did each one bounce?
2. How did you know?

Questions for the Players

1. How did the tennis ball feel to you after the basketball?
2. Which ball was the hardest to catch?
3. What color was the beach ball?
4. Why did you choose your ball to bounce?

If the group appears interested and space permits, you may suggest that the class play an imaginary baseball game. This is vigorous and challenging.

ACTIVITY 2.2

ANYTHING CAN BECOME SOMETHING ELSE

Objective: To stimulate the imagination with sense memory

Suggestions for the Teacher

Place six or seven chairs in a semicircle at the front of the room. Divide the class into groups of six or seven. Each group will have a turn while the other groups watch. Ask the first group to come forward and sit down, facing the class.

Give a blackboard eraser (or another small, nondescript object) to the first child, asking him or her to handle it as though it were a particular object (for example, a diamond bracelet). The child passes it along to the next child, who passes it to the next until everyone has had a turn.

Ask each player to:

1. Handle it
2. Examine it carefully
3. React to it
4. Then hand it to the person next to you

Some of the objects that the teacher may suggest are:

1. A beautiful diamond bracelet
2. A kitten with soft fur
3. A dirty, torn wallet
4. A glass filled to the brim with water
5. A sharp knife
6. A tiny glass bead

Questions for the Observers

1. How did we know that they were holding a bracelet and that it was valuable?
2. What was different about the way they handled the kitten?
3. Would you have known they had a wallet? Why?
4. What were some of the ways the players showed what they were doing?

Questions for the Players

1. What was the hardest one? Why?
2. What did the wallet look like? Describe it.
3. You were careful not to drop any of the objects, yet you treated them differently. Why?

4. Describe the kitten. What color was it? How did you feel when you held it?

The idea of this game is to stimulate the imagination and help young players understand that it is not the object but their own imaginations that can turn a blackboard eraser into a bracelet, a kitten, a wallet, and so on.

By the time each group has had a turn, every child will have participated. The questions following the playing will help them discover new ways of seeing, handling, and reacting to the suggested objects. Although a simple activity, this is a good early step in using the imagination creatively.

ACTIVITY 2.3

ADD A MOVEMENT

Children in the middle and upper grades enjoy the challenge of this game and become skilled at playing it.

Objective: To strengthen concentration and increase awareness as the players think of different movements

Suggestions for the Teacher

Unless the group is very large, all class members can play at one time. The more children there are in the group, the harder the game becomes.

Have the players form a circle so they can see one another easily. Then ask one child to move a part of his or her body.

The second child repeats the first movement and adds a second. The third child repeats both motions and adds a third. Everyone in the circle adds a movement. By the time each child has had a turn, there will be a great variety of movements.

Players in the middle grades love to see how many times they can go around the circle, remembering all the movements in order.

ACTIVITY 2.4

KEYS

Concentration and organization go hand in hand.

Objective: To take players a step beyond concentration into the organization of their ideas

Suggestions for the Teacher

Bring in a large collection of keys: door keys, old keys, suitcase keys, skeleton keys, large keys, souvenir keys.

Give a key to each child in the group. After all the children have had a chance to examine their keys, ask the following questions:

1. What kind of key do you have?
2. What kind of door (or lid) do you think it will open?
3. Imagine what you will find when you open it.
4. Think about your key for a minute or two; then use it, and let us see what you have found.

The children may need more than a minute to decide what doors their keys will open and plan how to show it. When all are ready (this will probably not take long), give each child a turn to use his or her key.

Questions for the Observers

1. Could you see what the players found?
2. How did you know?
3. What were some of the interesting things they did with their keys?

Questions for the Players

1. Were the observers right about what you discovered?
2. What made you decide where you were and what door your key would open?
3. Would you like to make a play from your discovery?

"Keys" may be used simply as a game or may be extended, leading to the creation of an original play or a piece of creative writing.

3
DEVELOPING
BODY AWARENESS AND
SPATIAL PERCEPTION

Movement is a natural response to a stimulus and an important element of drama. Theatre began with movement; its origins were closely linked with religious and magical rites. The elements of conflict, character, plot, and dialogue gradually were added. With these additions, theatre as an art form was born.

Primitive peoples—in attempting to order their universe, explain natural phenomena, and pray to their gods—used rhythmic movement to express themselves. In time, this movement evolved into dance. An entire tribe might take part, or perhaps only the most skilled dancers. As the movements were repeated, they took on special meanings. These meanings were understood by both performers and spectators and were taught to the young, thus serving an educational as well as a religious purpose.

CHILDREN AND MOVEMENT

Creative movement deals with the elements of dance but is more spontaneous. Children move naturally; by encouraging such movement, the teacher can help children to express themselves through physical activity, thereby creating their own styles of movement, gaining confidence in their bodies, and developing spatial awareness. It is easy to move from creative movement to either dance or drama.

Drama differs from dance because it involves a linguistic element; the older the players, the greater the dependence on words to communicate meaning. The teacher of creative drama hopes to develop children's ability and ease in the use of both verbal and nonverbal expression; starting early is an important factor in achieving these goals. A child's posture reflects how he or she feels, regardless of what may be said. We read much about "body language" these days. This form of nonverbal expression includes any posture as well as reflexive or nonreflexive movement of the body that conveys emotion to the observer. Although most of the writing on body language concerns adults, the attitudes and feelings of children are just as clearly revealed by their movements and facial expressions. A teacher can learn much about the members of a class from the postures that the children assume and the use they make of the various parts of their bodies.

In addition, there is the physical pleasure a child derives from moving, a pleasure that leads into play, dance, sports, and exercise for its own sake. Today, unfortunately, television constantly bombards the eyes and ears of children, giving information of all kinds, it is true, but at the expense of movement and natural creative response. In bringing children indoors, television helps to make them passive spectators rather than active participants in games and sports in open areas. Most children enjoy moving their bodies and discovering different ways of exploring a space. As they gain physical control, they prefer running to walking and enjoy finding new methods of locomotion that are energetic and fast. Running, skipping, galloping, hopping, jumping, leaping, and rolling stretch the muscles and help children gain a mastery of their bodies as they try out all the different things they can do with them. Because movement is so natural an expression, it is the ideal way of beginning work in creative drama.

Children with language problems also tend to find great satisfaction in movement. The physicality of dance and movement circumvents their disadvantages in verbal skills, thus providing another reason for its inclusion, particularly in the beginning.

BEGINNING CLASSES IN MOVEMENT

Teachers of older children find that their goals may be reached more easily and quickly if they begin with physical activity instead of a verbal approach. Actors call these activities "warm-ups" and claim that they are an effective way to relax and tone the muscles of their backs, legs, arms, and necks in preparation for a performance. Through rhythmic exercise, a group can be drawn together and released as individuals in an objective and pleasurable way.

Classes in movement are most successful when taught in a large room, where children have plenty of space in which to move freely. Too large an area, such as a gymnasium or a playground, presents problems, however, as large, unconfined space often leads to chaos, dispersing the group rather than bringing it together. Therefore, boundaries should be established and maintained.

Piano accompaniment is an asset, if the teacher can play or has an accompanist; if not, a drum is perfectly satisfactory. Later on, recorded music will help suggest mood and characterization. In the beginning and for most purposes, percussion instruments are all the leader needs to give the beat and suggest or change rhythms. One advantage of the drum is that it permits the leader to move about freely and watch the group.

In a movement class, it is usually a good idea to begin work with the entire group, unless it is so large or the room is so small that the participants will bump into one another. In that case, the leader should divide the class into two groups, working first with one and then with the other, and alternating every few minutes in order to hold the children's interest. After gathering the children into a large circle, the leader should beat on a drum a good rhythm for walking. When everyone is moving easily and without self-consciousness, the beat can be changed to something faster, such as a trot or a run. Shifting the rhythm to a gallop, a skip, a hop, a jump, and then back to a slow walk not only stimulates good exercise, but also holds the attention as the children listen for the changes. Why rhythmic movement first? Because it encourages spontaneity within a disciplined framework. This is the goal of the teacher of creative drama as well as the teacher of dance.

As teachers, we have tended to think of creative drama as being concerned primarily with the development of intellectual and linguistic abilities, whereas we have thought of movement as being concerned with the control and use of the body. Actually, movement and body language are a part of drama. It is the combined mental, physical, vocal, and emotional involvement that distinguishes drama from all other art forms and gives it its special value.

Peter Slade uses the term *natural dance* to describe dance that is not tied to a set of rules or complicated techniques, but is improvised and personal in style. He further identifies it as the bridge between the primi-

Class in movement. (Courtesy of Lucille Paolillo, Children's Centre for the Creative Arts, Adelphi University; photograph by George Meyer)

tive and the sophisticated or between natural inclination and a disciplined art form.[1]

INSTRUMENTS

Although it was stated that the drum is the most commonly used instrument when working on rhythms, other instruments add variety and are not difficult to obtain. Some of these are triangles, bells, and gongs for metal sounds; sticks and castanets for wood sounds; and shaking instruments such as maracas, or gourds with pebbles inside. Imaginative leaders and groups will find or invent other instruments. Actually, trying out different objects to discover what sounds they make is an exercise in itself and one that most children enjoy.

One of the values of using different instruments is the discovery of the qualities of sound they produce. This, in turn, helps the student to feel the rhythm in a special way. For example, slow drumbeats might suggest waves washing up on the shore of a lake, whereas castanets might bring hailstones or raindrops to mind. In telling a story in movement, the use of several percussion instruments will stimulate the imagination, often giving different results from those obtained with the use of a drum.

Records and tapes are excellent, of course; percussion instruments are recommended primarily because the teacher has complete control over them—stopping, starting, and changing the rhythm, according to the immediate need. The terms *legato* and *staccato* can be introduced at this time; they have special meanings, which describe rhythms clearly and, incidentally, add to a growing vocabulary.

RHYTHMIC ACTIVITIES

The following activities are designed to help the student discover the drama in movement. In the early stages, the teacher works within the group, moving out when the participants are secure and able to move without this support. He or she does not *show* the group what to do, but supports, in every way possible, honest effort, involvement, and the development of individual ideas.

"Snail" is a good beginning game for establishing a common rhythm. Have the group line up in single file, each child putting his or her hands on the shoulders of the person in front. The leader moves to the center of the room, with the line following. Chanting "snail, snail, snail, snail,"

[1] Peter Slade, *Natural Dance* (London: Hodder and Stoughton, 1979).

Extension. (Courtesy of Rachel Carr; photograph by Edward Kimball)

the group moves into a shell-like, spiral formation. When the players can move in no farther, they reverse and move back into their original circle.

Rhythms can suggest people working or moving in unison. Try drumbeats to suggest formation of:

1. An assembly line
2. A marching band
3. Robots
4. Motorcycles
5. Athletes warming up
6. Workers using picks
7. Joggers

"Statues" is a favorite game with many children. Players follow the music, inventing gestures with arms, head, and body as they move around the room. When the music or drumbeat stops (without warning), everyone freezes into a statue. (Note the various poses). When the music starts again, all the players move, making new gestures. This can be repeated several times or as long as the interest holds.

MOVEMENT ACTIVITIES

The preceding activities were especially concerned with rhythm and the use of the body. All movement is concerned, however, with *where* and *how* the body is used. *Where* the body moves refers to:

1. Level (high, low, or medium)
2. Direction (forward, backward, left, right, or diagonally)
3. Shape of the movement

How the body moves refers to:

1. Energy (much or little)
2. Time (sudden or sustained)
3. Flow (free or tight)

Activities 3.1 to 3.3 deal with basic body movement and expressing images and ideas in movement.

PARTNER ACTIVITIES

So far, the activities have been planned for the whole class or for large groups. Working in pairs or with partners is more difficult because the movements must be synchronized. Working with a partner helps each child move from group work to individual work without feeling self-conscious. Try the following simple exercises as a starter.

Each member of the group takes a partner. Have the members of each pair put their hands on each other's shoulders and then push to see who is the stronger.

Next try the theatre game of having one person lead another whose eyes are closed. Have the class walk around the room in pairs until all are moving easily together. Reverse roles, and try it again.

One of the partners goes to one end of the room; the second partner, to the other. To the beat of the drum, they:

1. Walk toward each other, meet, and part
2. Walk toward each other, meet, and clash
3. Walk toward each other, meet, and go off together

Have one partner begin a movement, and the other partner pick it up and continue it.

Have one partner begin to make or do something, and the other partner complete it.

TELLING STORIES IN MOVEMENT

Pure dance has no describable story. Mime, on the contrary, uses movement to narrate or describe. Mime can range from the classic form, which captures the essence of a person or an action, to the imitative form, which reproduces an action realistically. There is a trend at the present time to add sound to mime; this is a new direction in an old art form.

Children enjoy making up stories that involve a variety of rhythms. For example, a story might go something like this: "I went for a *walk* in the park. It was a lovely morning, and I *skipped* happily down a path. Soon I met an old man, *shuffling* along with a pack on his back. Next I met some pigeons, *strutting* across the path in search of food." This can go on as long as the group wants, adding persons and animals with clearly observable gaits. The teacher, working with the children, suggests the rhythms with drumbeats. A little practice and the story will take on embellishments, providing a rich opportunity for imaginative ideas and ways of showing them.

Myths and legends lend themselves to mime and mimetic movement, for they are generally simple in plot and deal with universal themes and feelings. The more complicated the narrative, the less easy it is to dance or mime, and therefore the greater the temptation to use words to explain it. Because of their simplicity, the stories in Activities 3.4 and 3.5 can be told in dance, mime, or with improvised dialogue. Have the class try telling them in all three ways.

SUMMARY

Movement—the basis of play, ritual, games, dance, and theatre—is a natural beginning for work in creative drama. Physically, the whole body is involved: torso, arms, legs, head, and neck. Through the use of the body, muscles are stretched and relaxed. Posture and coordination improve with regular exercise. Because the entire group can take part at one time, the possibility of self-consciousness is lessened. Persons of all ages and backgrounds usually find it easier at first to become involved in drama through movement rather than through verbalization. This is particularly true of young children, children for whom English is a second language, and persons with special problems and needs. In the rhythms and patterns of a child's movement, the problems in his or her inner life often are revealed. This is why movement and dance are recommended as treatment, serving both diagnostic and therapeutic purposes.

Imitation and observation are as much a part of movement as is creativity. The leader encourages imagination but discourages cliché. Through movement, therefore, children experience both discipline and freedom. By moving into the rituals of the group (and here the word *rituals* is used in its broadest sense), each child has a feeling of belonging. Rhythm, that underlying flow and beat, captures the mover in an experience both objective and pleasurable. Taught together, rhythms and dramatic play provide a sound foundation for acting. "Dance-drama" encompasses the disciplines of both arts and thus is a powerful tool for creative expression.

ACTIVITY 3.1

USE OF THE BODY

Objective: To discover where *and* how *the body is used*

Suggestions for the Teacher

Have the group experiment with the following kinds of movement. First, *where* movement takes place.

1. *Low movement:* caterpillar, duck, seal, shallow pool of water, young plant emerging from the earth
2. *High movement:* airplane, high cloud, person on stilts, tightrope walker, kite
3. *Horizontal movement:* swinging bell, elephant's trunk, lion pacing in a cage, someone paddling a canoe, someone on a swing
4. *Up-and-down movement:* seesaw, airplane, bird, bat, ball bouncing, elevator, falling star, jack-in-the-box, rocket, piece of machinery

Next try the following to show *how* movement takes place.

1. *Fast movement:* arrow, fire engine, express train, leaf in a storm, jet plane, speedboat, race horse, top, skateboard
2. *Slow movement:* clock, farm horse, melting ice, tugboat, turtle, freight train pulling out of the station, movie in slow motion
3. *Turning movement:* curling smoke, merry-go-round, revolving door, spool of thread, figure skating, top
4. *Strong, heavy movement:* chopping wood, bulldozer, tank, stormy waves, digging in concrete
5. *Soft, light movement:* balloon, butterfly, flickering candle, soap bubble, kitten, kite, elf, leaf
6. *Sharp movement:* bucking bronco, cuckoo clock, cricket, grasshopper, juggler, woodpecker
7. *Floppy, loose movement:* clothes on a line, rag doll, mop, loose sail, straw hat blowing down the street, long hair blowing, flag in the breeze
8. *Smooth movement:* airplane, cat, fish swimming, syrup pouring, skating, rainbow forming, automobile on a thruway
9. *Twisted movement:* octopus, pretzel, knot, piece of driftwood, crumpled paper, tangled chain

Finally, a *change* in movement.

1. A candle standing tall and straight burns down to a pool of wax
2. A piece of elastic, stretched and then released

3. A paper drifting to the sidewalk and then picked up by a sudden gust of wind
4. A board slowly breaking away from the side of an old building and then falling off
5. A toy train moving rapidly, running down, and stopping; then being rewound and repeating the sequence

ACTIVITY 3.2

EXPRESSION THROUGH BODY MOVEMENT

Objective: To express images that suggest being, using, *and* feeling *through movement*

Suggestions for the Teacher

Discuss the exercise first, so that the children are clear about what they are doing.

Read the words slowly, giving the children time to *be*, to *use*, and to *feel* each element.

1. Water
Being: bubbles, rushing water, rain, whirlpool, quiet pool, surf
Using: blowing bubbles, carrying water, hosing the lawn, water-skiing, wading in shallow water
Feeling: weightlessness of floating, walking in water, walking against the tide
2. Fire
Being: bonfire blazing, forest fire raging, smoke puffing, match being lighted
Using: building a fire, putting out a fire, being warmed by a fire
Feeling: hot, warm, and sleepy from a fire, choking from the smoke of a fire
3. Air
Being: soft summer air with only a slight breeze blowing
Using: pumping air into a tire, blowing up a balloon, breathing good, clean air
Feeling: warm air, cold air, polluted air, pleasant cool air

ACTIVITY 3.3

EXPRESSION IN DANCE

The ideas may be expressed quite differently, or they may be expressed in much the same way, depending on the person moving. Each student must move as he or she feels, for there is no right or wrong way. At this stage, sincere involvement is the most important thing.

Objective: To express ideas in dance

Suggestions for the Teacher

Ask the children to try the following after you have given the directions slowly, one idea at a time.

1. Offering a prayer
   Giving thanks
   Asking for rain in a time of drought
2. Casting a magic spell on someone
   Being under a magic spell
   Trying to throw off a magic spell
3. Feeling frightened
   Investigating the cause of your fear
   Feeling relief at discovering that your fear was groundless
4. Feeling joyful
   Showing what has made you so happy
   Sharing your joy with others
5. Feeling very angry
   Showing what has made you so angry
   Resolving your anger by doing something about it

If this activity has been interesting to the class, it may be extended by combining the three parts of it in order to create a simple story.

ACTIVITY 3.4

DRAMATIZATION IN MOVEMENT

Players of any age will find "The Pasta Pot" to be a humorous tale that can be handled in a variety of ways, depending on the interpretation.

Objective: To tell a story in movement

Suggestions for the Teacher

Familiarize the children with the story. Focus on the action of the story: beginning, middle, and end. Check the space and have them use it to best advantage. Accept the children's interpretations, helping them to express themselves in their own ways.

The teacher may either tell the story first or read it aloud while the children dance or mime it. With the help of a drum and other instruments, children will find appropriate rhythms and movements by which to tell the story. Try out some movements.

1. Decide what best expresses the old witch, Nona.
2. How would Anthony move and show his feelings: curiosity, delight, dismay, helplessness, relief, enjoyment of the dance at the end?
3. How would you suggest pasta boiling in a pot? running over? rolling out the door?
4. What are the neighbors like? What are their feelings?
5. Can you make up a group dance at the end? The players may want to use a folk dance here instead of creating one.

THE PASTA POT

The witch Nona had a magic pasta pot. One day, as she put the pot on the stove, her servant, Anthony, heard her chanting the words, "Boil and bubble, pasta pot. Make me some pasta, nice and hot." What Anthony did not see were the three magic kisses that Nona threw at the pot when she had eaten her fill.

Then, telling him to stay and guard the cottage, but not to touch the pot, Nona left. She had no more than gone out the door, however, when Anthony, eager to see if the magic worked for him, looked at the pot and chanted the words he had heard her say. No sooner were the words out of his mouth than the water began to boil and the pot to fill up with pasta. Anthony was greatly pleased with himself and ate heartily, but to his dismay, the pasta continued to roll out of the pot. He couldn't stop it!

The neighbors, seeing the pasta rolling out the door of the cottage, rushed in to find out what was happening. They all tried to stop it, but it only kept on coming. At this moment, Nona returned. She threw three magic kisses in the direction of the pot, and at once, the pasta stopped. She gave Anthony a lecture for disobeying her; then, seeing how frightened he had been, she forgave him. They and their neighbors joined together in a dance.

ACTIVITY 3.5

MYTHS IN MOVEMENT

The Hawaiian Islands are rich in myths and legends, some of which offer excellent material for movement and creative dance. "The Story of Ma-ui" is one of them. Players of all ages will find ideas that can be expressed physically, perhaps even better than vocally—certainly, just as well. The story is simple and direct, with a theme reminiscent of those of folk tales around the world.

Objective: To tell a story in movement

Suggestions for the Teacher

Many different movements and rhythms can be found in this story. One way to begin is with a discussion of all the movements that are mentioned. Then the entire group can work on them together, using a drumbeat to set the rhythms. A warm-up composed of walking, running, jumping, stretching, curling up, falling, and rising might precede work on the story. Some of the rhythmic patterns that the group might try next are:

1. The sun, racing across the sky
2. The flowers, stretching and trying to grow, and then wilting and withering
3. The fishermen, casting their lines and pulling them in as the sun goes down
4. The people, trudging back to their homes, exhausted and cold
5. Ma-ui, climbing the mountain and jumping to catch the sun's ray
6. The sun, slowing down in its course across the sky
7. The slower rhythms found at the end of the story

After the class has worked on the movements long enough to become free and thoroughly acquainted with the story, they will be ready to try playing it in its entirety. While the tale can be told in pantomime or improvised with spontaneous dialogue, "The Story of Ma-ui" can be beautifully conveyed through dance or simple creative movement. Older groups may want to add a Hawaiian dance at the end or to combine speech and movement. There is no best way to handle it; it was included in this chapter because it offers unusual opportunities for creative movement for children in the middle and upper grades.

Not all stories can be expressed equally well in dance or creative movement. Those that depend primarily on the spoken language obviously cannot, although reading them aloud while the children move or dance is a possible way of handling them. Again, whether the story is better told this way or with improvised dialogue depends on the amount and importance of physical action.

THE STORY OF MA-UI

There was a time, long ago, when the sun raced across the skies of Hawaii so rapidly that the fruit had no time to ripen on the vines, and the fishermen could not catch any fish. The days were short, and the nights were long. The earth was so cold and dark that plants froze on their stems. These beautiful islands, as we know them today, were inhospitable to life, and the people wondered how much longer they would exist or where they could go if they left. One day, a small boy named Ma-ui decided that he would catch the sun and make it slow down. Then perhaps the plants and trees would have time to grow and mature, and the fishermen could wait for a catch before it was night again. He told his grandmother of his plan. At first, she feared for his life and tried to dissuade him; but when he begged her not to stop him, she gave him a magic stick and a piece of rope and fearfully bade him good-bye.

The next day, Ma-ui climbed to the top of Mount Haleakala to wait for the sun to rise. The trip was long and hard, but at last, Ma-ui stood where he could see the day break. When the first ray of sun appeared on the mountaintop, Ma-ui jumped high in the air. Quickly, he threw his rope around the ray and wrestled with it. Finally, with the help of his magic stick, he mastered it and tied it to the twisted trunk of a tree. Then he made it promise to slow down, or he would not let it escape. The sun saw the magic stick in the small boy's hand and promised never to race across the skies over Hawaii again. From that day forth, the flowers blossomed, and the trees grew straight and tall. The fruit ripened on the vines, and the fishermen had time to catch the fish so that the people had plenty to eat again.

4

FROM MOVEMENT
TO MIME

Pantomime is the art of conveying ideas without words. Children enjoy pantomime, which is an excellent way to introduce creative drama to the young child. Since many of her thoughts are spoken entirely through the body, the 5- or 6-year-old finds pantomime to be a natural means of expression. Group pantomimes of the simplest sort challenge the imagination and sharpen awareness.

For older children, pantomime is advocated because it encourages the use of the entire body and relieves the players of having to think of dialogue. With older children, also, group pantomime should precede individual work. Familiar activities such as playing ball, flying kites, running for a bus, or hunting for a lost object get the group on its feet and moving freely. If the entire class works at one time, self-consciousness disappears, and involvement is hastened. About 15 or 20 minutes of this sort of activity, changed frequently enough to hold the group's interest, makes for relaxation and readiness to move on to a more challenging assignment.

Others for whom pantomime is especially satisfying are children who do not speak English or who have speech problems. The child who has an idea but not the words to express it can convey meaning, often very successfully, through body language. I have had speech-handicapped students of all ages present characters, stories, and ideas in pantomime with clarity and artistry. Another benefit, in addition to the obvious one of building self-confidence, is motivation for skill in the language arts.

Having succeeded in sign language, children are encouraged to express themselves in words and writing as well.

Pantomime, incidentally, has become a familiar art form in the past 10 or 15 years. One of the benefits of television is the opportunity it affords all persons to enjoy the performing arts, including skilled professional mime.

PRACTICAL CONSIDERATIONS

CLASS SIZE

While movement classes can be carried on successfully with almost any number, pantomime requires a group of no more than 15 to 20 participants. If a class is very large, the teacher should make every effort to divide it, so that half the group is involved in another activity at that hour. Pantomime demands individual attention, and every child should be ensured the opportunity of participation each time the class meets. This is true whatever the age level, for growth results from repeated experiences that increase in difficulty.

LENGTH OF CLASS PERIOD

The length and frequency of class meetings depend on the situation and the age of the players. With very young children, daily classes for 10 to 15 minutes are ideal, whereas with older children, 2 or 3 meetings a week for 45 to 60 minutes work well. Some schools schedule drama classes only once a week; this is less desirable but may be the only possible arrangement. High-school students and young adults can be absorbed for as long as two hours, but in general, more frequent meetings of shorter length are preferable for children of the middle grades.

In schools in which creative drama is a part of the curriculum, the teacher can look forward to regular meetings throughout the year. Where it is not, it is up to the classroom teacher to introduce it whenever and however possible. It probably will be handled in connection with other subjects, which, if imaginatively done, can be of value as a tool for teaching and a creative experience for the class.

PLAYING SPACE

A stage is generally used for formal rehearsals, whereas a large room is more desirable for creative drama. If a large room is not available, a classroom in which all the chairs have been pushed aside will do. Space makes for freedom; a small or cramped area inhibits it. As was said in

Chapter 3, however, too large an area can present other problems, particularly for a beginning or an uncontrolled group. Boundaries are needed, as the leader soon discovers; there is greater freedom where there are clear boundaries of both time and space than where there are neither. An auditorium with a stage and chairs is least desirable as a playing space for a beginning group of any age, since it inevitably leads to a concept of performance with stage techniques before the players are ready for it. Under any circumstances, seating children on the floor in a semicircle so that all can see, hear, and be heard is the most satisfactory arrangement.

SOUND AND MOTION STORIES

Joanna Kraus, who devised the technique of the so-called sound and motion story, has provided a helpful approach to pantomime. It requires minimal participation, yet involves the players in describing action through the use of the body and some limited sound while seated. It also provides a means of participation in a room where the desks are fastened to the floor. The imagination is stimulated, creating some freedom within the boundaries of the space, time, or ability of the class to handle more demanding material. If a class enjoys sound and motion stories, the teacher can find stories that lend themselves to the technique and can mark suitable places for the participation. The story in Activity 4.1 is loved by children in the middle grades. Perhaps because the story is modern, or a contrast to the folk and fairy tales with which they are familiar, the children enjoy a situation that they can easily visualize.

SENSORY IMAGES

With a sound and motion story as a warm-up, the class is now ready for some specific exercises involving the five senses (Activities 4.2–4.5). They can be done on any level; the results will reflect the players' own experiences. It is sensory memory that we are interested in, rather than skill. Our lives are enriched by so much that we take for granted—our five senses.

ACTIONS IN PANTOMIME

There is no right or wrong order and no prescribed length of time to spend on any one activity. Generally speaking, the older the players,

Professionals teach children the art of mime. (Courtesy of Nancy Weiss McQuide, Milwaukee Imagination Theatre)

the longer their attention span. A pantomime that is guaranteed to capture the interest of everyone, regardless of age, is that of making or doing something (Activity 4.6). In the beginning, the teacher will offer suggestions, but most fourth graders have good ideas of their own.

Pantomimes of activities will grow more complicated and more interesting when players put them into new situations, such as those suggested in Activity 4.7.

EMOTIONS IN PANTOMIME

Feelings are bound to creep into the situations. The teacher may want to discuss feelings at this point in preparation for the next step. What feelings does the class think of? Their responses often include many more than were expected. Anger, fear, hatred, sorrow, happiness, excitement, pride, curiosity, vanity, anticipation, and depression are some that I have heard children of 9 and 10 describe. This is a good time to do some pantomimes in which strong feelings are motivation for action or are involved in the situations (Activity 4.8).

MOOD AND PANTOMIME

Mood can be created in countless ways, including the use of pictures, colors, light, music, and rhythms. The following ideas have been put into practice successfully with widely varying results.

The teacher selects a picture or photograph with people in it that will evoke a strong emotional reaction. If the picture is realistic, the teacher might, after all in the group have had a chance to look at it closely, ask such questions as:

1. Who is in the picture?
2. Why do you think this person is there?
3. What is he or she doing? feeling? Why?

The discussion that results will lead into possibilities for pantomime or even improvisation, if the group is ready for it. A story can be built from the meanings and mood that the children find in the picture.

Instead of a composition in which persons are represented, a picture of a place may be shown. Country roads, city streets, the platform of a railroad station, a deserted house, a stretch of empty beach, woodlands—all are springboards if the mood evoked is one that kindles the emotions and arouses the curiosity.

1. Where do you think this is?
2. Why is no one around?
3. What feelings do you have when you look at it?
4. What is there about it that makes you feel this way?

After some discussion, the leader will be ready to continue with questions leading to a scene laid in the place portrayed.

1. Who might come along?
2. Where are they going?
3. Do they meet anyone?
4. What do they talk about? do? feel?

In very little time, most groups will people the canvas with characters, often involving them in an imaginative situation laid in the scene depicted. For example, a deserted house could take the group in several directions. It might be the site of buried treasure (still a favorite theme of 8- to 10-year-olds), important documents, or a fascinating archeological discovery. It might be the home that a family has had to leave sorrowfully. Why? What has happened? Perhaps a son or daughter returns to say a last good-bye. Perhaps he or she meets a friend or finds something left behind, something meaningful. It might be the home of a famous man, who has come back after an absence of many years to see his old neighborhood once more.

1. Does anyone see him?
2. Does anyone recognize him? What happens if they do?
3. How does he feel about his home? the reception he is given?
4. How do his old neighbors react?

Instead of a realistic painting, an abstract composition might be shown. Color, dark and light contrasts, design, brush strokes—all will stimulate imaginative response. Not what the picture may *mean* objectively, but what it means to the viewer, is the aim of this exercise. Younger children tend to respond to an abstract composition more quickly than do older players, perhaps because they do not feel the need for realistic detail and appreciate the fact that the artist's expression is direct and free, as is their own. Movement, rather than story, will usually be the reaction to this experience, although some children move naturally from physical movement into character.

As stated in Chapter 3, music is a powerful stimulus to creativity. Use of rhythms to suggest kinds of movement, characters, or animals is a popular and highly successful way of working. From this to the heightening of characterization is a natural next step. Actually, only the beat of a drum is necessary, although music, particularly if the leader is able to play the piano, can enrich the activity. Recordings of orchestral music are extremely effective means of establishing mood and may be used as were pictures to stimulate the imagination, in a pattern of listening, reacting, and responding. A leader with no formal background in music can guide the group, not in the sense of a lesson in music appreciation, of course, but in the sense of encouraging listening and imaginative response. Again, young children seem to respond more spontaneously to music than do older children, who have learned to be concerned with structure, theme, and melody. Careful selection of the music to be used is necessary. Thereafter, the procedure is much the same as that followed with the pictures.

1. How does the music make you feel? Show us.
2. Where are you?
3. Who are you?
4. Are there others with you?
5. What is happening?

To create a story from music takes time, but after several experiences in listening and responding, the group will be ready to proceed with the creation of characters, an original situation suggested by the music, and perhaps some dialogue. Again, music is the way to induce the flow of creative energy and, because of its abstract quality, may produce a mood more readily than do other stimuli.

CHARACTERIZATION

Until now, we have been pantomiming activities and working to induce mood or feeling. The next step is characterization. Some participants already will have suggested characters different from themselves, but the teacher can use either these familiar exercises or new ones to start the group thinking in terms of characterization.

Again, situations involving groups are a good way to begin (Activity 4.9).

PANTOMIME SUGGESTED BY OTHER MEANS

A variation in pantomimic activities is the use of inanimate objects as a springboard. Most children love to *be* a mechanical device or familiar appliance and then ask the observers whether they can guess what they were. Activity 4.10 presents a different kind of problem solving, and often children from whom one least expects a creative response come up with wonderful ideas. The values lie in (1) sharpening the children's power of observation, (2) challenging the children's inventiveness, and (3) strengthening teamwork (when two or more children work together).

CREATING A PLAY FROM A SUGGESTION

Now that the class has had considerable experience in pantomime, it is ready to go a step further: the creation of a play, starting with a character, an idea, an object, or a location but not a plot. The children have had situations suggested to them, but Activity 4.11 leaves that part up to them.

Some teachers find that children's acting a story while it is read aloud is a good transition from pantomime to dramatization. Many stories can be handled in this way, although some lend themselves to it better than others. It is also an opportunity to enjoy good literature. By the time a group has worked on a story, it has heard the words many times and, it is hoped, has absorbed the meaning underlying them.

One of the best stories I have found for players of all ages is "Pandora's Box" (Activity 4.12). It is especially good to use at this juncture because movement and mime are important, yet the situation is one with which fifth and sixth graders can identify. Educationally, it is sound because it builds on the learnings dealt with so far—imagination, movement, pantomime, motivation for adding words—and provides an opportunity for discussion.

SUMMARY

Pantomime, while good practice at any time, is usually the most satisfactory way of beginning work in creative drama. Although it is not necessary to follow a prescribed program of exercises, it is easier for many groups to begin with familiar activities and then move on to mood or feeling and, finally, characterization. By starting with movement and then advancing to pantomime, the players learn to express themselves through bodily action, without the additional problem of dialogue. Younger children accept this as a natural means of expression, and older children and adults find it easier to begin with pantomime than with improvisation or formal acting. Pantomime sharpens perception and stimulates the imagination as the players try to remember how actions are done and what objects are like, in terms of size, weight, and shape. Recalling emotion demands concentration and involvement: How do you feel when you are happy, tired, angry, excited, or anxious? Close observation of people is a means of developing believable characters whose bearing, movement, and gestures belong to them and whose behavior seems appropriate. Although pantomime is considered here as a medium of expression, it may become an art form in itself. Mimes such as Marcel Marceau have demonstrated its power to communicate with people of all ages and backgrounds, when a high level of artistry is achieved.

ACTIVITY 4.1

SOUND AND MOTION STORIES

"The Night the Elephants Marched on New York" could tie in with a circus theme. Or it could be a stimulus to finding stories and local anecdotes in the news to write or tell and to discovering good places for sounds and actions. I like to use sound and motion stories for "starters," going on to improvisation and a total involvement after the limited participation required by this technique.

Objective: To involve the entire class in minimal participation in pantomime

Suggestions for the Teacher

Explain to the class what a "sound and motion story" is: *S* calls for sound; *M* calls for motion. When you raise your *right* hand, it means to make a sound that the word suggests. When you raise your *left* hand, it means to make a movement or mime an action that the word suggests. The class will get onto it quickly.

Read the story slowly, taking care to pause to allow the class to make the sound or the motion as it comes up. This is a story that children often want to repeat on another day.

THE NIGHT THE ELEPHANTS MARCHED ON NEW YORK*
JOANNA KRAUS

There they were, stranded in a railway yard in New Jersey, two hundred animals from Gambelli Brothers Circus.

Thirteen miles away in President Gambelli's New York City office, the phone rang. (S)

"What! What! I can barely hear you," President Gambelli yelled into the telephone.

From the other end of the wire came the sound of nineteen hungry elephants. (S) The chief animal trainer was trying to explain, but President Gambelli could only hear half of what he said.

". . . railway strike . . . in the yard at South Kearney, New Jersey . . . can't get the animals through to New York City . . . two o'clock opening tomorrow. . . ."

President Gambelli heard the roars of nine lions and fifteen tigers in the background. (S)

"I'll do what I can," called President Gambelli and hung up the receiver. (M)

* Joanna H. Kraus, *Sound and Motion Stories* (Rowayton, Conn.: New Plays, 1971), pp. 8–11.

He paced his office. On the wall was a large poster of a circus elephant which he knew thousands of school children had seen. He knew thousands of mothers, fathers, aunts, and uncles had bought tickets for the two o'clock performance of the Gambelli Brothers Circus.

Violetta, his assistant, rushed in with the morning papers and put them on his desk. He picked up the first newspaper. (M) "Rail Strike," announced the headlines. He picked up the second newspaper. (M) Large black letters spelled out the disaster. "Nationwide Rail Strike. Country Comes to a Halt."

"If the animals don't arrive on time, there won't be a circus," he said to Violetta. "Do you know there are over two hundred animals in the unit stranded in South Kearney, New Jersey!" Luigi Gambelli put his head in his hands. (M) How was he going to move two hundred animals by two o'clock tomorrow?

"We could put the smaller animals in vans, if we can find some," Violetta suggested, "but eight-thousand-pound elephants . . . I don't know. There won't be a van big enough anywhere."

"It sounded like the jungle when the chief trainer telephoned me. We've got to do something fast," answered President Gambelli.

"JUNGLE! That's it. That's where they're from—any kid knows that," said Violetta excitedly. "Well, it's only about thirteen miles from South Kearney to midtown Manhattan. In India the elephants walk farther than that."

"But they don't have rush hour traffic in the jungle," he reminded Violetta. Then Luigi Gambelli threw back his shoulders and looked sternly at the pile of newspapers on his desk. (M) "Gambelli Brothers Circus has never missed a performance, and it's not going to now! Get the governor on the phone, and then the mayor! I will *not* disappoint all those children."

The governor found vans to carry the smaller animals. He authorized a yellow permit slip for the larger animals to march to Lincoln Tunnel. (M) The mayor authorized a blue permit slip for the animals to finish their march to Madison Square Garden on the public streets of New York City.

Late that night the gorillas, lions, panthers, and tigers were sent in huge vans across the Hudson River over the George Washington Bridge.

President Gambelli, the chief animal trainer, and his assistants lined up the elephants, trunk to tail, and chained them together. As they worked they fastened each chain carefully. (M) When the elephants moved, you could hear the clinking of the heavy metal chains. (S) At the end of the line was a baby elephant. Tied to her tail were a zebra, a llama, and a Shetland pony.

The chief animal trainer carefully guided the lead elephant by the ear with his bull hook. (M)

A few miles from Lincoln Tunnel, a grocer rushed out to the street. "Luigi Gambelli," he said, "I heard about the animal march on the radio. You and the elephants are invited to have supper in my store." Nineteen elephants flapped their ears happily, as the grocer and his two children fed them thirty-nine cents a pound peanuts and fed carrots to the other animals.

A little later Miss Page, the Lincoln Tunnel toll booth attendant, waved hello to the motorists she recognized who drove through the tunnel every night at that hour. (M)

It was nearly eleven o'clock. Soon she could go home too. At her feet her pet dog, Bouncer, was dozing and dreaming of a bone. (S) For a few minutes there were no cars and she glanced at the new report forms she had to fill out. After "Accidents" she wrote "None." After "Unusual Events" she sighed and wrote "None."

Suddenly Bouncer pricked up his ears and let out a low growl. (S) Miss Page looked up startled. (M) She listened carefully, then looked uncomfortably about. (M) She could not see a car or a person. But way down at the end of the tunnel there was a noise that sounded like a movie she had just seen on television. The movie had been all about the jungle. The sound grew louder . . . and louder, as it got nearer and nearer. (S)

A minute later President Gambelli, the chief animal trainer, and his assistants arrived at the toll booth. Miss Page could only stare at them. President Gambelli took off his hat. (M) "Gambelli Brothers Circus," he explained. "They're part of a mixed animal act," the chief animal trainer added.

Miss Page looked quickly through the pages of *Traffic Rules, Regulations and Toll Rates*. There were twelve categories of vehicles in the little green book. "But there's nothing here about elephants," she told them. Then she turned back to the page on Class 2 Vehicles: "Animals, ridden, led or herded, and motorcycles." "Fifty cents an elephant," she said.

President Gambelli counted out nine crisp new dollar bills. (M) The chief animal trainer counted out five dimes. (M) "What about the zebra, the llama, and the Shetland pony?" the animal trainer asked.

Miss Page and Bouncer leaned out of the booth. (M) Neither had ever seen a zebra, a llama, or a Shetland pony before. Timidly,

Miss Page put out her hand and patted the pony. (M) "Aw, let them have a free ride," she said. "I know there's nothing in the regulations about zebras, llamas, and Shetland ponies."

After they had thanked her, they marched away. Miss Page could hear the elephants trumpeting at the end of the tunnel. (S) She picked up her report. Next to "Unusual Events," she scratched out the word "None." (M) Miss Page wrote rapidly. (M) She could still hear the sounds of nineteen elephants, one zebra, one llama, and one Shetland pony marching away. (S) "They'll never believe it," she said to Bouncer.

The next day at two o'clock exactly, Gambelli Brothers Circus opened. There were loud trumpets as the house lights dimmed. (S) The news photographers snapped pictures of Luigi Gambelli standing with the mayor and the governor. (M) President Gambelli told the press, "Gambelli Brothers Circus has never missed a performance."

ACTIVITY 4.2

USING OUR FIVE SENSES

Objective: To discover our senses by imagining situations in which we use them

Suggestions for the Teacher

One way of beginning is with a general discussion of the ways in which we find out what is going on around us. What are our five senses? (Sight, hearing, touch, smell, taste)

Try the following exercises in groups.

1. *Sight:* Hide something small in the room. Then have the class look for it.
2. *Hearing:* Ask the children to listen for a minute to all the sounds they can hear, inside and outside the room. They will be amazed at the number of sounds they pay no attention to when they are not listening.
3. *Touch:* Have them touch as many surfaces as possible within range of where they are sitting. Describe them.
4. *Smell:* See what, if any, smells they detect. There probably will be some that they normally disregard, such as lunch being prepared, chalk dust, cleaning fluid, and gasoline if the room is near a parking lot.
5. *Taste:* The last is difficult if there is no food in the room. It may have to be done purely in pantomime, recalling taste. In other words, imagine that you are eating an ice-cream cone, a popcorn ball, and so on.

After the children have done the group pantomimes, try some individual ones that explore the sense of sight.

1. Imagine that you have dropped a straight pin on the rug and try to find it.
2. Look for a box of cookies that your mother says she put in the cupboard. You may have one when you find the box.
3. Look for your little black kitten, who is hiding somewhere in the living room.
4. You cannot find a library book that must be returned today. Look for it in your room.
5. Look at a display of fireworks from the window in your house. It grows larger and more colorful each time a rocket goes up.

ACTIVITY 4.3

THE SENSE OF HEARING

Objective: To explore the sense of hearing through pantomime

Suggestions for the Teacher

You are continuing the topic of the five senses. Now you will explore hearing through individual pantomimes.

1. You think that you hear a kitten mewing somewhere near you. Listen and try to discover the direction from which it is coming; then go find the kitten.
2. You are listening to the radio and hear three pieces: the first, you know and like very much; the second is very strange, and you do not know whether you are going to like it; the third, you do not like. Change the order to see if we can tell which is which.
3. You are reading quietly when there is a sudden crash outside in the street! What is it? Go to the window and find out.
4. Someone calls you on the telephone. You know the voice but cannot remember whose it is. Let us see you finally realize who is calling.
5. Your mother calls you from work or wherever she is and tells you to run an errand for her before she gets home. You have a poor connection and have a hard time getting the message.

ACTIVITY 4.4

THE SENSE OF TOUCH

Objective: To explore the sense of touch through pantomime

Suggestions for the Teacher

Explore touch through individual pantomimes.

1. You go into an empty room and try to find your cardigan sweater.
2. You are blindfolded and are playing a game in which you must pin a tail on a donkey where the right place is marked by a small piece of felt.

ACTIVITY 4.5

___

THE SENSE OF SMELL

Objective: To explore the sense of smell through pantomime

Suggestions for the Teacher

Try this group of individual pantomimes for the sense of smell.

1. You smell smoke. Is it a fireplace? a fire in a building? your imagination?
2. You are passing a bakery, and some delicious cakes and cookies are just coming out of the oven. Let us see your reaction.
3. Your mother is making something for dinner that you have never had before. You first smell it, then try to determine whether you know what it is, and finally try to decide whether you think you will like it. What is your conclusion?
4. You are "sniffing" perfumes at the drugstore counter, where they are placed for customers. There is some difference among the various ones but not a lot. Let us see which ones you prefer.
5. Make up an odor to see if we can tell what it is by your reactions to it.

By now, the class is getting used to expressing reactions through mime. Have them prepare pantomimes of their own for the sense of taste. Have the observers guess what the mime is tasting.

ACTIVITY 4.6

PERFORMING AN ACTION IN PANTOMIME

Objective: To help players sustain attention and organize ideas as they pantomime an action

Suggestions for the Teacher

Have the children push back their chairs in order to create a large playing space in the middle of the room. Suggest some of the following activities, which are designed for individuals.

1. Trying on a Hallowe'en costume
2. Blowing up balloons for a party
3. Gathering leaves for a science project
4. Wrapping a package
5. Carrying home a shopping bag with several breakable items in it (for example, eggs)

Next suggest some activities that involve two characters.

1. A clerk and a customer in a clothing store
2. A police officer trying to show a traveler who does not speak English how to get to a bus uptown
3. A shoe salesperson and a customer, who is fussy
4. Two children having a picnic lunch in the park
5. Two children playing ball in the street

When working with children in inner-city neighborhoods, suggest activities that are most common to those environments. Also, when working with country children, avoid activities that may be unknown to them. Besides giving them material with which they are familiar, this procedure helps children to regard their own experiences and communities more positively.

ACTIVITY 4.7

___

TELLING A STORY IN PANTOMIME

Objective: To carry "Performing an Action in Pantomime" further by creating a simple plot for which the action pantomimes were a preparation

Suggestions for the Teacher

Have the children push back their chairs in order to create a playing space in the middle of the room. Suggest the following activities, which are to be done by two or three children. They will need some planning, so give the groups a few minutes in which to organize the details and decide who will play what parts.

1. Your class is having a party. You are on the committee to prepare for it. What is the holiday or special occasion? What kind of decorations, refreshments, and games are you having? You finish and are pleased with the results just as your class returns from gym.

2. You and one or two of your friends are on your way to school when you see a puppy that has been hurt. If you stop to get help or take the puppy to a vet, you will be tardy. On the other hand, if you go off and leave it, no one may come along to take care of it. This is a problem; what do you do?

3. A fussy customer comes into a shoe store. The salesperson is having a difficult time trying to find out exactly what he or she wants. While the customer is there, a child comes in and wants to see some shoes for camp. He or she is in a hurry, but the other customer is taking up so much time that the salesperson cannot pay attention to the child. How does it all turn out?

4. Two children are playing ball in the street. Suddenly, the ball bounces off the pavement and goes through a neighbor's window. The neighbor appears and is very angry. What happens?

5. You are in a gift shop with many breakable items. The shop is crowded, and somehow your sweater catches on a glass vase, which falls on the floor and breaks. The clerk comes over to see what happened. What do you do? How does it turn out?

ACTIVITY 4.8

EXPRESSING FEELINGS IN PANTOMIME

Objective: To express feelings in pantomime

Suggestions for the Teacher

Have the children move the chairs irregularly about the room. (Irregular placement will stimulate the imagination.)

Read the situation slowly, so that the class hears and understands what it is going to do. Any number of children can take part in the pantomimes, but it is wise to limit groups to five or six. The more groups there are, the more difficult it is to avoid confusion.

1. A group of children are in an elevator in a large department store. They push the button for the main floor, but instead of stopping there, the elevator goes down to the subbasement. At first the children are frightened. Then they become curious and cautiously begin to explore the halls and large storage rooms. They find boxes of window decorations, Christmas decorations, manikins, bolts of material, and goods sold in the store. Suddenly, a man calls out, "Who's down here?" It's a maintenance man, who has come to check for any employees who may have been in the subbasement when the elevator went out of service. He sees the children and leads them up a staircase to the main floor.

2. A group of people get into an elevator in a big downtown building. Suddenly, it stops between floors. Their poise turns to fear as the operator pushes one button and then another—and nothing happens. Suddenly, she gets the elevator started, and it takes the passengers to the ground level.

3. You are a group of children who come into your schoolroom one morning and find a monkey scampering about. First you are startled, and then amused by his antics. Finally, the man who has lost him comes in and catches him, taking him away. You are sorry to see him go as he waves good-bye to you from his owner's shoulder.

4. You are sitting in a movie. First you are watching a very dull short subject. How do you feel when it seems to be going on forever? Then it changes to a hilariously funny cartoon. How do you react? At last, the feature begins, and you are absorbed.

ACTIVITY 4.9
_____

CREATING A CHARACTER IN PANTOMIME

Objective: To work on characterization

Suggestions for the Teacher

Until now, characterization has not been stressed in our emphasis on action, sensory memory, feelings, and mood. The following situations stress characters whom the children will enjoy creating.

1. You are a group of people waiting for a guide to a city monument or a place of historical interest. (Select a site in your community with which the children are familiar.) You represent visitors from various cities throughout The United States and perhaps abroad. Let us see if we can determine who you are and perhaps even where you come from.

2. You are customers in a toy department, doing your Christmas shopping. One of you is a grandmother buying a toy for her granddaughter, aged three; another is a father buying skates for his son; a third is a girl who has saved her babysitting money to buy a game for her sister. Others are buying gifts under $5 for children in an orphanage, a hospital, or a community center. Decisions must be demonstrated and characters created by the ways you go about your shopping.

3. You are pilgrims who have gone to a shrine where, once a year, one wish is said to be granted. Decide who you are and what it is you want. You might be a crippled man who wants to walk again, a poet who wants very much to have her work published, or a young mother who wants her sick baby to be cured. (The teacher may wish to play with the group and be the statue at the shrine who indicates which wish is to be granted. This is a good situation to pantomime because it offers an opportunity to work on both characterization and strong motivation.)

Here are some individual pantomimes that stress character.

1. You are a robber who is entering a house at night. While you are there, the owners of the house return unexpectedly. You listen and finally make your escape, having stolen nothing.

2. You are a neighborhood gossip. You have a party line, and one of your favorite pastimes is listening in on other people's conversations. This afternoon, you hear some very good news, some bad news, and then some remarks about yourself and your habit of listening in on your neighbors. How do you react? What do you do?

3. You are a child who has wanted a dog for a long time. One day, you overhear your parents talking about it in the next room. Your mother does not want a dog, but your father thinks that it is time you had one. They discuss reasons for and against getting you a dog. How do you react to their arguments, and what is the final decision?

4. Two of you are a customer and a storekeeper in a shop in a foreign country. You do not know each other's language. The customer decides, in advance, on three things he needs to buy and tries to convey what they are to the clerk, through pantomime. Who are you? What are the three things? How does it turn out? (This is an exercise that the entire class can do in pairs.)

Another exercise is to do one action as three different people.

1. You go into a restaurant to order a meal. Do it as:
   a. A teen-age boy who is very hungry
   b. A middle-aged woman who has very little appetite and sees nothing on the menu that she wants
   c. A very poor man who is hungry but must limit his choice to what he can afford
2. You are trying on dresses in a shop. Do it as:
   a. A very fat woman who has trouble being fitted
   b. A young girl who is looking for a pretty dress to wear to a dance
   c. A secretary who is trying to find the most appropriate dress to wear on her first day at work in a new job
3. You are visiting an art museum. Do it as:
   a. An artist who knows the painter whose work is on display
   b. A woman who thinks she should go to museums but does not appreciate the pictures
   c. An elderly man who has been ill and is enjoying visiting his favorite museum for the first time in many months
4. You are exercising in a gymnasium. Do it as:
   a. A young woman who loves athletics
   b. A fat man whose doctor has advised him to exercise to lose weight
   c. A child who has never seen gymnasium equipment before

ACTIVITY 4.10

CREATING INANIMATE OBJECTS IN PANTOMIME

Objective: To invent from a different kind of springboard—the inanimate

Suggestions for the Teacher

Some exercises are fun to do and stimulate inventiveness, but they have nothing to do with familiar actions, moods, or characters. The following ideas are good as a change and may be introduced any time you feel that the group needs a new type of stimulation.

1. Each person in the group represents an item found in a kitchen: a toaster, a knife, a pancake turner, a dishwasher, etc. Some items may require two or three players. Imagination and ingenuity are stimulated by thinking in a new direction. There is no right or wrong!

2. Assign each person a color and ask that it be suggested by means of movement, attitude, or characterization. This, incidentally, may be followed with an improvisation in which the color becomes a person. For example, Mr. White, Mrs. Black, Mrs. Blue, Mr. Green, Mr. Red, and Mrs. Yellow might be people at a reception. What are they like? How do they talk? How can we distinguish one from another?

3. Each person selects a property and acts according to what it suggests to him or her. The following are usually good for stimulating imaginative reactions: a gnarled stick, a ruler, a gold bracelet, a broken dish, a sponge. Again, the players do not use the properties; they become characters suggested by the objects' qualities.

4. Have the group listen to orchestral music. Suggest that the children try to identify the various instruments. Then have them *be* the instruments—not the musicians playing them, but the instruments themselves. If they are enjoying the exercise, suggest that each child select a different instrument to be until a whole orchestra has been assembled. This activity probably will not last longer than one session, but it is fun and a means of stretching the imagination.

5. Discuss growth and growing. It is suggested that the group members conceive of themselves as seeds, buried deep in the earth. It is dark, and they are quiet. Then spring arrives, with rain, sun, and wind. What happens to the seeds? Do they break through the earth? Can we feel them push and grow? As summer comes, the plants grow taller. What are they going to be—flowers or trees? tall or short? bushy? weak or strong? Feel the warm rain, the hot sun, the breeze blowing, the final push to maturity. Poetry written about the springtime ties in well with this exercise.

6. Either you or the class composes a story in which a variety of sounds are listed and described. It is great fun to act out the sounds and/or what is making them. For example, one child wrote the following narration for the others to act.

I woke up in the morning to the sound of my ALARM CLOCK going off. I opened my CLOSET DOOR, which squeaked. Then I turned on the FAUCET, and the water made a rushing sound in the sink. After that, I ran downstairs to breakfast. The coffee was PERKING in the pot. The BACON was frying in a pan. The TOAST popped up in the toaster. The RADIO was playing, but the MUSIC was drowned out by the STATIC.

Outside, I heard my father MOWING the lawn, and an AIR-PLANE was flying low overhead. It was going to be hot, and my mother turned on the FAN. Suddenly, down the street, I heard the noise of the SCHOOL BUS, its engine chugging. I ran out the front DOOR, which slammed, and I ran down the walk, my SHOES clattering. My DOG barked as I climbed aboard a very noisy BUS.

Such an exercise as this stimulates awareness as well as imagination in the attempt to suggest or reproduce sounds and the objects making them.

7. Mirror images are popular and great fun for actors of all ages. Two players face each other, one being a person and the other, the mirror image. Whatever the person does, the image must reproduce precisely. With practice, this can become a skilled performance, challenging to the players and fascinating to the observers. Greater awareness as well as the ability to work together are developed in the process.

ACTIVITY 4.11
_____

CREATING A PLOT IN PANTOMIME

Objective: To create a plot with characters who motivate the action

Suggestions for the Teacher

The following situations are suggested as starting places to set children thinking. The less experienced the group, the more preliminary work in the form of pantomime and discussion is needed. Group pantomimes related to the situation stimulate movement, whereas discussion of the topic and questions about it help to stir the imagination. When all the children seem to be ready, divide the class into several small groups to develop simple narratives. Each group will come up with its own ideas about plot and characters. This can be a one-time activity or the beginning of a creative play done entirely in pantomime.

1. A beggar comes to the door
2. A house is for sale
3. The tallest sunflower in town
4. A magic sandal
5. A bracelet in an alley
6. A puppy in a box left in a doorway
7. The surprise in a box of Crackerjacks

TELLING A STORY IN PANTOMIME

"Pandora's Box" may be part of a unit on ancient Greece and Rome, or it may be used simply because it is a good story and involves so much movement and mime. The amount of background the children have will determine how much explanation is needed before reading the story.

Objective: To enact a story while the teacher reads it and then engage in a group discussion before replaying

Suggestions for the Teacher

Read the story aloud, and then follow with a class discussion of the "evils" and troubles that human beings experience.

1. Ask the class what evil spirits are in the box.
2. Then plan how the evil spirits will escape. Will they jump out? run out? move out slowly, suspicious of Pandora? How do they move? act?
3. Have the children try being the evil spirits, escaping and running through the room, spreading the troubles that they represent.
4. Try adding sounds to the movement and speech appropriate to the characters.
5. When the structure and characters seem to be well in hand, the children can decide what roles they would like to take and enact them.

Discussion and a second playing, changing parts, should follow. The second playing usually brings more detail and a deeper understanding. Because this is a favorite story with great possibilities for discussion, it can easily be extended, leading into questions of disobedience or wrongdoing and its consequences. Children, who are naturally curious, identify with Pandora's plight, and the simple plot makes it an easy story for improvisation.

A discussion of Hope is appropriate for some groups. If so, talk about:

1. What we mean by a *hopeful* feeling. Is it the same as a *wish*?
2. What have you *hoped* for?
3. How does *hope* help people?
4. Why do you think that Hope was in the box with the evils?

PANDORA'S BOX

The people of ancient Greece had many gods, who, they believed, lived on Mount Olympus. When the people needed an explanation for something they could not understand—war, disease, storms, or unusual happenings—they thought that the gods were angry and had caused them. Indeed, they made their gods very much like human beings. Some were kind; some, wise; others, quick-tempered, spiteful, and jealous. The most powerful of the gods was Zeus, the king.

One day, Zeus looked down on the earth and decided to create a place of beauty and order where human beings, animals, and all growing things could live together in peace. The first two people he created were called Epimetheus and Pandora. They were given a beautiful garden in which to live and were told to enjoy themselves. There was one thing, Zeus said, that they must not do and that was to open a small box, which he left in their care. The two promised, and all went well for a while. Often, however, Pandora would look at the box, wondering what might be inside and why she was forbidden to open it. One day, when Epimetheus was out, she could stand it no longer. She bent over the box and, to her amazement, heard strange noises coming from inside it. She thought she heard voices calling to her, "Let us out! Let us out, Pandora! Please, let us out!"

"How I should like to know what is inside," thought Pandora. "I can't see what harm there would be in taking just one little peek."

Cautiously, she opened the lid a crack. Then, without warning, dozens of ugly little creatures flew out of the box. Disease, war, anger, jealousy, deceit, hunger—every evil in the world was let loose.

"Oh, what have I done!" cried Pandora. She tried to force them back into the box, but it was too late. They only flew at her angrily and refused to be shut up again. Hearing the commotion, Zeus looked down from Mount Olympus. When he saw what had happened, he was very angry. "Pandora and Epimetheus, you have disobeyed me. You have done the one thing I asked you never to do. You must leave the garden and never return."

Pandora and Epimetheus were very sad. Then Pandora looked at her husband and said, "Do you suppose there might be something else in the box that would help us? Something more than evil spirits?"

"The harm has been done," replied Epimetheus. "You may as well look again."

So once more, Pandora went to the box and raised the lid. A white figure slowly rose from the bottom of the box and spoke to her gently. "I am Hope," said the little creature. "No matter what evils overtake you, know that I will always be here to comfort and help you."

And that was how it happened that Hope came into the world to give comfort and strength when bad times seem too much for human beings to bear.

5
IMPROVISATION: CHARACTERS MOVE AND SPEAK

I hear; I forget—I see; I remember—I do; I understand.

—CHINESE PROVERB

Improvisation is difficult at first. Dialogue does not flow easily, even when it has been preceded by much work in pantomime and a thorough understanding of the situation or story. With practice, however, words do begin to come, and young players discover the possibilities of character development when oral language is added. Dialogue is apt to be brief and scanty at first, but usually begins to flow rapidly once children become accustomed to it. Players age 7 and older enjoy the opportunity of using words to further a story and more fully describe the characters they are portraying. It is a good idea to begin with simple situations in order to get accustomed to using dialogue before attempting more ambitious material.

Many of the situations suggested in Chapter 4 can be used for improvisation, although they were designed with movement in mind. Frequently, children begin to add dialogue of their own free will, as they feel the need to express ideas in words. When this happens, the leader accepts it as a natural progression from one step to the next. Young children, players for whom English is a second language, or older students who lack self-confidence usually wait until they are urged to try adding dialogue. The teacher should not expect too much in the beginning and should accept whatever is offered, knowing that more will be forthcoming the next time. I recall a sixth-grade class that was acting *The Song of Roland*. Although the children were fond of the story and well oriented to the background, the first time they played it, one scene went like this:

Hello, Roland.

Will you marry me?

Why, Roland, I'd love to.

The final playing, after several children had tried and discussed it, was a charming scene with all the necessary exposition and appropriate vocabulary.

IMPROVISATIONS BASED ON SITUATIONS

Even the simplest stories present complications for the beginner, so some preliminary exercises are suggested (Activity 5.1). The purpose is to give emphasis to dialogue rather than to the memorization of plot. Just one scene of a story often can be improvised to advantage.

Sounds, incidentally, can stimulate imagination and lead the listener to the creation of an improvisation. For example, the teacher can beat a drum or tambourine, knock, ring bells, or make any other kind of sound. This works particularly well with younger children, but is also a good exercise to use from time to time with those who are older.

IMPROVISATIONS BASED ON OBJECTS

Not only situations and stories motivate improvisation; some very imaginative results can be obtained by the use of objects or properties.

An improvisation with unusual interest was developed from a whistle by a very imaginative group of 10 year olds. They decided that it was a policeman's whistle, made of silver and bearing an inscription. They laid the scene in his home on the day of his retirement from the force; the characters were the policeman, his wife, and his grandson. The policeman came in that evening, took off his whistle, looked at it nostalgically for a long time, and then laid it on the supper table. His grandson, coming into the room at that point, begged him to tell the story again of how he had received it. As the story began, there was a flashback scene, in which the policeman was rescuing a child from burning in a bonfire. He was honored for his bravery and given an inscribed silver whistle, which he treasured for the rest of his life. At the end of the story, the flashback scene faded, and some neighbors came in with a cake and presents for him. The improvisation was effective both in its good dramatic structure and in the reality of the characterizations.

Not every group is able to develop an improvisation to this degree, but occasionally one will; when it happens, it is an inspiration to the rest of the class. Incidentally, such an imaginative improvisation is almost always the result of the play's being based on familiar material so that the players are sure of the dialogue and can identify easily with the characters. Again, respect for the children's background and acceptance of the ideas that come out of it not only make for comfort, but also bring forth ideas that the teacher probably would not have thought of. Children of foreign background have a wealth of material on which to draw, but too often, it remains an untapped source because they have been made to feel that it is unworthy of consideration. Both the stories they have been told and the details of their everyday life contain the basic ingredients of drama. For example, one group of boys, who lived in a housing project, played a scene in an elevator. The situation was simple but had reality. Two boys, having nothing to do, decided to ride up and down in the elevator, angering the tenants and almost causing a tragedy because one man on a high floor was ill and waiting for the doctor. The teacher did not know whether this had been an actual experience, but the situation contained reality, humor, and drama, with characters who were believable.

One final example of the use of properties was an improvisation done by a group of high-school girls. They were asked by the teacher to empty their purses and select the six most unusual or interesting objects. The objects they finally chose were a newspaper clipping, a snapshot, a lipstick in a Japanese case, a key ring with a red charm, a pocketknife, and a purse flashlight. Within minutes, they created a mystery, prompted by and making use of every one of the properties they had selected. There were six players, and their preparation time was approximately 10 minutes. Sixth graders with some experience in improvisation probably could do this, although it would be less well developed and finished than the same activity handled by teen-agers.

Activity 5.2 suggests improvisations based on objects.

IMPROVISATIONS FROM COSTUMES

Similar to the use of objects or props, and equally effective in stimulating ideas, is the use of articles of clothing. Such garments as hats, capes, aprons, shawls, tail coats, and jewelry suggest different kinds of characters. Innumerable examples could be given of situations that grew from characters developed this way. For example, to one boy, a tail coat suggested a musician who was down on his luck and playing his violin on a street corner for pennies. A feathered hat helped a little girl create a lady of fashionable pretensions and become a comic character in her extravagant dress and poor taste. A shawl suggested witches, grandmothers, people in disguise, or a scene set in very cold weather.

It is wise for the teacher on any level, working anywhere, to keep a supply of simple and sturdy costumes available for this kind of use. If children experience difficulty in getting into character, a piece of a costume may sometimes be all that is needed to provide the necessary incentive. Costume used in this way is not dressing the part, but is an aid to imaginative thinking (Activity 5.3).

IMPROVISATIONS BASED ON REAL PEOPLE

This is another approach to creating characters: from real people (Activity 5.4). Even fourth graders are amazingly perceptive, and fifth- and sixth-grade children are quick to think of persons to study and impersonate.

One girl offered as a character a woman who served the hot vegetables in the school cafeteria. Although the woman was bad-tempered, the girl had observed that she always was extremely generous in her servings and did her job more efficiently than anyone else. The group that chose her as a heroine for their story decided that she might have been a refugee. Because she had experienced hunger during that period in her life, she was determined that all plates would be generously filled, now that food was available. Her irritability they attributed to her own unhappy experiences and her separation from her family. The scene that the children improvised, using this particular character, was thoughtful, sympathetic, and interesting.

Another improvisation based on an actual person was the story of an elderly woman whom one child noticed every day, sitting on the front porch of her house. The group that chose her decided that she was really very rich but miserly and was saving her money for the day when her son came home. They agreed that he had gone into the army several years before and had not returned. Although he had been reported missing, his mother clung to the hope that he would come back some day, and so she sat on the porch—waiting by day and counting her money by night. The group decided to have him return, so the story had a happy ending.

A fantasy was the result of another character study. Two of the children described a well-dressed old man whom they saw coming home every morning around eight o'clock. They decided that he must have an interesting occupation and so made him a wizard, who helped the good people and punished the evil through the power of his magic cane. This became a modern fairy tale filled with highly imaginative incidents.

IMPROVISATIONS BASED ON CLUES

For groups that enjoy improvisation and have become good at it, some more demanding suggestions are given in Activity 5.5. The teacher may not want to introduce them until later. Making up original dialogue, in addition to creating plots, is difficult, and the springboards based on clues require more experience than many intermediate-grade children have. Classes that are ready will enjoy these mind stretchers.

GROUP IMPROVISATIONS

Improvisations for two or three children strengthen partner work. Activities 5.6 and 5.7 suggest a few, but the teacher can make up others related to the particular interests or experiences of the children. The community also makes a difference in how well the class can handle them or how much interest they hold.

IMPROVISATIONS SUGGESTED
BY CUSTOMS, TRADITIONS, AND HOLIDAYS

Anecdotes and traditions can also be used to stimulate thinking. National and regional customs often have interesting stories or personalities connected with them. If the teacher or even the students bring in material, it may contain dramatic possibilities.

One club group showed an unusual interest in holidays, so the teacher used this as a springboard for the entire year. She brought in stories about Hallowe'en, Thanksgiving, New Year's Day, Ground Hog Day, St. Valentine's Day, St. Patrick's Day, April Fools' Day, Memorial Day, and the Fourth of July. Sometimes the group acted out the stories she read to them; sometimes they made up stories of their own, suggested by the occasion. One day, they observed that there was no holiday in August. The result was an original play, which they called *A Holiday for August*. It was to be a festival of children's games, which developed into a particularly attractive summer pageant. August was the narrator, and he began by telling of his disappointment that no one had ever thought to put a holiday in his month. At the conclusion, he expressed his joy that the children had made him special with a festival of games played in his honor.

Television, films, and open discussion of heretofore taboo topics have affected the subject matter that has come into creative-drama sessions in recent years. While most children still enjoy working on the material the teacher brings in, their own experiences and problems often surface when they are given a chance to express their own ideas. Broken homes, divorce, racial discrimination, illness and death, values, and social issues of all kinds can be disturbing problems to children, problems that the leader must be prepared to deal with if or when they come up. This is to be expected in the fourth, fifth, and sixth grades. Activity 5.8 deals with issues of responsibility and of social concern.

"SEALED ORDERS"

"Sealed Orders" is great fun for children of the middle grades because of the mystery that surrounds it. Situations are written on slips of paper and put in a box. Each child pulls out a slip and has to obey the "sealed order" that he or she selects. For example, orders might be:

1. Pretend you are a burglar ordered by a gang to enter a house at night and find a valuable piece of jewelry. The owners are asleep in the house, so the job is dangerous.
2. Pretend you are a soldier who has been sent across enemy lines to secure a document for the government. Every step of the way is dangerous.
3. Pretend you are putting a gift in a box for a member of your family, who is asleep in a chair in the same room. It is his or her birthday, and the gift is a surprise, which you do not want to spoil.
4. Pretend your ball went over the fence into a yard guarded by a fierce dog. The dog is not in sight, and you hope that it is in the house; nevertheless, you must move quietly and with great caution in order to retrieve your ball without attracting attention.
5. Pretend you are on a treasure hunt along with several others. Suddenly, you spot the treasure but do not want anyone else to know where it is. Get it without their seeing you.

The more imaginative and "dangerous" the orders, the better the improvisation. If the class is large, it is difficult to think of enough different orders to go around. If you jot them down as you think of them, however, you will soon accumulate a supply. Children in the fifth and sixth grades often have wonderful ideas for orders. Suggest that they give you their ideas, and you will write them down; if the suggestions are not appropriate as written, you can rephrase or discuss them with the writers. In other words, help children to modify the order rather than reject their efforts. In this way, they will learn not only *what* works, but *why*.

ROLE PLAYING

Although role playing as therapy is not the job of the creative-drama teacher or the classroom teacher using creative-drama techniques, some teachers have tried it with reported success. The purpose is educative rather than therapeutic, and the situations examined are common to all. Human conflicts and the ways in which problems are solved can promote social growth. Family scenes, school situations, and playground incidents give opportunity for interaction and group discussion. Discussion is the most important aspect of role playing, according to some teachers, for it is during these periods that various points of view are presented and attitudes clarified. The teacher must accept all ideas, giving the boys and girls a chance to express themselves without fear of disapproval. He will pose such questions as: How do you think the father felt? the brother? the mother? What did the man next door think when you broke his window? How do you think he felt the third time it happened? If you were he, how would you feel?

Exchanging roles is a good way to put oneself in the shoes of another in order to understand a different point of view. One teacher gave a demonstration of role playing done with her group of junior-high-school girls, who lived in a neighborhood with a growing Puerto Rican population. The girls had had difficulty accepting the newcomers, and the teacher's introduction of role playing, as a way to help them understand the problem, led to the following impro-visation. The scene was the planning of a school party by a small clique. The committee wished to exclude the newcomers but could do so only by making them feel unwelcome. This led to a serious breakdown in group relations. The period spent in playing the situation reportedly did much to restore peace and communication. The problem was faced squarely, and the girls were able to discuss their own attitudes and feelings. Later on, when the improvisation was done as a demonstration for a class of university students, it made a tremendous impression. The insights expressed through the honesty of the players proved the value of the experiment. The teacher did not claim to be a therapist but was an intelligent and experienced classroom teacher who was deeply troubled about a situation that was interfering with the work of the class and the relations among the class members.

Peter Slade, in *Child Drama*, summarizes the use of role playing: "I would go so far as to say that one of the most important reasons for developing child drama in schools generally is not actually a therapeutic one but the even more constructive one of prevention."[1]

It must be pointed out that playing the part of a fictional character also demands identification. Exchange of parts gives all the players a chance to experience both sides of a conflict. Obviously, the real-life conflict that the group itself experiences is stronger than the fictional one, and the solution, if found, is of practical benefit; but the fictional situation, because it is more distanced, sometimes makes for greater objectivity.

IMPROVISATIONS SUGGESTED BY WORDS AND PHRASES

By the time children reach the intermediate grades, drama is related most closely to the language arts. The children's vocabularies have increased, and words have become more meaningful to them. Activities based on the use of language sharpen perception and stimulate interest in both spoken and written communication (Activity 5.9).

IMPROVISATIONS BASED ON STORIES

The most popular and, in many ways, most satisfactory form of improvisation for children is based on good stories. While making up original stories is a creative exercise, a group endeavor rarely achieves the excellence of a story that has stood the test of time or was written by a fine author. Improvising from a story is a way of introducing literature, and when a story is well chosen, it offers good opportunities for acting. Chapter 7 discusses the ways in which both simple and more complicated stories may be approached.

Good stories on any level should have literary quality, worthwhile ideas, correct information, and dramatic value. Children up to the ages of 10 and 11 like fairy tales and legends. Older children may still enjoy these but tend to prefer adventures, biographies, and stories of real life. Frequently, the last, because of their length, have to be cut or the incidents rearranged. This is a learning experience that, if the group has had some experience, should not be too difficult.

Groups sometimes want to act plays that they have seen. This can be a worthwhile activity, although the tendency is to try to do it exactly as

[1] Peter Slade, *Child Drama* (London: University of London Press, 1954), p. 119.

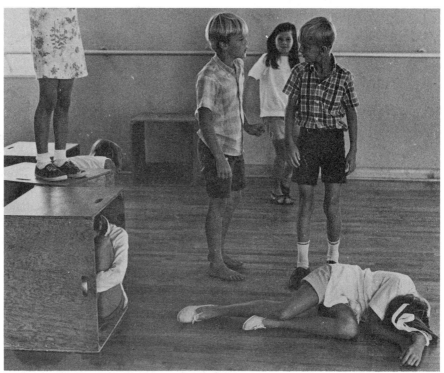

Children improvise. (Courtesy of Coleman A. Jennings, University of Texas at Austin; photograph by Alan Smith)

it was presented on the stage. Nevertheless, working on a reenactment of a play can be a valuable period of time spent with a good piece of literature and is to be preferred to the reproduction of television shows or enactment of stories from comic books.

In order to present the right story, the leader must, above all, know the group well. One leader, who was later to achieve remarkable success, told of her first experience as a young teacher at a settlement house in an inner-city area. Nothing she brought to the children in her drama group captured their interest. Improvisation seemed an impossible goal, although group members were alert and lively when she saw them on the street. Finally, she hit on the idea of asking them to tell her stories they knew. Hesitantly at first, then willingly, legends and family anecdotes came. She tried enacting them. Not only was the material a success, but the group doubled in size. Parents began to look in. Before the end of the year, an activity that had seemed doomed to failure became the most popular in the settlement. Some years later, the settlement house's drama department was to achieve nationwide recognition as an arts center. The search for material had led to the children themselves. Their cultural heritage and their creative use of it under intelligent and sensitive guidance was the first step.

SUMMARY

Improvisation is the creation of a situation in which characters speak spontaneously. There are many ways of introducing improvisation, but some groundwork in pantomime is the best preparation. Once the players have achieved a sense of security in movement, they are ready to add dialogue to their improvisations. Dialogue does not come easily at first, but continued practice with familiar material usually induces the flow. There are many points of departure, and some of the most successful are: improvisation from situations, objects, or properties; from sounds; from characters; and from ideas and stories. A good program makes use of all, although the teacher will be flexible in approach, using those methods that lead to the greatest success for the group. Stories should be chosen with care and include both familiar and new material. Although the teacher probably will want to start with the known, he or she will find improvisation an excellent opportunity to widen horizons by bringing in good literature with dramatic content.

ACTIVITY 5.1

SIMPLE IMPROVISATIONS BASED ON SITUATIONS

These simple improvisations may be done with children of various ages, although the backgrounds and locations of the players will determine the appropriateness. Some situations are better for older players or urban children.

Suggestions for the Teacher

1. Discuss the meaning of improvisation and how it differs from a prepared script and pantomime.
2. Divide the class into small groups. Have them prepare scenes to present to the class. When all agree they are ready, have them come forward, one group at a time, to share their scenes with the others. It is a good idea in the early stages of improvisation to accept all efforts, regardless of how short or inadequate the scenes may be. As time goes on, the results will be stronger.
3. Follow presentations with a brief class discussion, making sure that comments are positive. This can be accomplished if the teacher starts out with a positive comment. Any criticism should be constructive. This is the most important task for the leader at this stage. Children can be cruel, and their remarks may hurt a sensitive player.
4. Suggest some of the following situations:
    a. You are a group of people in a subway station. It is six o'clock in the evening. In the center of the station is a newsstand, at which newspapers, magazines, and candy are sold. It is run by a woman who has been there for many years. She knows the passengers who ride regularly and is interested in them and all the details of their daily lives. Decide on who you are going to be—a secretary, an actress, a businessman, a cleaning woman, a shopper, a policeman, a teen-ager, a stranger in town. Then let us learn all about you through your conversation with the proprietor of the newsstand, while you are waiting for your train.
    b. You are a committee from your school, assigned the job of selecting a gift for your teacher, who is retiring. Each of you has an idea of what you think is appropriate, and you have only a certain amount of money to spend. The scene takes place in a large gift shop. Let us know who you are and what you want to buy. What is the decision you finally make?
    c. You receive an invitation to a party, which you accept. Two

days later, you receive another invitation to a different party, which sounds much more exciting. You really want to go to the second party but you have already accepted the first invitation. What do you do? How do you feel about the decision you make?

d. You are in a Woolworth store, when you hear a crash behind you. An elderly man has accidentally bumped into a counter of glassware, knocking several pieces to the floor. The clerk is very angry. What do you do? How do the other customers react? What does the old man say? do? How does it end?

e. The scene is a small bakery. One of you is the owner; one of you is a child who helps him on Saturdays; and another is a beggar. It is not busy this particular morning, so the owner goes out for coffee. While he is gone, a beggar comes into the shop and asks for some bread. The girl (or boy) knows that she should not give away the bread, but she feels sorry for the old man. What do they say to each other? What does the owner say when he comes back? Try changing parts in this improvisation to see if it will turn out differently.

At least four of these situations have implications for discussion. After playing them, the class may easily be engaged in exploring the social aspects of the improvisations. Thus the activity serves several purposes: work on language arts through improvised dialogue, personal development through drama, and reflection on recognizable social problems that concern children.

IMPROVISATIONS SUGGESTED BY OBJECTS

Suggestions for the Teacher

Put an object in the center of the circle where all the players can see it. Ask them to look at it, without speaking, for three or four minutes and try to think of a story about it: Where might it have come from? How did it get here? What does it make *you* think of? Each of you will have an original story to tell; tell it.

Divide the class into groups of three or four. Present an object, and ask each group to make up an improvisation about it. Perhaps the property is a wooden spoon. When a wooden spoon was used with one class, the following ideas were suggested and these situations were improvised.

1. The scene was a settler's cabin over 100 years ago. The family had very few household items, and so they prized each one. Among them was a wooden spoon. In this scene, it was used to stir batter for corn bread, and then washed and put carefully away.

2. The scene was a museum and the spoon, a relic from the Indians who once inhabited the region. The characters were the curator of the museum and two children who were visiting it. The curator answered their questions by telling the history of the spoon.

3. The scene was a cave. Three boys were hiking and found the spoon. They used it to dig and discovered an old box of coins that had been buried there. They took the old spoon home with them for good luck.

4. The scene was an industrial-arts class. The boys were making things of wood, and a blind boy carved the spoon. It was so well done that the teacher said she would display it as one of the best things made in her class that year.

5. The scene was a dump. The old wooden spoon was the speaker as he told the other pieces of trash how he had been used and handed down from one generation to the next. Finally, his family became rich and threw him away because they considered him to be too old and ugly to be of further use to them.

Any object can function as a springboard, and no two groups will see it in exactly the same way. Among the kinds of properties that suggest ideas are:

1. A velvet jewelry box	5. A straw hat
2. An artificial rose	6. A cane
3. A foreign coin	7. A quill pen
4. A feather duster	8. An old dog collar

ACTIVITY 5.3

IMPROVISATIONS FROM COSTUMES

Suggestions for the Teacher

Put an assortment of garments (shawls, sashes, hats, aprons, and capes) and jewelry (large, cheap necklaces and bracelets) on a table and have each member of the class select one item from it. Then ask each child to create a character that the piece of clothing suggests. When everyone is ready, have them demonstrate their characters. This is fun, and some very imaginative results may be expected.

Next, suggest that they get together in pairs and create a situation. (These will be short and perhaps disappointing, but remember that it is the beginning of characterization with speech added, a more difficult assignment than pantomime.)

Another idea is to have 8 or 10 children, wearing their pieces of clothing, be people in a public place, such as a bus terminal or a community center. While this reduces the verbal contribution, it may cause some confusion. If it does, do not let it go on; commend what went well and quickly shift to something easier. Later on, the class will be ready for a large group activity of this kind.

Try this. The scene is a department store. The customers, wearing their garments, come in singly or in pairs. Here is a chance for you to be the clerk, if you want to join in the improvisation. Participating in this way is fun, and the children enjoy it. Incidentally, should there be a student teacher in the room, he or she can be a great asset. Most college students are more than willing to help "in role," and it strengthens the children to have them there. Should there be more than one student teacher in the class, they can work with small groups on improvisation; this helps to keep order as well as to assist the children in structuring their scenes.

ACTIVITY 5.4

IMPROVISATIONS SUGGESTED BY REAL PEOPLE

Suggestions for the Teacher

To create from a character, ask members of the class to think of particularly interesting persons whom they have noticed that day or sometime during the week. This is followed by questions:

1. Who was it?
2. What was he or she doing? talking about? wearing?
3. How old was the person?
4. What special thing attracted your attention?

ACTIVITY 5.5

IMPROVISATIONS FROM CLUES

More experienced players enjoy creating improvisations from clues.

Suggestions for the Teacher

Ask the children what kinds of persons they can imagine with these clues. Create a character who is suggested by:

1. Raw vegetables
2. A cane
3. A book
4. Coca-Cola
5. A hair dryer
6. Television

7. A hat
8. A fur piece
9. A checkbook
10. A belt
11. A stick
12. A bag

Another exercise that appeals to most children in the fifth and sixth grades and is conducive to imaginative planning is improvisation from proverbs. One way is to divide the class into four or five groups, each group taking the same proverb. I can guarantee that you will not get two improvisations alike!

Another way is to give each group a different proverb; or ask them if they know any proverbs not in this list.

1. A fool and his money are soon parted.
2. Early to bed and early to rise makes a man healthy, wealthy, and wise.
3. If you're tired of a friend, lend him money.
4. Pride goeth before a fall.
5. A stitch in time saves nine.
6. Necessity is the mother of invention.
7. A rolling stone gathers no moss.
8. A bird in the hand is worth two in the bush.

ACTIVITY 5.6

IMPROVISATIONS FOR TWO CHILDREN

Suggestions for the Teacher

Suggest that pairs of children imagine themselves in the following situations.

1. You receive a letter in the mail, telling you that you have won first prize in a poster contest. Tell your mother the good news.

2. Your dog has been hit by a car. When you come home from school, your mother meets you and tells you what has happened.

3. You and a friend are going on a trip by yourselves to your uncle's house in another city. It involves changing trains. The first train is delayed, however, causing you to miss the second. What do you do? Are there other trains? Is there any other way of getting to your uncle's house?

4. You are working at a booth for your school or church bazaar. It has been very busy until a few minutes ago. You decide to count the money you have taken in. When you open the box, you are shocked to find it empty. At that moment you notice a boy (or girl) from your class hanging around the booth next to yours. Could he (or she) have taken the money? Should you say something? How do you handle it?

5. This is the same situation as situation 4, except that now the woman in charge of cash for the bazaar stops at your booth to collect your money. She suspects you of taking it. How do you and she handle this very unpleasant situation? How does it end?

6. A salesman comes to the door. He insists on demonstrating a vacuum cleaner, although you tell him that you have one. How do you handle the situation?

7. Your aunt, who is always very generous with you, has taken you downtown to buy a jacket for your birthday. She likes one that you don't like at all. You like another jacket, which happens to be very expensive. You hate to ask her for it, even though you know she can afford it. How do you and she work it out? (There are several possible solutions.)

8. You are away at camp. You discover that one of your bunk mates has hidden a big box of cookies under his cot. It is forbidden to keep food in tents, but the brownies look delicious and you would really like one. Just as you have pulled out the box and are taking a brownie, your bunk mate walks in. What does he say to you? How do you answer him? What about the rule regarding perishable food? How does the situation work out?

ACTIVITY 5.7

IMPROVISATIONS FOR THREE CHILDREN

Suggestions for the Teacher

Suggest that groups of three children imagine themselves in the following situations.

1. You and your friend are going to the playground. Your little sister wants to go with you, but if she does, you cannot go into the area reserved for older children. What do you do?

2. You are delivering papers. You throw one toward a house, but instead of landing on the porch, it breaks a window. Both the husband and wife who own the house run out to see what has happened.

3. You and a friend are in the playground late one afternoon. A man you don't know comes along and offers you money to deliver a package for him. He holds out more money than you have ever had before, but you are suspicious and do not want to deal with him. He then offers you even more money, which is tempting because Christmas is coming. What do you say? do? How do you get out of it, or do you? (This is a tough situation but not an uncommon one. Therefore it gives the teacher an opportunity to discuss the dangers of the situation and the difficulties of handling temptation.)

4. You tried out for a leading part in a play but were put in the chorus. You try to be a good sport when you talk to the teacher and to the girl who was cast in the part you wanted.

5. You see the girl across the aisle cheat on a test when the teacher steps out of the room. He suspects that there has been cheating and asks you and the girl to stay after class so that he can find out about it. What does each one of you say and do?

6. You are delivering flowers for a neighborhood florist. On this particular day, you are carrying a very large plant, and you lose the address. You think you remember it, however, so you go to what you hope is the right door. It is the wrong address, but the person who answers the door accepts the plant and then discovers the mistake. You have left by that time. How do you, the florist, and the customer work things out?

7. Three of you are getting refreshments ready for a party. It is said that "too many cooks spoil the broth." This happens when all of you put salt in the chocolate pudding, thinking that it is sugar and needs sweetening. This can be a very funny situation.

8. Your two best friends are running for president of your class. The

three of you meet on the playground. What do you say? How do you handle the situation?

9. You are at the checkout counter of a supermarket. The cashier is checking off your items when you realize that you forgot to get the milk. You run back for it. This annoys the person behind you. Then you discover that you do not have enough money to pay the bill, so you have to return some items. By this time, both the cashier and the person behind you are annoyed. You put the things back on the shelves and return, but when you pick up your shopping bag, which the cashier has packed for you, it splits open. Now you are angry too. This makes all three of you laugh; suddenly the annoying situation becomes funny!

10. You are at a street fair when suddenly you hear an announcement over the loudspeaker that you hold the winning number of the biggest prize—a bicycle! When you reach the announcer, however, you see another child who claims that he or she has the winning number. Which of you has it? Did one of you misunderstand? Was it a misprint on the ticket? What will the solution be? You, the announcer, and the other child must settle it.

ACTIVITY 5.8

IMPROVISATIONS INVOLVING
MORAL AND ETHICAL CONFLICTS OR SOCIAL ATTITUDES

Objective: To improvise a situation and then follow with open discussion

Suggestions for the Teacher

Relate each situation slowly and carefully, suggesting that the children think about the various options they have for completing it.

Each situation is good for a serious discussion involving responsibility, morality, values, social concerns, and attitudes. Children in the middle grades are perceptive and fair-minded, and readily enter into discussion on such subjects. Thus the improvisation is extended with, we hope, lasting implications for social attitudes and behavior.

1. You are in a gift shop in a terminal. Over the glass and china counter, there is a sign that says if you break anything, you will have to pay for it. Your sweater sleeve accidentally catches a glass dish, and it falls to the floor and breaks. It is so noisy in the terminal that no one sees or hears it. What are you going to do?
   a. Go to the clerk with the broken pieces and explain what happened.
   b. Decide to do nothing, hoping you can get away with it.

2. Your class is competing in a play festival. The group about to go on is very good. Suddenly, you see their most important prop lying on the floor outside the stage door. You realize that if they lose it they will not be able to replace it, and any substitute prop will probably upset the actors. What are you going to do?
   a. Pick up the prop and give it to the stage manager.
   b. Hide the prop in a trash basket, in an effort to make the group do less than its best.

3. You are invited to a party in a very beautiful home. Your mother says that you should dress up, but your friends say that they are going to wear blue jeans. One of them claims that she has no dress clothes. What will you do?
   a. Try to persuade your friends to dress up.
   b. Dress up; then change into blue jeans at the last minute.
   c. Wear your best clothes and find that everyone else is dressed casually.

4. You are buying a birthday present for your sister or brother. You know exactly what she or he wants. You find two gifts, one cheap and the other expensive. You also see something you want for yourself. If you buy the expensive item, it will take all your money. If

you buy the cheap item, there will be enough money left for you to get what you want too.

   a. You decide on the expensive gift.

   b. You decide on the cheap gift and get yourself what you want as well.

5. Just before a game, you fall and hurt your knee. You do not know whether the injury is going to ruin your playing. What do you do?

   a. Say nothing about it and play. The knee lets you down.

   b. Explain and stay out of the game. The team is angry and upset.

6. There has been a bad flood in your neighborhood, and many families have had to leave their homes quickly. Your mother invites some people to stay in your house until the crisis is over.

   a. One of them is a boy or girl you dislike.

   b. You have to give up your room to a family.

   c. You decide to help in any way you can.

ACTIVITY 5.9

EXTENDING PHRASES INTO STORIES

"Extending Phrases into Stories" can be a serious lesson in creative writing or simply *fun* at the end of a long day. Children in the middle and upper grades love mystery stories and the supernatural and will enjoy this activity as they might enjoy a game.

Objective: To create a situation or simple story from colorful phrases

Suggestions for the Teacher

Write the following phrases on the blackboard:

1. The howling wind
2. Creaking stairs
3. A screeching owl
4. Rapid footsteps
5. A dark, lonely street
6. Squeaking hinges
7. A shadowy figure
8. A bell ringing in the night
9. A radio that suddenly plays by itself

Then ask the class to put the phrases into sentences. (For example, "The frightened boy walked down *a dark, lonely street.* He heard *squeaking hinges.* . . .") Next, extend the sentences into stories. Finally, the class selects one of the stories to act. (There may not be one that is playable; if so, settle for storytelling. The children will enjoy that almost as much.)

6

DRAMATIC STRUCTURE:
THE PLAY TAKES SHAPE

If teachers are going to help children create plays, they need some knowledge of the structure and fundamental elements that distinguish the play from other forms of literature. This is also helpful when discussing plays that the class attends. While there is no established formula for writing a play, there are certain elements that are useful to know.

STRUCTURE AND ELEMENTS OF A PLAY

Most important, a play is to be played. Until it finds life on a stage, it is not a play. There are not many plays for child audiences that meet the criteria of good dramatic literature. This is because the field is new, and few professional playwrights have been attracted to it. Those who have been are educators as well as playwrights and therefore understand children's interests and concerns. Charlotte Chorpenning, Aurand Harris, Joanna Kraus, Flora Atkin, and Suzan Zeder are among the best-known and most successful American children's playwrights. While we are not concerned in this text with formal production or the printed script, we are concerned that children in the middle grades who want to create a play with a beginning, a middle, and an end have some knowledge of the form by which plays are shaped. For this reason, some attention is given to dramatic terminology and definition.

Children are not concerned with a linear structure. Their plays may

95

move backward or forward in time; absent characters may suddenly reappear without explanation; and action in different times and places may take place simultaneously. This is not because children lack a sense of order but because they do not yet know the conventions of playwriting. Children have a logic of their own, but they need help in communicating their work to others. In giving them a concept of structure, teachers are helping them to express ideas, improvise dialogue, and eventually perhaps write plays of their own. We do not basically change their work; we provide technical assistance when they need it. Far from stifling their creativity, this knowledge will stimulate it. Given boundaries, children are always freer to express themselves than they are with no boundaries or form to follow.

CHARACTERS

A play involves characters. It is their conflict that holds our attention, and it is through them that the playwright delivers the message. Whether tragic or comic, loveable or despised, a character must be believable and belong to the play. Even in fantasy, a character must have reality; a witch or a ghost, for example, although unrealistic in itself, must compel our belief through the consistency of its behavior.

The hero or heroine should be someone with whom the audience can identify. Whatever his or her faults or human weaknesses, our sympathy must be aroused, making us care what happens. Characters should be admirable in some way, but we must accept them as real and their actions as true to life.

Characters should react to one another in a natural way. Although it is clearly established to whom the story belongs, there are other characters in the play who help to advance the plot through their involvement with it and their relationship to the hero or heroine. A skillful playwright develops character and situation through interaction. Sometimes many characters are needed to tell a story; sometimes it is better done with one or two. The fewer there are, the greater their responsibility for telling the story, and the more the audience learns about them. The playwright must let the audience know:

1. Age of the characters
2. Interests
3. Occupations
4. Members of the family and the characters' relationships to them
5. Social relationships
6. Appearance
7. Qualities of character and personality

DIALOGUE

Dialogue is the lines spoken in the play. Good dialogue should belong to the characters, both in content and in manner of speech. A noblewoman will not talk like a peasant, nor will a country boy talk like a prince. While dialogue must, of course, be understood, the speech patterns of the characters must not be sacrificed. For example, a character of little education who comes from a particular region will use colloquial speech or appropriate dialect.

Dialogue advances the plot. The playwright's job is to tell the story as economically as possible through the words of the characters. A soliloquy, in which only one person speaks, is a device used occasionally; but in general, it is through conversation between two or more persons that characters are revealed and the plot is unfolded.

THEME

The theme is the underlying thought or basic idea on which the play rests. Not every play has a well-defined theme; it may, however, be the most important element. If there is a theme, the story both springs from and expresses it.

PLOT

The plot is the story. It may be simple or complex, but what happens between the opening scene and the final curtain is the action we call story or plot.

CONFLICT

Conflict is the basis of drama. Without conflict, there is no resolution; with conflict, the interest is sustained to the end. The successful playwright resolves the conflict in a way that is satisfying and acceptable.

CLIMAX

The climax is the high point of the play. This scene usually comes somewhere near the end, after which there is an untangling, or resolution.

DENOUEMENT

The denouement is the portion of the play that follows the climax. It may be long or short, depending on the number of situations that need straightening out. In a children's play, the denouement and climax are often one, since children are satisfied once the conflict is settled, and long explanations at this point do not interest them. This is a term that teachers would not introduce at this stage; it is included here because it is the place in a play where the child audience invariably becomes restless. The conflict has been resolved, and the story has come to an end; for the child audience, there is nothing more of interest, and it is time to go home.

ACTS

Acts are the major divisions in a play. Short plays are generally written in one act. Longer plays may be divided into two, three, or even five acts, depending on the plot and the need to break it into parts.

SCENES

Scenes are divisions within acts and are most often used to indicate a different time or place. A play does not have to have any particular number of scenes; the time covered and the locations in which the action takes place determine them. Many one-act plays are written in a single scene because they are concerned with a single action or plot.

FLASHBACK SCENES

Flashback scenes sometimes are used to show an important event that happened at an earlier time, before the play began. The flashback is a device that helps to explain the behavior or attitudes of characters more dramatically than by merely telling about them. While teachers would not use the technical term with children, it is important for teachers to know it because children often use this device in their own playmaking.

NARRATOR

The narrator is a person who tells or reads an exposition that ties the incidents together. It is a useful device when an extended period of time or a variety of scenes are included, and is also a way of bridging the gap between actors and audience. It is frequently used in children's plays.

Planning the scenes. (Courtesy of the Creative Arts Team, New York University)

TYPES OF PLAYS

COMEDY

Comedy is defined as a play that ends satisfactorily for the hero or heroine. Comedy is generally funny, but humor is not essential. There are several kinds of comedy: slapstick, or broad comedy; comedy of

character, of action, of situation, and of dialogue. While children respond to slapstick, they can enjoy the more subtle forms, and older
children learn to appreciate wit and comic dialogue.

TRAGEDY

Tragedy is defined as a play that ends with the defeat or death of the
main character. Although fashions in playwriting change according to
the times and public taste, the downfall of the hero or heroine places
a play in the category of tragedy.

TELEVISION, FILM, AND THEATRE

Because television is so often confused with theatre in the minds of
children, a word should be said about theatre and television as separate
art forms. Theatre differs from film and television in several important
respects, primarily in structure; however, the majority of children are
far more familiar with television than they are with theatre. In fact, many
children have never experienced a live performance before they enter
school and then only when a play is given in assembly. While it is not
the purpose of this text to discuss the subject at length, the fact that
television is such an important part of our lives renders it worthy of
mention as an educational medium and a popular form of
entertainment.

To appreciate theatre, it is necessary to understand the similarities
and differences between it and film and to recognize the values of each.
The accompanying chart shows the major components of the performing
arts and the ways in which each of the three media handles them. Although opera, instrumental music, and dance are also performing arts,
they are intentionally excluded here.

	Theatre	Film	Television
Content	Dramatized stories, theatre-in-education programs Musicals and plays with music	Dramatized stories Documentaries Educational films	Dramatized stories Documentaries Serials Cartoons and animations
Actors	Live performers Small casts, perform- ing on a stage or in a special area	Filmed performers Large casts, often crowds	Filmed performers, taped or live for the camera Casts smaller than for film but larger than for stage play

	Theatre	Film	Television
Structure	Play is divided into acts and scenes; length is from 30 or 40 minutes to 2 hours with an intermission	Play flows without intermission; length is from 60 to 90 minutes (occasionally longer)	Program is interrupted by commercials; length is from 30 minutes to 1 hour (occasionally longer)
Production	Stage with scenery, costumes, properties, lights, sound effects Performance in a theatre, school, or community center	Large screen with indoor and outdoor settings; can be elaborate because camera is not limited to a small area; play often filmed "on location" in the actual setting of the story	Small screen designed for home use or schoolroom; plays filmed in studio or "on location," depending on story
Values	Direct communication with audience Performance often altered depending on audience and circumstances	Large variety possible, e.g., documentaries and educational films; can be shown repeatedly	Same values as film but programs are seldom repeated ("re-run") and are not usually available for rent or sale

Because films and television programs are presented on screen, they are more distanced from the viewer than is theatre. The relationship that exists between actor and audience in the theatre does not and cannot exist in a film or a television program, fine as it may be. For the same reason, there is no variation between one performance and another, as there is in theatre, where audiences vary in composition and response. But when material is filmed rather than limited by the confines of a stage, it has almost unlimited flexibility. Television makes possible many programs that could not be done on the stage—for example, documentaries and plays requiring elaborate technical effects. The videotape is also a boon to the teacher of the middle and upper grades, not as a substitute for the staged play, but as an enrichment when appropriate. Historical events and geographical regions come alive on the screen, broadening children's horizons and illuminating curriculum content. While many aspects of television and film are open to question, evaluation of programs must be made on an individual basis, for unquestionably there are as many of value as there are of poor quality.

My own conviction is that the amount of time children spend watching television is far more harmful than the actual programming. It is time that should be spent out of doors, in physical activities, in reading, and in enjoying family life rather than in passive viewing. Again, however, this is a matter of selection. There are programs with rich content and interesting format that offer worthwhile entertainment. It is up to us—parents and teachers—to guide children in their choices, rather than letting them watch indiscriminately whatever comes on the screen.

DRAMATIZATION OF A CHILDREN'S STORY

The script *The Three Wishes* is included as an example of a well-known children's story that contains the basic elements of a play:

1. A plot that holds interest
2. Plenty of action
3. A worthwhile theme
4. Characters who motivate the plot
5. Conflict
6. Humor
7. Climax and quick and satisfactory end

THE THREE WISHES
(An Old Tale)
Dramatized by Nellie McCaslin

Characters

Joanna, *an old peasant woman*

Peter, *her husband*

A Stranger, *a young man with an air of mystery about him*

The scene is a small cottage. In the room are a table, chairs, a cupboard, and a fireplace. Down right, there is a door leading to the outside. As the curtain rises, JOANNA, an old woman with a discontented expression on her face, is sweeping the hearth.

JOANNA: As if I could ever sweep all the dust and dirt from the hearth with this broom. (*She examines it.*) As many twigs fall from it as I have swept up. The old man will have to make me another, if he expects me to keep the house clean. (*She sweeps again for a moment, then stops and leans on the broom.*) Or better yet, if we had a servant girl, she could do all the cleaning. Think how that would be! To do nothing all day like our neighbor but sit in a chair by the fire and watch someone else do the work. Oh, why has the old man never earned enough to keep just one servant girl? Not five like the Duke. Nor four like our neighbor. Not even two like the simplest farmer. But one. Just one servant girl would be all I'd ask. (*She sighs.*) Oh, well, if the good man has not made his fortune yet, he never will now. And we'll end our lives just as we began them—poor peasants in a cottage. (*She puts the broom in a corner and begins to set the table for supper. While she is doing this,* PETER, *her husband, comes in. He steps wearily through the doorway, then stops, leaning on a stout stick.*)

PETER: (*sniffs*) What! Supper not on the table? What have you been doing all day while I worked in the fields?

JOANNA: What do you expect with no one to help me? If we had a servant girl now, the supper would be ready and waiting.

PETER: And if I had a donkey to carry the plow, I'd not be so tired. I could climb on his back when the day's work was done and ride home in comfort.

JOANNA: A donkey? Why not wish for a horse? We could get a cart then and both of us drive out together on Sunday.

PETER: (*sitting by the hearth and continuing eagerly*) Yes, a strong brown horse like our neighbor's. I'd want one like his. Then I could plant a garden that brought in some money. In time, I could buy another horse. With a team, there's no telling how much we could earn.

JOANNA: Well, we haven't even one donkey. So pull up your chair, and I'll have supper on the table in a minute.

PETER: (*sitting at the table*) Cabbage soup again?

JOANNA: (*bringing the pot to the table and ladling out the soup*) What did you expect? Meat and white bread like the Duke? Cabbage is the only thing in the garden.

PETER: (*eating it hungrily*) It's good. Though it would be better if you'd had a bone to cook with it.

JOANNA: A bone means meat. When have we had a roast with a bone left to flavor the soup? (*She sits down and tastes her soup. Then she takes a piece of bread.*) White bread now, instead of black. That would help.

PETER: White bread with butter, eh, wife?

JOANNA: (*eagerly*) When I stopped at our neighbor's today with the basket of cabbages to sell, I caught a glimpse of the kitchen. Such things as they were fixing for dinner! Cakes, butter, cream, and a goose roasting on the spit.

PETER: Ah, well, we are poor folk, Joanna. We could wish till the end of our days and nothing would come of it. (*At this moment, a voice is heard from the fireplace.*)

STRANGER: Nothing would come of it? Are you sure, Peter? Are you sure, Joanna?

PETER: Who was that?

JOANNA: Was that you, Peter?

PETER: (*getting up*) I'd swear I heard a voice.

STRANGER: (*coming out of the fireplace*) And so you did. (*He brushes off his clothes.*) Now, then, what was that you were saying?

PETER: (*startled*) Oh, nothing. Nothing important.

STRANGER: Come, now, Peter, Joanna. You were wishing for a well-stocked larder, I think.

JOANNA: Well, yes, we were.

STRANGER: Are you sure that's all that you wish for?

PETER: (*eagerly*) Oh no. If I had a donkey now—

JOANNA: Not a donkey, Peter, a horse. So we could ride in a carriage together.

PETER: And plow a garden that went from here to that forest.

STRANGER: I'll tell you what. I've been listening to the two of you for some time, and I'm about to make you a gift.

PETER: What kind of a gift?

JOANNA: Who are you? And how did you come here?

STRANGER: Let's say I'm a stranger who heard you in passing. (*He walks around the table, and they look at him in wonder.*) Oh, I'm not a rich man, if that's what you're thinking. Though I do have strange powers.

PETER: What kind of powers?

STRANGER: I'll show you. Yes, I'm going to give you three wishes.

PETER: (*repeating the words after him, stupidly*) Three wishes?

STRANGER: Yes. But I must warn you, you'll have only three wishes between you. So watch out you don't waste them.

PETER: (*joyfully*) You mean, if I wished for a donkey, I'd get one?

JOANNA: No, Peter, a horse, not a donkey.

STRANGER: Sh! That's what I mean. Be careful. When you've used the three wishes up, there'll be no more of them. Think of what you want most.

PETER: And they'll be granted, no matter how great the request?

STRANGER: They'll be granted, never fear. But only the three. So watch out, Peter.
(*The* STRANGER *moves back to the hearth and disappears as the old couple talk excitedly together.*)

PETER: Did you hear that, Joanna? Why, I can wish for a team of horses with a carriage to boot!

JOANNA: And a house!

PETER: Or a castle! With a kitchen as big as this room.

JOANNA: Filled with all sorts of good things to eat. (*She turns to speak to the* STRANGER.) Must we use all three wishes at once or can we save one for—Why, where has he gone? He's not here, Peter.

PETER: (*rubbing his eyes*) Vanished as suddenly as he appeared. Do you suppose we just dreamed this?

JOANNA: No, of course not. How could we both dream the same thing? And at the same time? He must have gone out the door while we were talking. Let's go after him.
(*The two old people go quickly to the door but do not see him.*)

JOANNA: He's nowhere in sight. You go down the road, Peter. He may have gone round the bend.

PETER: All right. (*He disappears from sight, calling.*) Hey, hey, there!

JOANNA: Gone before we even had a chance to thank him. He was standing right here. (*Puzzled, she stands in the middle of the room for a moment.*) We might have asked him to supper. I wish we'd—(*She claps her hands over her mouth.*) Just in time. Now, then, what to wish for?
(PETER *comes in the door and goes to his chair.*)

PETER: Not a sign of him anywhere. You don't think, wife—

JOANNA: That we only imagined him? No, I don't. He said he had magic powers. Therefore, why couldn't he disappear like smoke in the breeze? (*She has an idea.*) Up the chimney, perhaps? (*She goes to the hearth and looks up the chimney.*) Not there, either. Come, Peter. Let's sit down and think of three things to wish for.

PETER: Well, I still think a horse would be—

JOANNA: Sh! Remember what he said. Don't wish till we've thought of everything we need. I'd say a house, instead of this cottage.

PETER: Or a castle with barns—

JOANNA: And servants—

PETER: And fine dresses for you—

JOANNA: And a gold-headed cane for you to lean on when you're tired.

PETER: Wait! We can't waste a wish on a cane. Why not wish me young and strong again? Then I'd have no use for a cane.

JOANNA: (*excited*) Both of us young again, Peter! As we were when we first moved into this cottage. My hair would be black. And when I put on my fine clothes, I'd be as beautiful as the Duke's daughter.

PETER: We mustn't be hasty. Let's eat our soup and then after supper, we'll decide. (*He takes a spoonful of soup.*) It's cold.

JOANNA: And why shouldn't it be? Sitting out in these bowls. (*She takes a spoonful.*) Oh, I wish we had sausage to go with it.
             (*No sooner has she said the words than a sausage is on her plate.*)

PETER: Oh, Joanna, see what you've done! Only two wishes left!

JOANNA: I didn't mean to do it.

PETER: (*angrily*) You've thrown away one-third of our fortune, Joanna. I wish that sausage were on the end of your nose! (*At once, the sausage is hanging from her nose. She puts her hands up and feels it.*)

JOANNA: Peter!

PETER: I'm sorry, Joanna. I was angry. I didn't think. Here, let me pull it off.

JOANNA: It's stuck tight. I'm trying.

PETER: (*Going over to her, he pulls and pulls.*) It certainly seems to be stuck there. Come, let's both pull.
             (*They both pull, but the sausage refuses to budge.*)
             It seems as if the harder we pull, the faster it sticks. I have it! I'll cut it off.

JOANNA: No, Peter. You might cut my nose.
             (PETER *gets a huge knife and comes toward her.*)

PETER: I'll be careful. Let me try.

JOANNA: (*running away from him*) No, no. Leave me alone.

PETER: Perhaps if I cut it off just below—about here?

JOANNA: I don't want even half a sausage on the end of my nose. (*wailing*) Oh, Peter, what shall I do?

PETER: Just one wish left. Shall it be a house or the horses and carriage?

JOANNA: I can't go about with a sausage hanging on my nose. No matter how rich we were, people would laugh.

PETER: We could tie a scarf over your face.

JOANNA: Every time I stepped out of the house?

PETER: Perhaps no one would notice—

JOANNA: Oh, Peter, how would you like to have a sausage hanging down over your chin?

PETER: It may go away.

JOANNA: It won't, I know. Oh, Peter, there's just one thing to do.

PETER: You mean—

JOANNA: Yes. To wish it off. Are you willing?

PETER: I guess you're right. (*They look at each other.*) We were both foolish.

PETER & (*together*) We wish the sausage off her/my nose. (*Mi-*
JOANNA: *raculously the sausage comes off in* JOANNA'S *hand.*)

JOANNA: There. (*sadly*) All three wishes gone. And we're no better off than we were.

PETER: Except, perhaps—Come, wife, let us eat our supper and be grateful that no harm was done. After all, we do have soup in our bowls—

JOANNA: And a roof over our heads—

PETER: And strength enough to work in the fields.

JOANNA: And each other.

PETER: And, who knows, perhaps some day he will come again. The next time— (*He and* JOANNA *look at each other and laugh.*) (*The curtain falls.*)

The business of the sausage, incidentally, provides excellent material for pantomime, and it is suggested that this part be improvised by itself.

Where does one go to find good stories for creative drama and playmaking? There are a number of sources. The children's room of the public library is usually the best, and the creative-drama teacher will be wise to become familiar with its shelves. Also, go to the children themselves. What are their favorite books and stories? What are their interests? Have any of them stories of their own to share? Family stories, stories with ethnic backgrounds, stories that no one else knows. There is a creative-writing contest held every two or three years in New York City entitled "Stories My Grandparents Told Me," which could be a rich resource for dramatization.[1] Lively characters, amusing and touching anecdotes, customs of other lands, and experiences of immigrants in the United States are fodder for the playwright and actor. And, of equal

---

[1] Conducted by the Police Athletic League of New York; Kitty Kirby, Director of Performing Arts.

importance, they help build the children's respect for one another's cultural backgrounds.

DRAMATIZATION OF LEGENDARY MATERIAL

Myths, legends, and folk tales are particularly good for playmaking. These stories have been told and retold over the years, so that the story line is clear and easily followed. Characters generally are well defined; have complete relevance to the plot; and—even in the case of the supernatural—have credibility. The theme is usually strong, for one generation has passed the tale along to the next, carefully, if unconsciously, preserving the values of the culture. Primitive creation myths, explaining natural phenomena, are particularly good today in the face of our expanding body of information about the universe and the new kinds of questions we are asking.

A group might dramatize a well-known myth or legend, or, through the study of legendary material, develop a play of its own. Children enjoy thinking of ways to explain phenomena, sayings, or characters for which they have no ready answers. Because an activity of this sort involves creative writing as well as creative playing, it is a way in which drama can be integrated naturally into the curriculum. Younger children might want to find their own explanations for such things as the Man in the Moon, Ground Hog Day, Jack Frost, candles on a birthday cake, or local jokes and customs. Older children find intellectual stimulation in the study and dramatization of myths and legends. They may also want to try their hands at the writing of original science fiction. Our space age, far more familiar and acceptable to young people than we often realize, can be a powerful force for imaginative writing.

Holidays often have interesting origins, which would make good material with which to construct a play. Hallowe'en is a good example.

Hallowe'en

Of all the holidays, Hallowe'en must certainly be one of the top favorites of children. Their fascination with the supernatural; the dressing up in fanciful and grotesque costumes; the parties, games, tricks, and treats (all to be forgiven in the spirit of the occasion) make for a holiday with appeal for every age. Even the commercialization of Hallowe'en in the form of ready-made costumes, masks, and crepe-paper decorations and of packages of candy corn in the supermarket have not spoiled its appeal, although it has perhaps shifted the emphasis. At any rate, Hallowe'en as a suggestion for dramatization is guaranteed to elicit an enthusiastic response from the most resistant group. Let us take a look at Hallowe'en to see what some of the possibilities are.

Its roots go back to antiquity, thus providing a rich source of information for playmaking as well as the fun and the social activities associated with its celebration. As a holiday, therefore, Hallowe'en enjoys great popularity because it offers interesting content, action, and an opportunity for dressing up. Fifth and sixth graders, with the help of the teacher, can learn about play structure through the process of building a creative drama from source material concerning this holiday.

The customs associated with Hallowe'en spring mostly from three distinct sources: pagan, Roman, and Christian. The strongest influence was probably the pagan. Each year, the Druids of northern and western Europe celebrated two feasts—Beltane, on May 1, and Samhain, on October 31. The latter was a fall festival, held after the harvest had been gathered, thus marking the end of summer and the beginning of winter. The Druids' new year began on November 1, so that Hallowe'en was actually New Year's Eve. Fortune-telling was a popular custom on this holiday, as people were eager to learn what the new year held.

The Druids believed that the spirits of persons who had died the previous year walked the earth on this night. They lighted bonfires in order to frighten away the evil spirits. It is thought that the candle in a pumpkin is a descendant of this custom. One legend has it that a rogue named Jack was caught playing tricks on the devil. As punishment, Jack was doomed to walk the earth forever, carrying a pumpkin lantern to light his way.

In order to ward off evil spirits and to imitate them and so frighten other people, many persons took to the wearing of costumes and masks. This led to playing tricks, mixing fun with fear and superstition.

In Rome, the festivities were mainly in the form of feasts honoring the goddess of fruits, Pomona. When the Romans invaded Britain, they brought their customs with them. The traditional use of fruits and vegetables (apples, corn, nuts) may be derived from the intermingling of Druid and Roman celebrations.

During the Middle Ages, the Christians observed All Saints' Day, or Allhallows, which falls on November 1. The eve of that day is October 31, which became known as Hallowe'en, or Allhallows Eve. There is little, if any, Christian significance left; for most people, Hallowe'en is a secular celebration, retaining only the outward trappings of ancient customs and rituals. Witches, ghosts, goblins, cats, bats, and pumpkins come to mind when we hear the word *Hallowe'en*. (Recently, collecting money for UNICEF has replaced gathering the traditional candy "treats" in many communities.)

Because so much information is available and much of it is not generally known, Hallowe'en is a good choice for a program that can be researched, improvised, written, and, if desired, performed for the enjoyment of others. The tasks involved would be:

1. Looking up information about Hallowe'en (the amount dependent on the age of the group and the time that can be devoted to it)
2. Improvising legendary material with the greatest appeal for the children
3. Developing a program or play by the group based on the information found
4. (Optional) Writing a script that has come out of the research and improvisation

Should this prove to be something that the children want to perform for others, it will lead naturally into the next stage: a play for an audience. What we are concerned with here, however, is an understanding of dramatic structure, obtained through the process of creating an original play or group project.

St. Valentine's Day

St. Valentine's Day, like many of our celebrations, is also ancient in origin and popular with children. While at least two St. Valentines are known to have existed, and the name was popular in Roman times, the man who was probably the inspiration for the sending of affectionate messages was a Roman priest, martyred in A.D. 270. The holiday named for him may have been derived from a pagan feast, but by medieval times, it had become associated with lovers, often unfortunate or unhappy.

In western Europe, St. Valentine's Day was celebrated on February 14 with the exchange of romantic or comic messages. According to one legend, St. Valentine sent loving notes to his friends while he was in prison. Actually, we know very little about him beyond the fact that he became the patron saint of lovers. Today, he is best remembered for having given his name to a popular minor holiday.

The first commercial greeting cards produced in the United States were made in 1840 by a woman named Esther A. Howland. Today, millions of Valentine cards are sold each year. Many are also made by schoolchildren for their families and friends.

Activity 6.1 suggests some projects for St. Valentine's Day.

LOCAL HISTORY AND LEGEND

Local folklore is another rich source of material for dramatization and one that is too infrequently tapped. Whether it be tales of Native Amer-

icans, early settlers, actual events, oral history, superstitions, or neighborhood gossip, it is fascinating to children, who bring it to life by
studying and then enacting it (Activity 6.2).

USING A VIDEO CAMERA

When video equipment is available, improvisations and plays may be
taped. Older children can learn to operate the machine, which adds to
their learning. Major values in the use of video are:

1. The play or scene that has been prepared can be captured on film
   and viewed by the players, who enjoy seeing their work.
2. The tape can be viewed many times and shared with parents and
   other classes.
3. The children can see where they need improvement: personal involvement, speech, body movement, knowledge of the material,
   structure of the play, etc.
4. By seeing both the film and the live play, the class can examine
   the differences between live theatre and film.
5. The young filmmakers benefit by working on the technical aspects.
   If the classroom teacher is familiar with video, he or she can teach
   the children how to use it. If not, there are probably others on the
   faculty who will be glad to help.

Video adds another dimension to the study of drama/theatre. While
encouraging "movie stars" is to be avoided, taping classwork or a class
play is a valid project in our high-tech society (Activity 6.3).

SUMMARY

Although the study of dramatic structure belongs to the upper rather
than to the middle grades, it is a part of playmaking on any level. The
advancement of plot and the development of character depend on a
structure of some sort. Younger players, unfamiliar with theatre conventions, often invent highly imaginative forms, and this is not to be
discouraged. The main thing to keep in mind is that some structure is
necessary to create order out of the profusion of ideas that a lively group
offers. Breaking a story into scenes, finding the climax, listing the necessary characters, deciding where additional characters can be added
or where extraneous material can be cut—all develop critical judgment
and a sense of organization in young players.
   The dramatization of a favorite story makes different demands on the
group and is much easier to write than an original play. To begin with,

there is a plot, which supplies the basic structure. Characters are clearly defined but must be given appropriate dialogue. In a play, dialogue serves three major functions: to describe the characters; to further the action; and to help show the time, place, and circumstances in which the story takes place. Because the players do not have to create an original narrative, they can focus their attention on characterization and dialogue.

ACTIVITY 6.1

ST. VALENTINE'S DAY

Objective: To create a program or play for St. Valentine's Day based on material about it

Suggestions for the Teacher

As the holiday approaches, children are busy making and buying valentines; therefore, any background material you bring in will find a receptive audience.

Questions you might ask are:

1. Does anyone know who St. Valentine was?
2. Where did he live?
3. Did he send messages of affection to his friends?
4. Why do we celebrate St. Valentine's Day on February 14?
5. Do any other countries observe this holiday?
6. Does anyone have old valentines at home?

You might bring in stories about St. Valentine's Day. Have the class make valentines for families, friends, and sick persons. Suggest that they act out stories about the holiday. This can be a project that children in the third grade might want to share with parents or another class. The fact that St. Valentine's Day comes in February gives plenty of time for a class to become familiar with creative drama and to experience working together.

This project, or one like it, is an example of how creative drama can be used with social studies, literature, and art and how children gain from the social experience of working together and sharing that work with sympathetic, interested spectators.

ACTIVITY 6.2

MAKING PLAYS FROM LOCAL HISTORY

Objectives: To make use of local history and legend; to learn more about the region in which we live

Suggestions for the Teacher

You will know something of the history of your region. See what stories or historical material is available that is appropriate for your class and will appeal to them. Find pictures and, if possible, plan a field trip to the site of the action.

When the children are thoroughly acquainted with the material, suggest that they try enacting it. If there are no appropriate stories, here is your chance to use the daily life of the people; for instance, school, work, and building of roads or homes offer opportunities to learn basic dramatic structure in a natural way.

1. Story or substance
2. Beginning, middle, and end
3. Characters

These are the essential elements of a play. When material tells a story or contains substance that develops along clear dramatic lines from beginning to end and is enacted by characters, the result is a play. A work that represents research into a subject is often referred to as a *docudrama* to distinguish it from a play based on a plot. Creating a docudrama is an interesting way to learn about playmaking and is enjoyed by most children. A study of life in a particular region of the country or community may seem to lack dramatic conflict, but conflict is always present in the struggle for existence—the human being versus the environment, poverty, or social attitudes. It is more difficult to create an original drama of this kind, but it is worth the effort.

ACTIVITY 6.3

THE NEWSCAST

Children are familiar with the newscast format and enjoy being reporters. The project is ideal to share with parents and other groups.

Objective: To record a successful project on videotape

Suggestions for the Teacher

1. Choose an activity from this book that you and the class would like to film. This decision should be made after the students have worked on the project long enough to be sure of their continuing interest and the adaptability of the material to video.
2. Keep the program short and avoid an excessive number of props. (Fifteen minutes should be the maximum length of time for the finished product.)
3. Use an uncluttered space for filming—either the classroom or an all-purpose room rather than a stage.
4. Use either a story dramatized by the children or an activity in which creative drama is employed as a way of learning. For example, creating a newscast teaches children how to develop better written and oral communication.
    a. To prepare for the project, you should cut out from magazines or newspapers enough pictures to give one to each child.
    b. Allow 15 minutes for each person to write a news story suggested by his or her picture.
    c. Divide the class into groups of five or six. Then, using the newscast format, one group at a time can present its stories—each reporter reads his or her story in an imagined television studio.

This activity will take several class sessions, because it requires practice in expository writing, revision, and clear, expressive speech.

7

MAKING PLAYS
FROM STORIES

PLAYMAKING AS A CLASSROOM ACTIVITY

When the group has had experience with pantomime and improvisation and knows something about structure, it will be ready to attempt to dramatize a story. Children often have suggestions of their own regarding favorite stories that they want to dramatize. Regardless of how well they know the story, there is still some preliminary work to be done before improvisation begins. The teacher, well acquainted with the group by this time, knows the kind of material that has appeal and presents the fewest difficulties. Success is important to future work, so the teacher will want to select a story that he or she is relatively sure the group can handle.

There is a wealth of good literature readily available, which both group and teacher can enjoy and find worthy of their efforts. The stories in this chapter and the poems in Chapter 8 are illustrative of the kinds of material that groups in the intermediate grades have used successfully. Suggestions are offered as to ways in which material may be presented and handled. It should not be inferred that these are the only or even the best ways of using the material; they are merely examples of the thinking done by some groups.

Folk tales, legends, and fables are recommended material for use on all levels, although different age groups will view them according to their own maturity and experience. For young children, stories should be simplified in the telling, whereas in working with older children, greater emphasis can be given to characterization. Meanings and insights come with experience as well as age; hence a really good story spans many age levels.

When the teacher has decided on an appropriate story, he or she must decide whether it is better told or read. In general, telling the story is preferable because it establishes a closer rapport with the class and gives the teller a chance to observe reactions and to clarify any points that appear to puzzle the audience. This means being thoroughly familiar with the material; in fact, the beginning teacher will do well to practice telling the story aloud before presenting it to the group.

After the story has been told and all questions have been answered, the children are ready to begin planning how they will dramatize it. A discussion should include a review of the plot and descriptions of the characters. Then the class is ready to try playing it. Asking for volunteers is a good way to start. This gives the stronger class members a chance to try it first and the more timid an opportunity to become better acquainted with it before taking their turns. Casting is done on a voluntary basis the first two or three times. Later on, the leader may suggest that other children try various parts. For instance, he might say, "Lynne hasn't had a chance yet. How would you like to try the princess this time, Lynne?" Or, "John has been the cobbler. Let's give Alan a chance to play it. And you, John, be one of the townsfolk." Or, "I know David has a strong voice. How about letting him be the giant?" In other words, the teacher must be concerned with the development of each participant. Later on, when the group is ready to play the story for the last time, the leader might suggest those children who have brought the greatest reality to each part, but this is as close as the teacher comes to typecasting.

The situation may be played any number of times, but the replaying should not be interpreted as rehearsal. It is hoped, of course, that with each playing, the story will gain in substance and depth, there will be deeper insights, and the participants will develop greater freedom and self-confidence. The discussions preceding and following each playing are important aspects of creative drama, for it is during these periods that some of the most creative thinking takes place. Some questions that might precede the first playing are:

1. What do we want to tell?
2. Who are the people?
3. What are these people really like?
4. What are they doing when we first meet them?
5. Where does the first scene take place?
6. What kind of a house do they live in?

After the scene has been played once, more specific questions can guide the discussion:

1. Did the players tell the story?
2. What did you like about the opening scene?
3. Did the people show that they were excited (angry, unhappy, or whatever)?
4. When we play it again, can you think of anything that would improve it?
5. Was anything important left out?

In the course of a year, there are often delightful results, and both the teacher and the group may want to share them with others. There is no reason why this should not be done, provided public performance was not the original intention. More often, however, the initial results will be crude and superficial. Dialogue will be scanty, despite the most careful planning. To the experienced leader, this does not represent failure. It is an early stage in the development of the group and may, at that point, indicate real progress. Acceptance of the effort does not mean that the teacher is satisfied to remain at this level but that the efforts have been recognized. In time, the teacher will become more selective

Building a play from a favorite story. (Courtesy of the Creative Arts Team, New York University)

in what he or she accepts, but in the beginning will accept all ideas because they have been offered. It is important for all class members to feel that their ideas are worthy of consideration. In time, even 10- and 11-year-olds will learn to distinguish between contributions that advance the play and those that distract or have little to do with it.

STORIES FOR DRAMATIZATION

The legends, myths, and folk tales in Activities 7.1 to 7.5 have been selected because of their simplicity and appropriateness for dramatization.

SUMMARY

Because of the greater plot complications and length, the stories in this book are more demanding than are those selected for younger children. Characters are presented in greater depth; hence more time must be spent on their development. Most groups like to consider such questions as:

1. What is the character really like?
2. Why does the character behave as he or she does?
3. What do others think of the character? Why?
4. If the character is not like that, why do others think so?
5. How does the character change, or what has he or she learned as a result of his or her actions?

As the participants grow in experience, they will find new ways of telling the story. Some will want to use narrators; others, many scenes; and some may rearrange the sequence of events. Every group is unique, and the teacher learns to expect an endless variety of ways in which the same material can be handled and interpreted. The growing self-confidence of the players releases ideas, which lead to further thinking and experimentation. Each group, regardless of age, becomes more critical of its efforts as it strives for a higher level of accomplishment.

Legends, folk tales, myths, modern stories, and true stories provide material for dramatization. The rewards are twofold: the substance the material provides, and the ways in which it can be handled dramatically. Skills that are developed through making plays from stories include reading, listening, speaking, and organizing ideas.

Finally, teachers must keep in mind that

1. Children want to succeed. In the creative-drama class, where there is no right or wrong, success is possible.

2. Children want to relate to others, although they may not know how to go about it. In the creative-drama class, which is a communal art, cooperation is an essential element. Therefore, establishing a relationship with others is implicit.

3. Children want to learn, although they may resist being taught. In the creative-drama class, players are learning constantly while enjoying participation in our oldest art form.

ACTIVITY 7.1

INDIAN LEGENDS

"Blue Bonnets" is a favorite with children in the middle and upper grades. Many Indian legends are excellent for improvisation, but this one has a special appeal because it is the story of a child and her sacrifice for the community.

Objective: To make a play from a legend

Suggestions for the Teacher

This charming legend gives an opportunity for total group participation. Since movement is an important element, a good beginning can be made with a dance around the campfire. The use of a drum aids enormously in building rhythms, as the Indians move and dance and pray. You can, of course, begin by telling the story, but before dialogue is attempted, practice in rhythmic movement helps the players to become involved.

Discussion of the story and its theme should precede the playing, inasmuch as this will deepen the children's understanding of a people different in custom, yet like us in their human strengths and weaknesses. When the group is ready to begin, it is suggested that short scenes, rather than the whole story, be played first. For example, the opening scene, in which the Chief calls his people together and explains the seriousness of their situation, is quite enough for one sequence. Yellow Star's sacrifice is another. The players may conceive of the story as taking place in one act, with a break to indicate passage of time, or they may see it as a play in two or three scenes. Because it is a story in which any number may participate, playing it in the round is desirable, if possible. Players and observers are one, and are, therefore, involved to an unusual degree.

The part of Yellow Star is a favorite, but the Chief, the mother, and the selfish braves and squaws can be built into characters who are believable and interesting. If this story finds favor, you may wish to bring other Indian legends to class. Most of them require little more than space for playing, since they are concerned with human beings in conflict with nature and with human weaknesses familiar to all.

BLUE BONNETS

Yellow Star is a little Indian girl who lives with her father and mother in a village belonging to the Comanche tribe. As the story begins, the Chief calls his people together. He describes the trouble that has come to their village after many weeks without rain. The long drought has caused the brooks to dry up; vegetation is dying; and animals have left the parched plains in search of food. The people sit quietly in a circle around the campfire as they listen to their leader. Then they beat the drums and dance, praying to the Great Spirit for rain. At first, nothing happens. Then, suddenly, they hear the voice of the Great Spirit far in the distance. They stop, put down the drums, and listen: "You are being punished for your self-ishness and greed. You have lived in a land of plenty for many years, but your people have not shared with their brothers."

The Chief begs for mercy, but the Great Spirit replies, "I will forgive your tribe and send you the water you need only when one among you sacrifices on the campfire that which is dearest to his heart."

Excitedly, the braves talk together. They suggest that one give his horse, another his jewelry, and still another offer his beautiful young squaw to the Great Spirit. No one, however, is willing to make a sacrifice for the sake of his brothers, and so they move from the campfire and start slowly off toward their homes. The Chief calls them, "Come to this place again in the morning. By that time, one among you may have found the gift that will bring us all forgiveness."

The people slowly disappear, each hoping that someone will think of a way to save them. Only little Yellow Star remains. In her arms, she carries her fawn-skin doll, with its bonnet of blue-jay feathers. The doll is her dearest possession. She realizes that she must throw it into the fire to please the Great Spirit, but it is not easy to part with her only toy. Finally, she reaches her decision, as night falls on the village, and she tells the Great Spirit that she is ready to give that which is dearest to her heart. She watches the doll burn slowly; then, seeing the blue feather bonnet lying in the ashes, she picks it up and throws it into the flames. To her amaze-ment, the feathers do not burn, but become small blue flowers. Yellow Star knows, then, that the Great Spirit has accepted her gift, and with a light heart she runs home.

The next morning, all the Indians gather together, as their Chief has commanded, but where only last night there was a campfire, there is now a huge bed of blue flowers. The people are mystified, for they cannot understand how flowers could have sprung up in the hard, dry earth.

Yellow Star's mother tells the Chief about the doll. "Surely," she says, "it must be a sign. Hundreds of flowers now grow on ground that was trampled and dry."

The people, however, are unwilling to believe her story, for why should the Great Spirit be satisfied with so small a gift as a child's fawn-skin doll? At that moment, there is a roll of thunder in the distance. The Chief knows now that the Great Spirit has accepted Yellow Star's offering. Again, he asks his people to beat their drums and give thanks that they have at last been forgiven. The first raindrops fall.

ACTIVITY 7.2

GREEK MYTHS

Greek mythology is a rich source of material that can be successfully dramatized. One myth that has been used many times with success is the story of Prometheus, who stole fire from the gods. Basic human emotions and a dramatic story make it particularly appealing to children from 9 to 12. The idea of an uninhabited earth stirs their imagination and provides an unusual opportunity for creativity.

Objective: To make a play from a myth

Suggestions for the Teacher

The story must be told carefully and in considerable detail, since not all children will be familiar with it. Although Greek myths are readily available, a brief synopsis of "Prometheus" is given here, with suggestions as to ways in which it can be handled.

The discussion preceding the story can take many directions. It may begin with a consideration of human qualities and feelings. It may begin with occupations and some pantomime suggesting them. It may begin with an analysis of the characters in the story and their conflicts. Eventually, in whatever way the story is introduced, there must be a focus on the characters, their behavior, and the consequences of Prometheus's act.

As with "Blue Bonnets," the myth should be broken down into scenes before it is acted. Work in pantomime can easily be done with the whole group, for there is rich opportunity here. Together, the children can build a hut, hunt for food, plant a field, make a musical instrument (drum or pipe) and discover how to play it, and suggest the beginning of human thought processes. Each activity gives scope for imaginative pantomime. Children love playing the statues who come to life and learn to do the things for which they were intended. One whole period may easily be given over to these pantomime activities.

When the players are ready to begin on the story, they may wish to take turns playing gods and people. If playing in a large room, the children may conceive of one end of it as Mount Olympus and the other end as the earth. Or, if there is a platform, they may decide to locate Mount Olympus on a higher level. The plot calls for at least three scenes, although some groups may see it in five or six. More than one group has played it with a simultaneous setting, with Zeus and Athena observing and commenting, while Prometheus works. When this approach is used, the scenes may move back and forth without a break or scene division.

"Prometheus" is a story strong enough to hold the interest for several class sessions, with constructive discussion preceding and following each playing. If the group enjoys the story, other myths may be introduced, for there are many with fine dramatic action and values that children comprehend. Like the other stories in this chapter, "Prometheus" gains depth and detail with each new playing. The young demigod's sense of responsibility and compassion for his people begins to emerge, adding another dimension to the character. The conflict between the law of Zeus and the moral courage of Prometheus as he begins to feel for his men and women makes for powerful drama. The final playing can be most rewarding, as theme, story, character, and action are unified. The group that has become really involved in Prometheus's dilemma will have had a rich experience.

THE STORY OF PROMETHEUS

The Greek gods and goddesses were believed to have dwelt on Mount Olympus, high above the earth. Ruling over them was the mighty Zeus. Among the young demigods, most in favor with Zeus for his bravery in helping defeat the Titans, was Prometheus. One day Zeus and Athena, goddess of wisdom, were walking in the garden. They caught sight of Prometheus in the distance, looking down toward the earth. Zeus called to him and asked him what interested him, for he often had seen the young demigod staring down at the forests and mountains below.

Prometheus replied that he was troubled because the earth was so empty and silent, with no one moving about its surface. Zeus smiled and said that for some time, he had been considering a reward for the young demigod. "Prometheus," he suggested, "perhaps you would like to descend to the earth and fashion human beings out of soil." Prometheus was overjoyed.

"You are wise and kind," added Athena. "When you create them, remember to give them strong bodies, keen minds, and tender hearts. Let them also see that there is a need for beauty as well as for the necessities of life."

"You may give them any gifts you wish except the gift of fire," continued Zeus. "That alone belongs to the gods and must remain on Olympus. When you have fashioned and are satisfied with your work, I will come down to earth and blow the breath of life into their bodies."

Prometheus was eager to begin and went off swiftly. Working with power and skill, he modeled his first human being upright and powerful and called him "the Builder." Then he took more soil and made a second person, who was likewise tall and strong. Putting a few grains of corn in his hand, he named him "the Sower and Reaper." The third, he pronounced "the Hunter," and to that one he gave a stone. The fourth he called "the Musician." Finally, he finished his fifth, whom he proclaimed "the Thinker."

Scarcely had he stepped back to admire his efforts when the deep voice of Zeus was heard from Olympus. "We are pleased with your people, Prometheus. I shall now come down to blow life into them."

Miraculously, each statue came to life and breathed and moved and walked. As the days passed, Prometheus cared for his people and worked with them, teaching them to do the special jobs for which they had been created. They learned quickly and worked happily. One day, however, the seasons changed. The warm air was replaced by cold winds and snowy weather. The people were cold, and Prometheus was deeply disturbed as he watched them huddling together, trying to keep warm. Finally, he could bear it no longer. He knew he must give them fire.

When he called to Athena for help, she asked, "Do you care so much about your people, Prometheus?"

Prometheus declared that he did.

"Enough to risk the wrath of Zeus!" continued Athena. "He will surely punish you. The one thing he has forbidden them is fire."

"I have made my people, and I must help them, even though I suffer for it," replied Prometheus.

"Very well, then," said Athena, "I will help you find the fire to give them."

As swiftly as he had gone down to earth, Prometheus returned to Olympus to get the fire that he was determined his men and women should have. Then he called the five together and told them not to be frightened, but to learn to use their new gift. Just as he had taught them other things, he taught them how to use fire for warmth and for the cooking of food. He warned them never to let the fire go out. The people were fascinated with the many possibilities of fire, and were soon warm and comfortable again.

It was not long, however, before Zeus learned what had happened. Angrily, he told Prometheus that he had disobeyed and must be punished for his act.

"I am ready to accept my punishment, great Zeus," Prometheus replied, "for I cannot let my people suffer from the wind and cold."

"A gift that has been given cannot be recalled," continued the god. "Human beings now possess fire, but you must pay the price. I shall have you bound by chains to yonder mountain. There you must remain forever and serve as an example to those who dare to disobey my laws."

So saying, Zeus sent his messenger, Hephaestus, down to seize Prometheus and put him in chains. The people were grieved when they saw the dreadful thing that happened to their creator and teacher, but their hearts were filled with gratitude for his great gift to humankind.

ACTIVITY 7.3

A KOREAN TALE

The tales and legends of Korea are little known in this country. "The Magic Gourd" is not unlike many European folk tales in theme, although the setting, of course, differs.

Objective: To make a play from a folk tale

Suggestions for the Teacher

Most legendary material can be played creatively, but the value is enhanced by a study of the culture from which it came. Bringing in gourds and pictures of the countryside and learning about the life of the Korean peasants of a bygone day will help to give the story reality. Although the lesson of actions and their consequences is familiar, it invariably makes for good group discussion. And even though we are primarily concerned with drama, art can never be completely separated from its origin and social message.

THE MAGIC GOURD

Once upon a time in a village in Korea, there were two brothers, Nor Boo and Hoong Boo. The older brother, Nor Boo, was rich and selfish, while the younger brother, Hoong Boo, was poor but kind. Hoong Boo's wife and children lived in a tumble-down cottage with only one ragged blanket to keep them warm while they slept. Whenever Hoong Boo asked Nor Boo for clothing or food, the older brother refused, saying he could not afford to feed two families, although in actuality he had plenty.

One spring day, Hoong Boo noticed a tiny swallow with a broken leg. The kind-hearted peasant picked it up gently and put its bones together. Then he placed it in its nest. The next spring, the swallow returned and dropped a seed from a gourd on Hoong Boo's hand. As food was scarce, and Hoong Boo was touched by the gesture, he planted the seed. The following fall, there were three gigantic gourds growing outside his door, and Hoong Boo decided to eat them. He fetched a saw and slowly cut the first gourd open. To his amazement, instead of fruit, it was filled with gold. Stunned at the sight, he split open the second gourd, and this time glittering jewels poured out. Awe-stricken, he opened the third, which was the largest of them all. There was a sudden explosion.

When the smoke had cleared, Hoong Boo saw a mansion where his humble home had been, with servants moving about in it. He and his family were filled with happiness. They went inside and in no time were living in it as comfortably as if they had lived there all their lives. Now when Nor Boo heard the news, he was furious. He went over to his brother's home at once.

"Dear brother, the news has spread through the village. Tell me, how did you become rich so suddenly?"

"From a seed I planted. When I split open the gourds that grew from it, great riches poured out," answered the honest Hoong.

"Oh, come now, there must be more to it than that. After all, I am your brother. Remember all the things I have done for you? Surely you will share your good fortune with me. Tell me, where did you get the seed?"

Hoong Boo told him. "One day, a little swallow had broken its leg, and I set it for her. I didn't see her again until the next spring. She brought me the seed. When fall came, there were three gourds growing where I planted it. That is all I can tell you."

Nor Boo's eyes flashed greedily. "Thank you, brother, you will not regret this."

Nor Boo went home and waited and waited for a swallow to fall from its nest. Finally, losing his patience, he caught a swallow and broke its leg. Then he set it and went away. Sure enough, the next spring, the bird brought him a seed. Nor Boo could hardly wait to plant it, and he cared for it all that summer. Like his brother's vine, it produced gourds that grew and grew until it was harvest time. So one sunny day, with his saw in hand, Nor Boo cut open the first gourd. Suddenly, as it split open, a swarm of small ferocious insects jumped out and stung him.

"This must be a mistake," cried Nor Boo. Quickly cracking the second gourd, he was struck by a gust of foul-smelling dust.

"The third can't be any worse than this," he exclaimed, as he threw the third down on a rock.

At that, the earth shook violently, and a figure appeared. "How dare you break my brother's leg so you could get rich?" it boomed.

"Who are you?" asked the frightened Nor Boo.

"I am king of the swallows. When I heard what you had done, I came here to punish you."

"I will be kind—and generous—like my brother, I promise," the terrified Nor Boo shouted.

And, would you believe it, from that day on, Nor Boo became one of the kindest men in Korea.

ACTIVITY 7.4

A CHINESE LEGEND

"The Coins of Lin Foo," a legend from China, is particularly good for dramatization. It is included because of its flexibility, its many characters, and its engrossing story.

Suggestions for the Teacher

If the group is inexperienced, it will be wise to play the story just as it is, with no attempt to do it in the Chinese manner. Any number of children can take part, for although there are only a few main characters, there is great opportunity to add any number of villagers, farmers, and merchants at the fair. This will give everyone in the class a chance to work on pantomime and characterization and will help to set the mood. The magistrate's trick to discover the thief is enjoyed by children of every age, and a trial scene always makes for good drama.

Older and more experienced groups may want to play the story in the style of the Chinese theatre, adding to the cast a narrator and a property man. A study of the Chinese theatre should precede any attempt at dramatization. This legend ties in well with a unit on China, should a class be studying it in social studies. If the children want to share their work with another class, it is suggested that simple properties and possibly a panel or backdrop would be fun to make and would enhance the presentation.

THE COINS OF LIN FOO

There was once in a small village in the State of Tsin a lad named Lin Foo, who lived with his widowed mother, Wing Soong. After the father's death, hard times had come upon them, and they had been forced to leave their home and sell their plot of land. Wing Soong, in order to earn a living for herself and her son, made fritters each week, which Lin Foo took to the market to sell. How his mother wished that she might someday earn enough money to educate Lin Foo, for he was as bright as he was industrious!

On this particular morning, when Wing Soong handed him the basket of fritters, the boy asked if he might stay longer in the village, for there was to be a fair, and he wanted to join his friends and look around. "I should like to see the wares in the booths, the flags, and the little carved dragons and birds."

"Of course," said his mother. "Just mind you keep the money safe and do not stay so long that it grows dark before you reach home. You'd better be off now, for the way is long, and already the village will be crowded with the farmers and their carts."

Assuring her that he would be home before dark, Lin Foo set out for the village. There he spent a happy and profitable day. First he sold his basket of fritters and put the money in his pocket. Indeed, he had no trouble at all in selling the fritters, for the humble Wing Soong was known throughout the village for her fine cooking and fair prices. The lad went from booth to booth, finally deciding that the safest place for his money was under a stone near the entrance to the fairgrounds. If he did this, he thought to himself, he could move among the crowds to his heart's content, with no fear of the coins slipping out of his pocket and rolling away in the dust. Carefully, he placed the money under the stone and went off to join some village boys he knew. Finally, it was time to start for home. He bade his friends farewell and went to the stone under which he had hidden his money. But to his dismay, when he lifted it up, there was no money there. Lin Foo was sure that someone must have stolen it. Disconsolate, he sat down by the side of the road, wondering what he would tell his mother and what they would do without money for the coming week. While he was sitting there, An Li, the magistrate, came along; seeing the boy, he asked what was troubling him.

"Oh, master, I am a poor boy, whose mother makes fritters to sell on market day. She entrusted me to bring home the money, which I hid under this stone for safekeeping. When I came back just now to get it, I found it had been taken. And so I have neither money nor fritters to take home with me."

"Have you a father, my boy?" asked the magistrate.

The lad replied that he had not and that he lived alone with his mother, Wing Soong. He told the kindly man that all the money they had was what he got for the fritters. The magistrate questioned him further. "Did you put the money well out of sight?"

"Oh, yes, honored sir. No one could possibly have seen it."

"Is this the stone?"

The boy nodded his head.

Then An Li said, "I shall arrest this stone. You, boy, go on home. But return with your mother tomorrow morning at ten o'clock. I shall try to get your money back for you."

Lin Foo went home. After he had gone, the magistrate had his attendants summon all the villagers who were at the fair that day and order them to be present the next morning for the trial of the stone. He requested that the magistrate's table and chair, two stout bamboo sticks, and a large jar full of water be brought to the spot for the trial.

The following day, Lin Foo and his mother set out for the village. A crowd was already there by the time they arrived. Many of the people thought that An Li had lost his wits from too much study of the law. Some were willing to wait to see what the wise man had in mind. At length, An Li appeared with his attendants. He asked if the boy, Lin Foo, were present. Lin Foo stepped forward. Then he asked if the boy's mother were there also. Wing Soong bowed humbly. Finally, he asked if this was the stone that had stolen the coins. When the boy, mystified, replied that it was, An Li ordered his attendants to strike the stone 50 times with the bamboo sticks. Many people laughed, and some tapped their heads in ridicule. Angrily, An Li shouted, "Silence! You are showing contempt for this court. Each one of you shall be fined 20 li, which you must toss into this jar."

Soberly, the people filed past the jar in a circle and dropped in their coins. As the last man contributed his coin, the magistrate jumped up and shouted, "Arrest this man! He is the thief!"

There was a murmur of excitement and bewilderment in the crowd. They asked each other how the magistrate could know that this man was the thief or if, indeed, he was. Finally, An Li picked up the jar, which he showed to the crowd.

"Do you see here? When this man dropped his coin, these streaks of grease appeared on the surface of the water. Only that coin could have come from the basket that carried the fritters." Then he turned to the thief. "Where is the rest of the money?"

The thief pulled it unwillingly from his pocket. "Here it is, Your Honor."

An Li asked that the money be put in the jar with the rest, and then he announced that the court was dismissed. The villagers began to leave but not without expressing their amazement and respect for the magistrate's wisdom. When they had all gone, An Li handed the jar to Wing Soong. "There you are, my good woman. Your money is restored to you. I hope your son has learned his lesson—never to leave things of value foolishly in such a spot as this, thus tempting the dishonest folk who are watching to steal them."

Wing Soong took the coins gratefully. She thanked the wise magistrate for what he had done and for giving her twice the money the fritters had brought.

ACTIVITY 7.5

A BAHAMIAN FOLKTALE

Stories and legends from the Bahamas are almost unknown in this country. Yet, as in all places where people have lived, worked, played, and worshiped, a rich store of folklore exists. It waits only to be discovered.

Suggestions for the Teacher

"The Old Man and the Goombay Cat" makes wonderful material for creative playing. It gives information about the Bahamas in its description of the country, the plants, the foods, and the customs, including the legends told by the people. It could, therefore, be used in connection with a social-studies unit on the islands. It could also be played purely for the narrative. William T. is an appealing character, and the others can be more fully developed than they are in this account of his strange experience.

After the children have decided which characters are necessary to the telling and which others may be added, they are ready to decide on the scenes. If a large room is being used, one end can be William T.'s cabin; the other, the fishing cove. The middle of the room might be the village square. If the space is small, the scenes can follow in sequence. The procession at the end can be handled in a variety of ways. It can move around the playing space in a large circle or weave in and out, suggesting that it is going into different parts of the village.

All can try playing William T.—showing how he moves, walks, sits, runs, handles his fishing pots, and rescues the cat. When the class is thoroughly familiar with the story, it will want to go on to the enactment of scenes. Again, by allowing small groups to play bits of the story, you will give each an opportunity to contribute dialogue, characterization, and movement. Some groups can be villagers, creating individual characters and showing their love for William T. Classes handle the cat differently. One class wanted to have a child play the part when the cat becomes large. Another group used a "prop" cat in the scenes where it is small, but had a child play the cat when it grows to enormous proportions. Still another imagined it throughout, using offstage sounds when the cat and the parrot meet. This last was probably the most satisfactory solution, but it is good to let the class wrestle with the problem and come up with its own solution.

Some children chant the songs, although there is music that can be used. Superstition and the supernatural intrigue most children, so this aspect of the story usually has particular appeal. There is a rich opportunity here for learning and creative playing. The results will be as simple or as detailed as the children are able to make them.

THE OLD MAN AND THE GOOMBAY CAT*
KITTY KIRBY

Cat Island was home to William T. His father and grandfather were born there. William's father had sold fish by day and had given organ lessons to the island children by night. He had been a "church-going" man. And, like his father, William T. was also a fisherman and gave organ lessons; but now he was getting old and could no longer see the notes.

His wife was dead, and his two sons and daughter had left the island. His only companion was a parrot named Penny. Penny had flown into the old wooden house one day after a tropical storm had swept over the island. She had just flown through the window and adopted old William T. Many afternoons the children would stop by the old man's house to say hello to Penny. The children called William T. "Cousin Will-Yum," and loved to listen to stories of his boyhood. They would sit on the old wooden porch and listen attentively as William T. swung in his worn-out hammock and drew in long breaths of smoke from his pipe. Then he would begin:

"When I was about sixteen, I was one of the best sea divers on the island. My father used to take me out in his small boat to the coral reefs. There we would dive down into the clear, blue-green water into a sea-garden. It was still—so still—we would swim through coral caves with plants all around us. There were hornlike plants and sea fans that looked like feathers. Pink plumeworms with spindly flower petals danced like angels. And bright, jewel-like fish would swim all around us: red parrot fish, blue parrot fish, and silvery grunts."

As he spoke, little girls' eyes would shine brightly as they listened, but the boys would be fidgety and impatient.

"Tell us about the sea monsters and how you set yourself loose from the water octopus," the little boys would beg.

Penny knew these stories well, and would interrupt William T. each time he spoke of the sea fans, the grunts, and the parrot fish. Still, the children would never leave until the old man had finished his stories. Then, after picking some tamarinds from the century-old tamarind tree which shaded the old man's hut, the children would say good-bye to "Cousin Will-Yum" and Penny and leave.

William T. never needed a clock to wake him up in the mornings

* Published with the permission of the author. *Goombay* is an African word that originally meant the language spoken by slaves in the Bahamas. It was later used as the name of the carnival that takes place every June. This carnival, or festival, is similar to Mardi Gras and, like it, includes dancing in the streets, music, and feasting. Goombay Day is the first day, or opening, of the carnival, which, today, is a tourist attraction.

because every morning when the rooster crowed he knew it was time to get up and go fishing.

"Breakfast, Will-Yum Tee. Breakfast!" Penny squawked.

"Come, come, Penny. Give me some time to get hold of myself," answered the old man.

William T. fed Penny and fixed himself a bowl of hominy grits. Penny not only ate her own food, but she helped William T. with his, too.

"Such a glutton," said William T.

"Glutton, glutton!" repeated the parrot. "Yes, you are, but I don't know what I would do without you," said the old man as he put Penny back into her cage.

"Fish biting good today, Will-Yum Tee? Fish biting good today?" chattered Penny.

"Hope so, Penny. You know tomorrow is Goombay Day!" said the old man as he gathered up his fishing pots and said good-bye to the bird.

William T. started down the hilly steps and narrow lanes toward the fishing cove. He hoped that today would bring a good catch. He hadn't had much luck lately. Walking along, he passed barefoot boys and girls on their way to school. They reminded him of when he was a boy. Their faces broke into a smile when they saw him.

"Good morning, Cousin Will-Yum," said the children.

"Morn-in', children. Have a good lesson today and mind the teacher!" answered the old man.

The children giggled. William T. waved good-bye and continued on his way. He walked along the busy waterfront until he came to the edge of Rock Cove. Then he sat down on the warm, pink sand and took his shoes off because he had to wade a little before reaching his rock in the deep water.

"Fish biting good today, mon?" asked William T. as he climbed onto the rock.

"Hope so," answered the other old fishermen.

William T. sat down and began to bait his fishing-pot with pieces of conch.

"Mon, you still using that old fish-pot trap?" teased one of the fishermen.

"Never mind. 'Tis good enough," answered William T.

William T.'s father was known to have made the best triangle fishing-pot traps on the island. The method had been handed down to him from *his* father and he, in time, had taught it to William T. The old man was very proud of the fishing-pot trap and felt it was still good enough to use today. He was just about to lower his pot into the water when the cry of an animal brought him to his feet.

The tormented cry grew louder. Leaving his pot behind, William T. went to see what was wrong. He walked to a nearby rock that jutted out into the water. Not too far from there he saw newcomers. They were teenage boys and they were having lots of fun throwing rocks and pebbles at a scrawny, old, black cat.

"Stop it! Can't you see you are hurting a poor, helpless animal?" shouted William T.

"Go 'way, you silly old man!" said the boys as they continued to torment the cat. "This is a fisherman's rock. You can't even bait a trap. You are too old!"

Shoving one of the boys aside with his elbow, William T. butted the other two with his head. The youths were so amazed at the strength of the old man that they quickly ran to the other side of the rock. William T. looked down at the cat as it let out a mournful "meo-o-ow."

"They won't hurt you anymore," said the old man as he picked up the cat, and together they went back to his fishing spot.

The old man sat down and dropped his pot into the water. Then he and his newly found friend waited. The fish were not biting, and the old man had grown tired, so he pulled in his pot. The cat jumped into the wet pot and rolled over and over in it.

"Mon, you look like one big cat-ball!" said William T. laughingly. He laughed so loudly that all the other fishermen stopped to see what had happened.

"You catching cat instead of fish?" they teased jovially.

"Haven't seen a cat in a long time on the island," said another fisherman. "How did he get on the rock?"

"Don't know," answered William T. Then, looking at the cat, he kept on laughing as he watched it roll out of the pot.

With his head turning and his tail swishing, the cat pranced lightly over to one of the fishermen's baskets and with one swipe of his paw hooked a small porgy and ran back to William T.

"Tut, tut. That was not nice," said the old man, watching the cat devour its delicious fish. After finishing his meal, the cat licked his whiskers and strolled over to William T. Settling himself on the old man's lap, the cat purred and purred and soon fell asleep.

Once more the old man lowered his pot into the water and hooked the ends to the edge of a rock alongside him. He sat there gazing out at the ocean at the hundreds of fishing boats looming over the waters. William T. thought to himself:

"Mon, what big boats! And listen to the sound of those engines and young fishermen singing. Not like the little boats that me and my father used. They even got machines to help catch the fish. Look at the haul of Nassau groupers, jack-runners, margaret-fish, and the largest fresh conch that I've ever seen! You've got to be young and strong to carry all that load on your back. Big Goombay Day for them . . . and all that is left for us old fishermen are little fish that got away from the big nets."

He looked farther up the rock and saw more newcomers.

"I wonder how long it will be before they take over this rock?" he thought. "My father and grandfather fished here, so in a way I inherited this rock." Then he thought of the young boys telling him he was too old for fishing.

At that moment the cat stirred on the old man's lap. William T. stroked the furry body. Somehow he felt calmer, and as he gazed out into the ocean the ripples of the water made him feel drowsy, and he drifted off to sleep.

Many hours passed. The old man was awakened by the tapping of the cat's paw on his arm. He looked around and saw that everyone had gone.

"I'm glad you woke me," said William T.

The cat pushed the fishing-pot with his two large paws and swung the handle from side to side.

"All right, all right! I'll hurry!" said the old man as he pulled in his meager catch. Showing them to the cat, he said, "I did not catch much fish, but you were good company." The cat blinked his eyes and purred.

With the catch over his shoulder and the cat under his arm, William T. climbed off the rock and waded in the water until he reached the pink, sandy shore. The cat jumped from the old man's arms.

"Don't get lost again," said William T. as he waved good-bye to the cat.

After walking for some time, William T. felt he was being followed.

"Meo-ow, meo-ow."

William T. turned around, and there, nosing into some seashells and fishbone along the road, was the cat!

"You are following me. I'd like to take you home, but I'm a poor fisherman and already have a bird that I can barely feed."

"Meo-o-ow," replied the cat mournfully.

As William T. started to leave, he thought he saw teardrops falling from the cat's eyes, but then he thought of Penny. He was late with her supper. So he hurried on his way.

The sun, shining like a large copper ball, was dropping lower and lower behind the fertile green hills. Tourists riding in bright blue surreys, pulled by horses wearing straw hats, nodded their heads in greeting to the old man as he hurried along. The soft night winds rustled the palm leaves of the coconut trees that stood tall and majestic all over the island. The air was also warm and fragrant with the smell of thousands of hibiscus plants. And lamplighters, flickering in and out of trees, lit up the night with their twinkling lights.

The old man trudged up the rocky steps until he reached his house on the top of the hill. From the porch came the sound of Penny.

"Will-Yum Tee, Penny wants supper! You're late! You're late!" squawked the parrot.

"Just now, Penny, I'm coming," said William T. But the parrot just kept on talking.

"Will-Yum Tee! Will-Yum Tee. . . !"

William T. opened the door, found his oil lamp, and lit it. He then washed his hands and mixed some dilly seeds and pumpkin seeds together. Then he went outside to feed Penny, who was still being talkative. While the old man was feeding Penny, the cat was making his way soft-footed around the side of the house. The cat leaped through an open window and landed silently on the cracked, wooden floor. William T. said good-night to Penny and went inside to prepare his supper.

"MEO-O-OW!"

"My goodness, you followed me. And how did you get in here?" asked the old man.

The cat nodded his head up and down, swished his tail, and turned around. Then before William T. knew what was happening, the cat tore across the kitchen of the two-room house and stopped suddenly in front of the table. Looking up at the bowl of coconut milk, he meowed and meowed.

"So you are still hungry? I will share some of my supper with you," said the old man. He gave the cat some coconut milk, mixed some okra and rice with his meager catch of fish, and went outside to cook it in his coal stove. Finally, William T. and the cat sat down to eat their supper.

After the old man and his little friend had finished eating, the cat stretched his two front paws, brushed his whiskers, blinked a cat blink, and yawned. Then he strolled across the room and curled up in an old, worn-out chair. Staring straight at the old man, the pupils of his eyes grew large and bright. His mouth widened into a large grin. The fisherman noticed a strange look on the cat's face. Suddenly the wooden walls began to creak and the sound of bells and drums echoed throughout the room.

"Who's there? Who's there, mon?" he gasped.

William T. tried to get up, but he could not move. There rising up in front of him was an enormous cat of black, shimmering fur. His brilliant eyes, almost blinding the old man, were as green as the ocean. Around his neck he wore a necklace of coral seashells. His silvery whiskers sparkled as he smiled and swayed from side to side to the rhythm of the Goombay. The old man was dumbfounded and his mouth dropped open when the magnificent cat began to sing:

Goombay fish is very nice.
Eat it once, you eat it twice.
Mix it with some okra and rice.
Goombay fish is very nice.

Finally the fisherman found his voice. "A Goombay Cat!" he cried. "A Goombay Cat! Gracious! Heavens, am I dreaming?"

The singing and music stopped as suddenly as it had begun. William T. rubbed his eyes and looked again at the worn-out chair. There, staring and smiling, was the scrawny cat. Shaking nervously, William T. got up and went outside to see if Penny had heard the singing and music too, but the parrot was sleeping soundly.

"My mind must be playing tricks," said William T. to himself as he went back into the house. Gazing curiously at the cat, he patted the animal several times and found him a place to sleep. Then he went off to bed muttering to himself.

"I, I, I, must be get-ting old . . . very old."

The next morning William T. was awakened by a light weight on his chest and a tickling on his cheeks. It was the cat sitting there and blinking at him.

"Morn-in'," chuckled the old man as he rubbed his rugged cheeks. "Your whiskers tickled me."

The cat leaped forward, leaped up in the air, turned three somersaults, and landed with a bounce on the old wooden floor.

"Mon, what a cat! You're sure feeling good this morning."

Looking at the cat and studying him for a moment, he remembered last night. Should he tell his friends about what happened? Would they believe him if he told them about the cat? Or might they say: Cousin Will-Yum is getting old . . . very old. Then he thought to himself—how did the cat get on the rock? And why was this island named Cat Island? Did some strange cats live here long ago? He decided to keep all this to himself, but someday he would tell the story to the children.

Bracing his back, he sat up on the edge of the bed. As he went to put on his shoes the cat pounced at them, pulling at the shoestrings.

"Don't tan-ta-lize me, mon. Let me put my shoes on in peace. I gotta hurry 'cause today is Goombay Day!"

But the cat would not let go.

"Don't vex me," said the old man impatiently. Just then a squawk came from the porch.

"Will-Yum Tee! Will-Yum Tee! Don't forget my breakfast! You're late! You're late!" screeched Penny.

The cat let go of the shoestrings and perked his ears toward the sound. Before William T. could stop him, the cat ran to a hole in the screen door and eased himself through the opening onto the porch. Suddenly the cat caught sight of the beautiful red bird with her flowing tail of brilliant green and yellow feathers. His eyes grew wide and bright as he meo-o-owed loudly. Seeing the cat, Penny flapped her wings furiously as she scuttled wildly around in her cage. Her ruby-red eyes glared in panic.

"Will-Yum Tee! Will-Yum Tee! Hurry! Hurry!"

Thinking something dreadful had happened to Penny, William T. rushed outside; by now he was out of breath. He calmed down when he saw the cat just sitting there watching the wild performance of the bird.

"Come, come, Penny. He won't hurt you. He wants to be your friend."

Penny looked at William T. and then at the cat. With her beak held high, she moved to the corner of the cage.

"Come, Penny," he pleaded as he opened the cage door. Penny hesitated, then flew onto William T.'s shoulder, keeping an eye on the cat.

William T. was very happy and chuckled to himself as he went inside to prepare breakfast for his two friends. After breakfast was over, Penny quickly flew into her cage. She was very quiet. The cat followed William T. and watched him as he locked the cage door.

"Good-bye, Penny. I'll bring you some sweet benny-cake for Goombay."

The cat looked up at Penny and winked his eye, but Penny only flapped her wings. The old man gathered his fishing-pot trap and threw it over his shoulder. He put his last piece of conch, which he had to use as bait, into his pocket; then he and the cat started on their way to Rock Cove.

William T. had seen many a Goombay morning, but somehow there was a strange and happy feeling about this one. The sky was so blue and wide it seemed to run right into the blue-green water. You could not tell where the sky began and the ocean ended. He was so happy that he began to whistle an old familiar tune. Looking down at his little friend, who was strutting gracefully to the rhythm of the tune, he began to sing:

Got-ta catch fish, before big boats come.
Got-ta get it done, before the mid-day sun.
Got-ta catch fish to sell to ev-ry one.
Got-ta catch fish, before the big boats come.

As he was singing he looked up at the sky. Not a cloud was in sight, and the sky was bluer than he had ever seen it. He could feel the heat from the blazing sun burning through the soles of his shoes. The sweat was running down his face. The old man and his friend stopped to rest a while under a shady silk-cotton tree.

"Good morn-in', Cousin Will-Yum," said a group of women with shiny faces. They were carrying baskets on their heads filled to the brim with fruits: soursops, saperdilles, Spanish limes, cassavas, tamarinds, and sea grapes.

"You are early, Cousin Hilda, Rebecca, and Cousin Eunice," said the old man.

"Yes, 'cause it's Goombay Day!" answered the women, swinging their brightly colored, well-starched dresses. Everyone was moving so fast no one noticed Cousin Will-Yum's new friend.

"Come, come let us hurry," said the old man to the cat as they moved along with the crowd. Nearing the waterfront, he and the cat stopped at the Open-Straw Market.

"Big boat in today for Goombay, Cousin Will-Yum," hollered Auntie Hattie B. from her booth in the Open-Straw Market.

"Yes, child. I seen them big tourist ocean liners down by the Prince Charles stop. Lots of money mak-in' to you."

"We'll set up a table for you right by Cousin Eunice on the waterfront," she said.

"Where did you get the cat?" asked Cousin Hilda, noticing the cat for the first time.

"Found him yesterday on top of the rock," answered William T.

Leaving the Open-Straw Market, William T. passed brightly decorated straw booths running along the waterfront. The sun illuminated the blue-green water till it sparkled a jade green. Multicolored seashell beads, big straw pocketbooks, gaily colored straw dolls, and straw hats bedecked with seashells lined the booths.

Suddenly the smell of smothered conch and pigeon peas and rice filled the air. William T. knew he was near the Market Range, with its many booths full of steaming vegetables, sweet fruits, and dazzling pink and white conch shells. Cousin Charlie had his booth here.

Cousin Charlie was busy cooking conch smothered in tomato sauce, and pigeon peas, and rice for the festival. The succulent dish bubbled in a big, cast-iron skillet on an open fire.

The cat ran up to Cousin Charlie's stand, looked up, and meowed and meowed. He licked his whiskers and kept his eyes on the smothered conch.

"Mon, where did you find this cat?" asked Cousin Charlie. "Why, I haven't seen one for a long time on this island."

"He found *me*!" laughed William T.

Cousin Charlie fixed a plate of smothered conch and rice and gave it to the old man and the cat.

"Thank you. We will have a good lunch today," said William T. as he and his little friend pushed their way through the Market Range and headed for the waterfront. When William T. and the cat arrived at the fishing rock, he noticed that the cat's back was arched high, his ears were turned up, and he was switching his tail vigorously in signs of anger. It was then that he looked around only to see the young boys who had taunted the cat yesterday. They were fishing not too far from the old man's spot.

"Come, come. They won't bother you," said William T. as he sat down to bait his fishing trap.

The cat flexed his muscles, his tail stood straight up, and his eyes grew large and bright as he watched the fishing trap being lowered into the blue-green waters. William looked at the cat. He gasped when he saw that once more the cat was changing in size. He began to tremble and broke out in a cold sweat as harmonious sounds of bells and drums swelled across the ocean. At that moment a gigantic wave rose up and the great cat leaped into the oncoming billowing waves.

"Help! Help!" cried William T. "My cat is in the water!"

But the other fishermen were so frightened by the crashing of the water against the rocks that they did not hear his cry.

Suddenly the music stopped and the waters were calm again. William T. noticed the fishing-trap was still in place, but there was a heavy tugging on it. He tried to pull the trap up, but it would not give. Again he cried for help. Hearing his call, his fishing companions came to his rescue. Together they grabbed hold of the fishing-trap and began to pull and pull. All at once out of the water came the trap-pot filled with hundreds of beautiful fish shimmering in the sunlight. And there amidst the miraculous catch nestled the cat.

"My *cat*! My *cat*!" cried William T. But the fishermen were so amazed by the miraculous catch that they paid no attention to the cat.

"Mon, look at that catch! Biggest I've ever seen!" shouted one of the fishermen.

"Never seen so many fish in one haul," said another.

Tears of joy ran down William T.'s cheeks as he lifted the wet, shivering body out of the trap and cradled it under his tattered old coat.

"Are you all right, mon?" he whispered. The cat looked up at William T. and purred contentedly.

"Old man, how did you catch all those fish?" asked the teenage boys.

It was then that William T. looked at his fishing trap piled high with goggle-eyed fish: margaret fish, jack-runners, grunts, and Nassau group-ers. He was so happy that he could not speak for a moment. He just stood there staring at his catch. Then, remembering the boys' question, he looked down at the cat and said:

"Just luck, mon. Just luck."

"Will you sell us some of your catch?" asked one of the boys.

"*No!*" I will not sell you any of my catch . . . but I will give you some of them." He then shared many of his fish with his companions and the boys. The boys felt ashamed and sorry for the way they had treated the cat and the old man.

"May we help you carry your load off the rock?" asked the boys.

The cat purred; the old man smiled, and said he would like that very much.

News of Cousin William's catch spread all along the waterfront. Auntie Hattie B., Cousins Eunice, Hilda, and Rebecca, and all the women left the Goombay tables to see the great haul of fish. Even Cousin Charlie left the Market Range to see Cousin William's big catch. Children came from all over the island when they heard the news of the old man's catch. Now they danced around him, playing big bass drums and singing a song of the Goombay catch:

> Cous-in Will-Yum caught big catch!
> From the blue-green waters.
> He caught them in his fish-pot trap,
> From the blue-green waters.

While the children sang, the cat swished his tail to the rhythm of the song. William T. was so happy he began to sing too:

> Goombay Cat caught big fish.
> From the island wa-ters
> He caught them with a great big smile,
> From the island wa-ters.

The teenage boys walked tall, their heads held high, as they carried William T.'s catch to his table. William T. strutted proudly before them with the cat riding on his arm. It was a grand sight to see the joyous procession marching to their tables to begin the Goombay festival. Tables were quickly filled with fried chicken, coconut cakes, and other delectable dishes.

"Well, mon," said William T., setting the cat by his table. "It's time for us to fix our table."

The old man was about to pick up his fish-pot when he heard the sound of the Goombay song! It lasted for a brief second, and when William T. looked down again the cat was gone! Where his little friend had stood was a shiny, coral, seashell necklace. He picked it up slowly and he knew that his little friend was now gone forever.

However, William T. was not sad. The beautiful necklace was left by the Goombay Cat to remind him that miracles still happen and that he wasn't so very old after all.

New Words

Conch shell A large univalve shell of spiral appearance; a mollusk shell native to the Florida Keys and the Bahamas

Coral reef A hard structure secreted in or by the tissues of various marine organisms, serving as a support and place of abode

Cove A harbor with rocks where the natives fish

Jack-runner, grouper, water octopus, grunt Fish found in waters around the Bahamas

Sea fan A coral with fanlike branches

GOTTA CATCH FISH
KITTY KIRBY

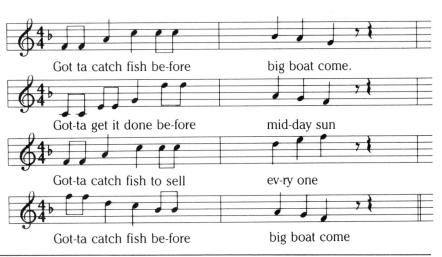

Got ta catch fish be-fore   big boat come.

Got-ta get it done be-fore   mid-day sun

Got-ta catch fish to sell   ev-ry one

Got-ta catch fish be-fore   big boat come

8

THE MANY
POSSIBILITIES
IN POETRY

Children like poetry. They are sensitive to the rhythm of poetry and enjoy the repetition of sounds, words, and phrases. The direct approach of the poet is not unlike their own; hence poetry, unless it has been spoiled for them, has a special appeal to children. The music and language, as well as the ideas, feelings, and images of poetry, reach children, capturing and stimulating their imagination. For this reason, poetry can be used in creative drama, often with highly successful results.

Many teachers find poetry a more satisfactory springboard than prose for introducing creative playing to a group. This is probably an individual matter, depending as much on the leader as on the participants. If teachers enjoy poetry themselves, they will find that it provides a rich source of material that can be used at all levels of experience and with all ages. For children, poetry and play go together quite naturally.

For these reasons, the possibilities in poetry as motivation are considered. What kinds of poems are usable? How can poetry and movement be combined? Has choral speaking any place in creative drama? For the answers to these questions, the teacher has only to go to the children themselves as they engage in their play. Many of their games are accompanied by chants, which are a form of choral speaking. Rhythm is basic in action games, while some games are played to verse, with the players often making up original stanzas. If we listen, we note the enjoyment of repetition, refrain, and the sounds of words. Only very much later does poetry become a literary form to be taken seriously, and when it does, the element of play, unfortunately, is too often lost, along with the enjoyment.

CHORAL SPEAKING

Because poetry lends itself so well to the group, let us begin this chapter with a consideration of choral speaking, its purposes and procedures. Choral reading or speaking is simply reading or reciting in unison under the direction of a leader. It is not a new technique, for people have engaged in it for centuries. It antedated the theatre in the presentation of ideas and became an important element of the Greek drama. Evidences of choral speaking have been found in the religious ceremonies and festivals of primitive peoples, and it is still used for ritualistic purposes in church services and on patriotic occasions. In the early twentieth century, moreover, it was recognized as one of the most effective methods of teaching the language arts and of improving speech habits.

In the past, choral speaking was used as an important means of communication and communion; today, it is an art form as well and is employed both ways by the theatre, the church, and the school. When working with older children or adults, choral speaking has three major purposes:

1. Learning (when the purpose is process and, therefore, is participant centered)
2. Performance (when the purpose is program and, therefore, is audience centered)
3. Enjoyment.

As with creative drama, it does not necessarily follow that the practice of choral speaking must result in performance. Practice has values of its own, whether or not the product is shared with others. Usually it is not.

VALUES

One of the values of choral speaking is that it can be used successfully regardless of space or class size. While a group of 20 or so is more desirable than one of 40 or 50, the larger number need not be a deterrent.

Many teachers consider the greatest value of choral speaking to be the opportunity it provides for speech improvement. Pitch, volume, rate, and tone quality are important to the effective interpretation of material. The need for clear diction is apparent when a group is reading aloud, whereas the practicing of speech sounds alone is often a tedious and unrelated exercise. During discussion, even young children will make suggestions as to how a poem should be recited. Vocal expression and clear enunciation of speech sounds are often acquired more easily and with greater motivation when the group works together on meaning.

A third value, which choral speaking shares with creative drama, is the opportunity it provides for cooperation. Choral speaking is a group activity, and thus directs each individual to a common goal. The·child with the strident voice learns to soften his tone, whereas the shy child can work for more volume without feeling self-conscious. Even the speech-handicapped child may recite without embarrassment, because she is not speaking alone and, therefore, is not conspicuous.

A fourth value of choral speaking is its suitability to any age level. It may be introduced in the kindergarten, but it is equally effective when used in high-school or college classes. Not all material is adaptable to choral work, but much is, and the major criterion is probably that it be enjoyed by the speakers themselves.

PROCEDURES

There are many ways to begin choral speaking. With older children who have had no experience in group reading, the teacher will not only select the material with care, but also give some thought in advance to its interpretation. Discussion of the meaning and of the various ways of reading the material in order to bring out the meaning gives pupils a part in planning the group reading. A second reading will reveal further meaning, as well as difficulties in phrasing and diction.

As the group becomes more experienced, it will offer suggestions as to those lines that may be most effectively taken by the whole group, by part of the group, and by individuals. Although a structured activity, choral speaking offers a real opportunity for creative thinking, as each group works out its own presentation. The teacher leads, indicating when to start, and watches the phrasing, emphases, and pauses suggested by the readers. The amount of time spent on a poem will vary, but it is more important to keep the enthusiasm alive than to work for perfection. With practice, the participants will grow increasingly sensitive to the demands of different kinds of material, and their results will improve in proportion to their understanding and enjoyment.

Most authorities on choral speaking suggest dividing the group into light and dark voices. This is not quite the same as a division into high and low, or soprano and alto, voices but has to do with quality and resonance as well as pitch. Some leaders, however, believe that a division in which there are both light and dark voices in each group makes for more interesting quality. However it is done, some division is necessary for any class of more than 10 children. Some poems can be read by three groups if the class is very large. These may include middle voices—although, again, it is the material that will suggest the groupings, rather than an arbitrary division.

WAYS OF READING

Unison.   In unisonous choral speaking, the whole group speaks together. Although the simplest technique in one sense, reciting in unison is the most difficult, since using all voices limits variation. It takes practice to achieve clear diction and make the reading interesting. Some poems, particularly short ones, are most effective when read or spoken by the entire class.

Antiphony.   In antiphonal speaking, each one of two groups takes certain parts. Many poems are more effective when recited in antiphony than in unison. The poem will dictate the way it may be read.

Cumulative.   The cumulative technique is used to build toward a climax, or certain high points in the poem. As the term suggests, cumulative choral speaking is the accumulation of voices, either of individuals or of groups.

Solo.   Lines or stanzas often call for individual speaking. Solo choral speaking can be an effective technique, as well as a way of giving an opportunity for individual participation.

Line-around.   Line-around choral speaking is solo work, in which each line is taken by a different person. Children enjoy this technique and are alert to the lines they have been assigned.

As the group progresses and attempts longer and more difficult material, it may suggest using several or all of these techniques in one poem. The results can be remarkably effective, encouraging attentiveness, self-discipline, and imaginative planning. Occasionally, sound effects can be added. Music, bells, drums, and vocal sounds, produced by the children themselves, provide an opportunity for further inventiveness.

POETRY FOR CHORAL SPEAKING

Because our primary concern is creative drama, poems that suggest movement or pantomime are presented in Activities 8.1, 8.3, and 8.5.

The poems in Activities 8.1 to 8.8 have been used successfully with many groups, combining choral speaking and activities suggested by the content or sounds of the poem. The first, "Happy New Year," is an old rhyme, suggesting the simplest kind of movement as a beginning. The group members can say the verse together, with one child acting the part of the caroler; or half the group can speak, with the other half playing the carolers. Perhaps the entire group will want to speak and move. There are various possibilities in even as short a rhyme as this.

HAPPY NEW YEAR

All	Happy New Year! Happy New Year!
Solo	I've come to wish you a Happy New Year.
	I've got a little pocket and it is very thin.
	Please give me a penny to put some money in.
	If you haven't got a penny, a halfpenny[1] will do.
	If you haven't got a halfpenny, well—
	God bless you!

Many years ago in England, children went caroling from house to house on New Year's Day. Their listeners gave them money, much as we give candy and apples for trick or treat on Hallowe'en. Whether or not they received a contribution, they sang or spoke, and this old rhyme has been handed down.

As the teacher works on choral speaking, its values soon become apparent. First of all, for most children, it's fun. In addition,

1. Choral speaking offers the timid child and the slow reader an opportunity to overcome his or her fear by being in a group, yet occasionally having a line to say alone.
2. It moves the aggressive child into the background within an acceptable structure.
3. It introduces children to new material and offers them an opportunity to repeat old and familiar works.

One word of caution: avoid excessive practice. Drilling for perfection can destroy the values of choral work and have a lasting negative effect.

POETRY AND DANCE

Poetry grew out of dance and song, and so these are natural companions. Inviting a dancer to the class—the dance teacher, perhaps older students who have had more dance experience than the class, or a

[1] Pronounced hā' pə nē.

professional dancer if one is available—adds another dimension when working with poems. Dance offers an abstract expression rather than the more literal interpretation of mime and improvisation. Dividing the class, with one half moving to the cadence and meaning of the poem and the other half speaking it, calls for imagination and cooperation.

Working on poetry first in mime and then in dance helps students experience it more fully. Lyric verse lends itself best to nonverbal interpretation, whereas narrative and dramatic verse stimulate the improvisation of dialogue. Some groups respond to poetry more readily than others but most will enjoy it, if the leader's approach is positive and enthusiastic.

A poet or a professional children's-theatre company that performs poetry may inspire children. One such company (Periwinkle Productions, of Monticello, New York) began playing poetry programs over 20 years ago and retains poetry performance as an important emphasis in an expanding theatrical repertory. In addition to poetry reading and performances, the company works in schools with teachers to encourage creative writing, principally poetry.

SUMMARY

Poetry is an effective springboard for improvisation; and improvisation, for poetry. The directness of verse motivates the players to a direct and imaginative response. For this reason, poetry is a good starting point for the beginner, although it can be used at any time with even the most advanced players. Because the sounds of poetry have as great an appeal as the content and mood, it is suggested that poetry be spoken as well as acted.

Choral speaking is a group art and can, therefore, be combined with creative drama if the teacher so wishes. Some of the reasons for including choral speaking are as follows:

1. It can be done with groups of any size and age.
2. It emphasizes group rather than individual effort.
3. It provides an opportunity to introduce poetry to a class.
4. It offers the shy or disabled child an opportunity to speak.
5. It promotes good habits of speech through enjoyable exercise, rather than drill.
6. It is fun.
7. It can be combined successfully with rhythmic movement and panto-mime.

Just as action songs are used with very young children as an approach to creative rhythms, so poetry may be used with older children to suggest mood, stimulate ideas, and begin the flow of creative energy. Chants and the repetition of words have a natural appeal. Thus poetry and nonsense verse may prove a successful method of introducing creative drama.

ACTIVITY 8.1

LEAVE HER, JOHNNY, LEAVE HER

The hearty spirit expressed in the ballad "Leave Her, Johnny, Leave Her" has an appeal for children of the intermediate grades. The swinging rhythm established by the solo speaker is picked up by the group, who use it in bodily and vocal expression. If children enjoy this ballad, they will probably enjoy other work songs, of which there are many.

Objective: *Speaking in unison while moving to verse*

Suggestions for the Teacher

Begin with a discussion of sea chanteys. Try to find recordings of chanteys and traditional sea ballads for the children to sing. "Leave Her, Johnny, Leave Her" is reported to be an old ballad that was saved for the last spell at the pumps before the sailors left the boat to go ashore.

Have the class feel the rhythm of the pump handles going up and down as they say the verse together. Then let a solo voice take the first and third lines while the rest of the group repeats the refrains. Finally, suggest that the chorus work the pumps rhythmically as they speak their lines. The repetition of words makes memorization easy.

LEAVE HER, JOHNNY, LEAVE HER
(TRADITIONAL)

Solo	I thought I heard the old man say,
Group	Leave her, Johnny, leave her!
Solo	You can go ashore and draw your pay,
Group	It's time for us to leave her.
Solo	Oh, the times are hard and the wages low,
Group	Leave her, Johnny, leave her!
Solo	I'll pack my bag and go below,
Group	It's time for us to leave her.
Solo	It's growl you may, but go you must,
Group	Leave her, Johnny, leave her!
Solo	It matters not whether you're first or last,
Group	It's time for us to leave her.
Solo	I'm getting thin and growing sad,
Group	Leave her, Johnny, leave her!
Solo	Since first I joined this wooden-clad,
Group	It's time for us to leave her.
Solo	I thought I heard the first mate say,
Group	Leave her, Johnny, leave her!
Solo	Just one more drag and then belay!
Group	It's time for us to leave her.

ACTIVITY 8.2
_____

THE PLAINT OF THE CAMEL

Objective: To give practice in articulation through choral speech

Suggestions for the Teacher

"The Plaint of the Camel," a nonsense poem, is fun to speak; it is also a fine study in "patter" work. It needs spirit in the telling and the capacity to maintain a light, animated tone and crisp, clean-cut articulation. All the fun will go if the speakers drawl, speak lifelessly and monotonously, or give feeble consonants. It is not speed that must be worked for, but neatness and agility of speech movements—the capacity to pass lightly but firmly from syllable to syllable and from word to word, taking time to give the meaning and the mood as well as to shape the sounds.

The poem can be spoken as line-around or as solo work. The first line of each stanza can be spoken by one voice; the second, by another; and the next two lines (which are almost always linked together), by a third. All the speakers might join in speaking the last three lines of each stanza. In stanza 4, there is a slight difference to this order. Because of the form in which this stanza is cast, it would seem best to give the first two lines to one speaker and the second two, to another. It is quite possible to choose a different set of single speakers for each verse, thus using 17 speakers; this practice is helpful as a preliminary to individual speaking.

THE PLAINT OF THE CAMEL*
CHARLES EDWARD CARRYL

Voice 1	Canary-birds feed on sugar and seed,
Voice 2	Parrots have crackers to crunch;
Voice 3	And as for the poodles, they tell me the noodles
	Have chickens and cream for their lunch.
Voice 4	But there's never a question
	About MY digestion—
	ANYTHING does for me!
Voice 5	Cats, you're aware, can repose in a chair,
Voice 6	Chickens can roost upon rails;
Voice 7	Puppies are able to sleep in a stable,
Voice 8	And oysters can slumber in pails.
Voice 4	But no one supposes
	A poor Camel dozes—
	ANY PLACE does for me!

* This poem appears in many anthologies. One of the easiest to find is Marjorie Gullan, *The Speech Choir* (New York: Harper & Row, 1937), pp. 153–154.

Voice 9	Lambs are enclosed where it's never exposed,
Voice 10	Coops are constructed for hens;
Voice 11	Kittens are treated to houses well heated,
Voice 12	And pigs are protected by pens.
Voice 4	But a Camel comes handy
	Wherever it's sandy—
	ANYWHERE does for me!
Voice 13	People would laugh if you rode a giraffe,
	Or mounted the back of an ox;
Voice 14	It's nobody's habit to ride on a rabbit,
	Or try to bestraddle a fox.
Voice 4	But as for a Camel, he's
	Ridden by families—
	ANY LOAD does for me!
Voice 15	A snake is as round as a hole in the ground;
Voice 16	Weasels are wavy and sleek;
Voice 17	And no alligator could ever be straighter
	Than lizards that live in a creek.
Voice 4	But a Camel's all lumpy
	And bumpy and humpy—
	ANY SHAPE does for me!

ACTIVITY 8.3

GET UP AND BAR THE DOOR

"Get Up and Bar the Door" is an old ballad that I have used successfully on every level, although children of the intermediate grades and junior high school enjoy it the most.

Objective: Speaking the verses in unison while four characters enact the story

Suggestions for the Teacher

Before putting the reading and the action together, it's a good idea to practice each separately. Have the class read the ballad aloud first. Next, let several pairs of students act it out, either in pantomime or with improvised dialogue—the poem by itself makes a good play. Finally, gradually meld words and action scene by scene.

This is such good drama that it bears repeating in a demonstration or a program for parents.

GET UP AND BAR THE DOOR

It fell about the Martinmas* time,
    And a gay time it was then,
When our goodwife got puddings to make,
    And she'd boiled them in the pan.

The wind so cauld blew south and north,
    And blew into the floor;
Quoth our goodman to our goodwife,
    "Gae up and bar the door."

"May hand is in my hyssyfscap,
    Goodman, as ye may see;
And it should nae be barred this hundred year,
    It'll no be barred by me."

They made a pact between them twa,
    They made it firm and sure,
That the first word whoe'er should speak,
    Should rise and bar the door.

Then by there came two gentlemen,
    At twelve o'clock at night,
And they could neither see house nor hall,
    Nor coal nor candle-light.

---

* St. Martin's Day, a church festival held on November 11, in commemoration of the saint (315?–399?)

"Now whether is this a rich man's house,
Or whether is it a poor?"
But ne'er a word wad one o' them speak,
For barring of the door.

And first they ate the white puddings,
And then they ate the black;
Tho' muckle thought the goodwife to hersel'
Yet ne'er a word she spake.

Then said the one unto the other,
"Here, man, take ye my knife;
Do ye take off the auld man's beard,
And I'll kiss the goodwife."

O up then started our goodman,
An angry man was he:
"Will ye kiss my wife before my eyes,
And scad me wi'pudding-bree?"

Then up and started our goodwife,
Gied three skips on the floor;
"Goodman, you've spoken the foremost word,
Get up and bar the door!"

ACTIVITY 8.4

THE PIRATE DON DURKE OF DOWDEE

Objective: To try a ballad with refrain, using light and dark voices

Suggestions for the Teacher

The nonsense ballad "The Pirate Don Durke of Dowdee" is excellent for the fun it gives by means of its swashbuckling and melodramatic style. It should be given with real dash and spirit, with a swinging rhythm and crisp speech. The contrast between the pirate's wickedness and his gorgeousness, noted in the first and last stanzas, must be given full value by all the voices. These two stanzas can be spoken by all the choir, and each of the rest of the stanzas can be spoken by a different individual or a different small group, all of the chorus joining in the last line of each stanza. The individual or small group speaking the verses also should speak the refrain, which is an integral part of the verse.

THE PIRATE DON DURKE OF DOWDEE*
MILDRED PLEW MEIGS

All voices	Ho, for the Pirate Don Durke of Dowdee! He was as wicked as wicked could be, But oh, he was perfectly gorgeous to see! The Pirate Don Durke of Dowdee.
Dark voices	His conscience, of course, was as black as a bat, But he had a floppety plume on his hat, And when he went walking it jiggled—like that!
All voices	The plume of the Pirate Dowdee.
Light voices	His coat it was crimson and cut with a slash, And often as ever he twirled his mustache, Deep down in the ocean the mermaids went splash,
All voices	Because of Don Durke of Dowdee.
Dark voices	Moreover, Dowdee had a purple tattoo, And stuck in his belt where he buckled it through Were a dagger, a dirk and a squizzamaroo,
All voices	For fierce was the Pirate Dowdee.
Light voices	So fearful he was he would shoot at a puff, And always at sea when the weather grew rough, He drank from a bottle and wrote on his cuff,
All voices	Did Pirate Don Durke of Dowdee.

* Marjorie Gullan, *The Speech Choir* (New York: Harper & Row, 1937), p. 90.

Dark voices   Oh, he had a cutlass that swung at his thigh,
                  And he had a parrot called Pepperkin Pye,
                  And a zigzaggy scar at the end of his eye,
All voices   Had Pirate Don Durke of Dowdee.

Light voices   He kept in a cavern, this buccaneer bold,
                  A curious chest that was covered with mould,
                  And all of his pockets were jingly with gold!
All voices   Oh jing! went the gold of Dowdee.

Dark voices   His conscience, of course, it was crook'd like a squash,
                  But both of his boots made a slickery slosh,
                  And he went through the world with a wonderful
                  swash,
All voices   Did Pirate Don Durke of Dowdee.

All voices   It's true he was wicked as wicked could be,
                  His sins they outnumbered a hundred and three,
                  But oh, he was perfectly gorgeous to see,
                  The Pirate Don Durke of Dowdee.

ACTIVITY 8.5

I HEAR AMERICA SINGING

*Objective: To speak or read a poem cumulatively, **with small groups or individuals performing the actions in pantomime***

Suggestions for the Teacher

"I Hear America Singing" is a splendid poem for both choral speaking and dramatization. The various characters and their occupations suggest pantomime to participants of all ages. If playing in a large room, the characters can be scattered about a circle, with any number taking part. Pantomime and speaking may be done simultaneously or separately, as the group prefers. The mood is powerful and usually acts as a unifying element.

I HEAR AMERICA SINGING*
WALT WHITMAN

Solo	I hear America singing, the varied carols I hear,
Add voices	Those of mechanics, each one singing his as it should be blithe and strong,
Add a voice	The carpenter singing his as he measures his plank or beam,
Add a voice	The mason singing his as he makes ready for work, or leaves off work,
Add a voice	The boatman singing what belongs to him in his boat, the deckhand singing on the steamboat deck,
Add a voice	The shoemaker singing as he sits on his bench, the hatter singing as he stands,
Add a voice	The wood-cutter's song, the ploughboy's on his way in the morning, or at noon intermission or at sundown,
Add a voice	The delicious singing of the mother, or of the young wife at work, or of the girl sewing or washing,
Add a voice	Each singing what belongs to him or her and to none else,
All	The day what belongs to the day—at night the party of young fellows, robust, friendly,
	Singing with open mouths their strong melodious songs.

* Walt Whitman, *Leaves of Grass* (Garden City, N.Y.: Doubleday).

ACTIVITY 8.6

ABRAHAM LINCOLN

Objective: To speak or read a poem aloud using a variety of voices and techniques

Suggestions for the Teacher

"Abraham Lincoln" is good for choral reading because of its combination of exposition and dialogue. Children in the middle grades are familiar with Lincoln, so that preparation for reading it is minimal. The spare, direct verse is expressive of the man and is easy for a group of young readers to handle.

ABRAHAM LINCOLN (1809–1865)*
ROSEMARY CARR AND STEPHEN VINCENT BENET

All voices	Lincoln was a long man, He liked out of doors. He liked the wind blowing, And the talk in country stores.
Light voices *Dark voices* *Several voices*	He liked telling stories, He liked telling jokes. "Abe's quite a character," Said quite a lot of folks.
Dark voices	Lots of folks in Springfield Saw him every day, Walking down the street In his gaunt, long way.
Light voices *Several voices*	Shawl around his shoulders, Letters in his hat. "That's Abe Lincoln," They thought no more than that.
Solo 1 *Solo 2* *Solo 3*	Knew that he was honest, Guessed that he was odd, Knew he had a cross wife Though she was a Todd.
Solo 4 *Solo 5*	Knew he had three little boys Who liked to shout and play, Knew he had a lot of debts It took him years to pay.

* Rosemary Carr and Stephen Vincent Benet, "Abraham Lincoln (1809–1865)," in May Hill Arbuthnot, ed., *Time for Poetry* (Glenview, Ill.: Scott, Foresman, 1961), pp. 41–42.

Solo 6	Knew his clothes and knew his house, "That's his office, here.
Solo 7	Blame good lawyer, on the whole, Though he's sort of queer."
Solo 8	"Sure he went to Congress, once, But he didn't stay.
Solo 9	Can't expect us all to be Smart as Henry Clay."*
Dark voices	"Need a man for troubled times? Well, I guess we do.
Light voices	Wonder who we'll ever find? Yes—I wonder who."
All voices	That is how they met and talked, Knowing and unknowing. Lincoln was the green pine. Lincoln kept on growing.

* Henry Clay was an American statesman and orator with a reputation for brilliance (1777–1852).

ACTIVITY 8.7

THE OWL AND THE PUSSY-CAT

Objective: To read an amusing verse with lightness, humor, and precision of articulation

Suggestions for the Teacher

Most of the children will be familiar with "The Owl and the Pussy-Cat" and will enjoy reading it aloud. Experiment with it. Try parts in unison, antiphonally, with solo voices, and cumulatively.

After trying it as suggested below, see what other arrangements can be made. After children have read or spoken a number of poems, they will have some ideas of their own.

THE OWL AND THE PUSSY-CAT
EDWARD LEAR

All voices

The Owl and the Pussy-Cat went to sea
In a beautiful pea-green boat,
They took some honey, and plenty of money
Wrapped up in a five-pound note.

Light voices

The Owl looked up to the stars above,
And sang to a small guitar,

Owl solo

"O lovely Pussy, O Pussy, my love,
What a beautiful Pussy you are,
You are,
You are!

All voices

What a beautiful Pussy you are!"

Pussy-cat solo

Pussy said to the Owl, "You elegant fowl,
How charmingly sweet you sing!
Oh! Let us be married, too long we have tarried:
But what shall we do for a ring?"

All voices

They sailed away, for a year and a day,
To the land where the Bong-tree grows;
And there in a wood a Piggy-wig stood,
With a ring at the end of his nose,
His nose,
His nose,
With a ring at the end of his nose.

Owl solo

"Dear Pig, are you willing to sell for one shilling
Your ring?"

Pig solo

Said the Piggy, "I will,"

Light voices

So they took it away, and were married next day
By the Turkey who lives on the hill.

Dark voices   They dined on mince and slices of quince,
                   Which they ate with a runcible spoon;
All voices   And hand in hand, on the edge of the sand,
                   They danced by the light of the moon,
                              The moon,
                              The moon,
                   They danced by the light of the moon.

Questions

1. What is a five-pound note? a shilling?
2. What is a runcible spoon?
3. Do you know any other verses by Edward Lear?

A program of verses by Edward Lear not only is fun, but stimulates imagination, humor, and ideas about reading them.

ACTIVITY 8.8

WHAT DO WE PLANT?

Objective: To read a poem aloud, trying various ways of expressing the ideas

Suggestions for the Teacher

"What Do We Plant?" has no place for solo work but suggests different ways of reading it. Have the class offer ideas and try them out. The children will come up with interesting effects and in the meantime will give thought to the uses of wood and of other natural resources and to our waste of or care for them. There are lessons in this poem as well as appreciation of the verse itself.

WHAT DO WE PLANT?
Henry Abbey

What do we plant when we plant the tree?
We plant the ship, which will cross the sea.
We plant the mast to carry the sails;
We plant the planks to withstand the gales—
The keep, the keelson, and beam and knee;
We plant the ship when we plant the tree.

What do we plant when we plant the tree?
We plant the houses for you and me.
We plant the rafters, the shingles, the floors,
We plant the studding, the lath, the doors,
The beams and siding, all parts that be;
We plant the house when we plant the tree.

What do we plant when we plant the tree?
A thousand things that we daily see;
We plant the spire that out-towers the crag,
We plant the staff for our country's flag,
We plant the shade, from the hot sun free;
We plant all these when we plant the tree.

9

PUPPETS AND MASKS

Puppets and masks are an important part of theatre history, predating by centuries the play as we know it. In many countries, puppetry enjoys the status of a fine art, designed and performed for adults, whereas in our country, it is generally regarded as children's entertainment. In recent years, however, there has been an awakened interest in puppetry as an art form, resulting in a new popularity, and its value as a teaching tool has been recognized. Besides providing alternatives or adjunct activities to creative drama, puppetry and mask making offer wonderful incentives for improvisation.

One could say that puppetry starts with dramatic play, when dolls and toys are manipulated to perform various roles and actions. The young child's game of peek-a-boo, with the hands hiding the face, illustrates an early concept of the mask. As children grow older, they assign both mask and puppet more specific functions and handle them with greater dexterity. Children's first awareness of the mask as a mask, however, probably occurs at about the age of 4 or 5, when they wear it as part of a Hallowe'en costume. Children of that age put on masks, confident that they are hidden from view and disguised as ghosts, witches, or monsters. Puppets and masks have much in common; in fact, they sometimes are indistinguishable from each other. In this chapter, some of the ways in which both can be made and combined with creative drama will be discussed.

PUPPETS

Many persons associate puppetry with the field of entertainment, although it is equally at home in the classroom. Today, with the popularity of the Muppets and other puppet characters on television, children learn about puppets at an early age and become acquainted with some of the techniques of handling them. This familiarity suggests to the teacher ways to include puppets either as special craft projects or as tools for teaching subjects other than arts and crafts. A further, and particularly valuable, use is the social or therapeutic one: through the puppet, a shy or troubled child is often able to express what she cannot state as herself. Best of all, perhaps, because these engaging little creatures are such fun to make and manipulate, they capture the child's attention and hold it in a variety of situations.

What is a puppet? Contrary to what many think, puppets are not dolls, although they often resemble them. Puppets are "actors" who come to life with the help of a puppeteer. Almost any object can be a puppet: a toy, a tool, a hairbrush, a lollipop, a spoon, a broom. Even the hand can be a puppet, if the "puppeteer" moves it and speaks so that the

The mouth. (Photograph by David Attie from Making Puppets Come Alive *by Larry Engler and Carol Fijan, Taplinger, 1973)*

hand appears to be doing the walking and talking. Just to prove it, try transforming a few common objects into puppets. Kneel behind a table and move an object along the edge of it. Keep moving. Here are a few things that can be used.

1. *A wooden spoon.* Make it walk, run, jump, and disappear.

2. *A toy.* A teddy bear or a rag doll, which are soft and move in different ways from the spoon, will do. Sometimes toys make fine puppets, but it is not a good idea to depend on them. The puppets you make yourself will almost always be better.

3. *A pencil, a ruler, a lollipop, an artificial flower.* They will become different characters when you start moving them. Now try holding one in each hand. What happens when a pencil and a ruler meet?

4. *Your own hands.* What can they do that the other things cannot do? Hands make wonderful movements. Let them walk, dance, jump, fight, bow, and march off.

Look around for some other objects that have not been mentioned. Invent actions for them and decide what kinds of characters they seem to be. Remember that *you* make the puppet. It is not alive until you move it.

MAKING PUPPETS

There are many different kinds of puppets. Some hang from strings; some are fastened to sticks called rods; and some slip over the hand like gloves. Some puppets are as tall as a person and must be pushed or moved from inside. Because the string puppet is the most complicated to make and manipulate, it is not recommended for the beginner or for the elementary-school classroom. The hand puppet, with its many variations, is the most satisfactory for any age level, and the classroom teacher will find it within his or her capabilities, regardless of previous experience. The hand puppet includes the bandana puppet, the finger puppet, the paper-bag puppet, the flat puppet, the shadow puppet, the sock puppet, and the glove puppet.

Just as a costume closet or box is handy to have for creative drama, so a supply of scrap materials is necessary for making puppets. You probably will not have to purchase anything because most of what you need will be in your own or the children's homes or in the school. Scraps of paper and fabrics, boxes of all sizes, sticks, Styrofoam, lollipops, apples, balls, and paper bags are usable. Ribbons, yarn, sewing materials, paper cups, paper napkins, discarded decorations, old socks, and gloves will find a use as somebody's puppet.

Bandana Puppet.   The easiest puppet to begin with is the bandana puppet. Place a bandana or cloth over the hand. Let the first, middle, and ring fingers be the head of the puppet, and put a rubber band around them for the neck. The thumb and little finger are the arms. Put rubber bands around them in order to hold the cloth in place. Imagine that the hand is the actor. Have the puppet clap its hands, shake its head, and fall down.

There are many more things you can do in making a bandana puppet. For instance, try cutting a hole in the middle of the bandana and poking the first finger through it. Next, take a Styrofoam ball with a hole scooped out for your finger and use it for a head. Heads can be made out of many things: a small paper cup, an apple (after cutting out the core), or a ball. The bandana puppet can be quickly made by the teacher, but making one is also within the capability of young children.

Finger Puppet.   The finger puppet is the smallest of all puppets. It slips over the finger and can be played with as it is or used with larger hand puppets to show different-size characters. For instance, a finger puppet might be an elf, with a hand puppet as a human being.

One way to make a finger puppet is to sew it of felt. First, make a pattern. Put the hand flat on a piece of paper and draw around the fingers with a pencil. Be sure to add a little extra material all the way around to allow for the sewing. Next, cut out the paper patterns and pin them on a piece of felt. You will have to cut two shapes for each puppet. Put the two shapes together and sew around the edges. Leave the bottom open for your finger.

Another way to make finger puppets is to cut the fingers off an old glove. White gloves are the best because puppet faces can be drawn

Bandana puppet.

Finger puppets.

on them. Slip the glove fingers over your own, and you will have five little puppets! Instead of drawing right on the puppets, you can cut paper circles and paint faces on them; when the paint is dry, the faces can be pasted on the puppets.

Paper-Bag Puppet.   The paper-bag puppet is one of the best puppets with which to begin because bags come in all sizes and are easily obtained. Also, if you happen to tear the bag, there are many more around.

Adults, children, giants, and elves can be suggested with different sizes of paper bags. Small bags fit on the hands, whereas big bags will go over the head. If a bag is worn on the head, holes will have to be cut out for the eyes and mouth. Next, paint or draw a face on the bag.

Paper-bag heads.

Flat Puppet.   The flat puppet is also often called the rod puppet. It is included here because it is easy to handle and can be used with other kinds of puppets. Flat puppets are a little like paper dolls. They can be cut out of lightweight cardboard, colored, and pasted onto tongue depressors or sticks. When the puppet is firmly attached to the stick, hold it in your hand just below the edge of the stage or table top. As it is moved, it will seem to be walking by itself. Animals make good flat puppets because you can draw only the side view.

If you would like to show your puppet moving in both directions, cut out two shapes and paste them together with the stick in between. Color both sides, and your person or animal can be moved from either left or right. One more advantage to flat puppets: they are easy to keep in good condition because they do not take up much space when put away in neat piles.

Shadow Puppet.   Flat puppets can be used for shadow shows also. In order to give a shadow show, all you need are some flat puppets, a sheet, and a lamp placed behind the sheet. When the puppets are moved behind the sheet, they cast shadows on it. The closer they are to the sheet, the stronger the shadow, or silhouette.

Shadow puppets may be made more exciting if parts of them within the outside boundaries are cut out and backed by colored gelatins. Stores that handle stage-lighting equipment carry relatively inexpensive gelatins in a variety of colors. Older children love the challenge of making these puppets, which in some ways resemble stained-glass windows. The strong light shining through the gelatin brings out the richness of the color, and creates a magical effect. Plastic shopping bags in bright colors also can be used effectively. In the oriental theatre, where shadow plays originated, one can still see performances using puppets made

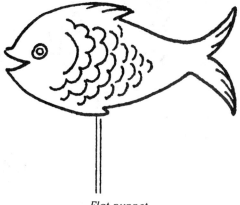

Flat puppet.

Shadow puppet.

of wood or hide decorated with elaborate openwork patterns. Older students enjoy making puppets of this kind with colored gelatin pasted over the open areas. The stylized result can be quite beautiful and effective.

Sock Puppet.   A sock makes a very good puppet because it stretches, yet does not slip off the hand. You can do many things with a sock puppet, such as making it into a mouth. Put one of your own old socks over your hand, with your fingers in the toe and your thumb in the heel. You now have the upper and lower jaws of a mouth. Bring them together in a big bite. By adding eyes and other markings, you can create a bird, a wolf, a crocodile, or a dragon. You can make a puppet mouth more exciting by sewing a lining of red felt inside it and adding another piece for a tongue. So many children's stories have animal characters that the "mouth" is a useful puppet to have on hand.

Glove Puppet.   The glove puppet requires more sewing than do the other types. It has to be cut out of two pieces of cloth and sewn together. It may also have a separate head. First, take a piece of strong cotton cloth and fold it in half. Felt is good because it does not ravel. Other

Sock puppet.

fabrics will do, however, so use those you have on hand, provided they are sturdy.

Cut a pattern of newspaper for your puppet. There should be a head and two arms, and the pattern must be large enough to fit the hand. Pin the pattern to the material and trace around it. Then remove the pattern and cut out the puppet. Keep the two pieces of cloth together and sew around the edges, remembering to leave the bottom open to allow the puppet to fit over your hand. A felt puppet is ready to use as it is. If softer material is used, it should be turned inside out before sewing. Under any circumstances, allowance must be made for the seam.

Children will want to put a face on the puppet. Eyes, nose, and mouth can be drawn or embroidered on it. Buttons make excellent eyes, and yarn makes good hair. A little stuffing makes the head rounder. If you want to make a separate head, a lightweight material, such as Styrofoam or papier-mâché, works well. After you have decorated the head, slip it over your first and second fingers, which are inside the puppet's body. Although it is harder to handle a puppet with a separate head than a puppet that is all in one piece, most children learn how to manage it with practice.

Giant Puppet.   Some puppeteers use puppets as tall as or even taller than themselves. These giant puppets must be made of lightweight material so they can be pushed from behind or inside or be carried. Unless you have a large area in which to perform, you probably will not be making life-size puppets; for those who want to try, however, here are some suggestions. An easy way is to put a paper-bag or papier-mâché head on a broomstick or pole. Then hang a blanket or cape on the

Glove puppet.

Giant puppets.

broomstick and have the manipulator hide inside the covering. He then can carry the stick as he, in fact, "merges" with the puppet.

Another way to make a giant puppet is to use a tall, narrow cardboard box. A face and clothes can be painted on the box, which the puppeteer pushes from behind. A variation of this, which can be very effective, is to decorate a piece of cardboard on one side and manipulate it from behind.

Sixth-grade children with plenty of space in which to work and help from the art or shop teacher can make giant puppets with chicken wire as an armature. This form, covered with papier-mâché, is an ambitious undertaking and poses the additional problem of storage. When so much time and effort has been put into a project, it is too bad not to keep the work, yet few schools have a place for creations of this magnitude.

Parade Puppet.   Parade puppets are actually giant puppets that are used on floats and in parades. Instead of being characters in a story, they may relate to a theme or holiday; for example, they could be made for Hallowe'en, the Chinese New Year, or whatever local event is being celebrated. One good reason for making them is the opportunity they offer for the class to work together in small groups of three or four. In not having to be concerned with a story or an enactment on a stage, the children can give all their attention to the huge figures. The main thing is to be sure that the structures are firm and that the puppets can be carried easily in the parade.

Big masks, incidentally, are fun to make and belong in the same procession. One rehearsal should be sufficient for participants to learn their places in the line and to be sure that they can manage their puppets, banners, or big masks.

Holding the Puppet

There are different ways of holding puppets, so it is suggested that you use the one that works best for you. Because some children have short fingers, they will have to experiment to find a comfortable way to hold the puppet. Some puppeteers put their first and second fingers in the neck, their fourth and fifth fingers in one arm, and their thumb in the other. Puppets can be held either in front of the body or over the head. Again, use whichever way is easier for you. If you are playing for a long time, it is usually more comfortable to work the puppet in front of your face. If you decide to hold your puppet that way, you will be seen by the audience. This does not matter. The audience will soon forget that you are there.

If you want to hang a curtain between you and the puppets, you will need a stage. A dark, lightweight piece of cloth at the back of the stage will hide you and make the puppets stand out. If the cloth is semitransparent, you can see through it without being seen by the audience.

SOME BASIC ACTIONS

Moving the puppet's head up and down means "yes." Shaking it from side to side means "no." When the puppet's hands point to itself, it means "me" or "mine." Moving one of its hands toward its body means "come here." Waving its hand may mean either "hello" or "goodbye."

Walking, running, and jumping can be suggested by the way you move the puppet across the stage. Try not to lift it in the air. You will soon get the knack of holding it down, so that it seems to be doing all the moving by itself.

When two persons are puppeteering together, the chances are that each is holding a puppet. This is more difficult than playing alone but it is also more fun. Each puppeteer has to make sure that the puppets do not bump into each other. Also, when one puppet is speaking, the other should remember to listen. Occasionally, there will be a scene for three puppets. This takes some doing, for three people will have to work together backstage, or one person will have to handle two puppets. It is a good idea at first to use stories that have no more than two characters on the stage at one time.

THE PUPPET STAGE

It is not necessary to have a stage, for puppets can act anywhere. All that is needed is a smooth surface about 3 feet long. A table, a coffee table, a bench, or a box will do. A cloth stretched across a wide doorway will partially hide the puppeteers. Another idea for a stage is a cardboard

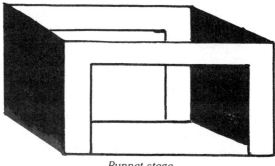

Puppet stage.

box with openings cut in the front and back. This can be placed on the bench or table. The puppets can be manipulated through the back opening.

SCENERY

Scenery is no more needed than is a stage, but sometimes the puppeteers may want it. A backdrop can be made of cardboard or stiff paper and fastened securely to the floor of the stage so that it will not fall down.

MUSIC

Music can be an effective part of a puppet production. It helps to establish mood and bridge scenes, and if dances and songs are included, it serves as accompaniment. Music never should be intrusive, for puppetry is primarily a visual medium; but, like the other theatre arts, puppetry can be enhanced by appropriate music. In general, recorder, guitar, or piano music is best. When children work with puppets, music should be used sparingly, if at all—unless the children are fairly experienced, and a tape recorder is handy. But children in the fifth and sixth grades are often skilled in the handling of technical equipment, and being responsible for the tapes adds another job to a class project.

STORIES FOR PUPPET PLAYS

It is a good idea to work without scripts because you have your hands full just moving the puppets. If you are very familiar with the story you are presenting, you can make up the dialogue as you go along, just as you do in creative drama. Besides, it will sound more natural if you do. While many stories that are good for creative playing are also good for puppetry, not all work well. One thing must be kept in mind: there is very little room backstage. Therefore, stick to stories in which no more than two or three characters are on stage at the same time. The scenes often can be arranged in order to have no more than two. Activities 9.1 to 9.3 present some examples.

PUPPETS AS TEACHING AIDS

Puppets also make excellent teaching aids because of their power to hold and sustain the attention of a class; and, in doing so, they facilitate learning. Unlike some curricular materials, puppets are not limited to any one area of study. They can be used to teach any subject, ranging from the language arts to science and math. They can be combined

A puppet play.

with other teaching materials, and they can be used alone. The value of puppets lies in their mobility, not in their beauty or complicated construction. Those made by teachers and children are usually more satisfactory than are commercial puppets. If puppets are purchased, however—and there are many on the market—they should be selected for their durability; the nonwashable and perishable should be avoided.

The degree of sophistication of puppets that students create depends, of course, on the age and previous experience of the students. While the simple puppets of young children can be wonderfully effective, experienced older groups find a challenge in making more elaborate ones. It cannot be repeated often enough, however, that a good puppet is one that can be manipulated easily; the most beautiful puppet in the world is a failure if it does not move easily and well. Another consideration, and an important one, is the child's perception of his or her work. In other words, "it is not what the puppet looks like that counts but rather how the child feels about the puppet . . . a rabbit puppet made by a child does not have to look like a real rabbit—the child needs only to believe in it. . . ."[1]

---

[1] Tamara Hunt and Nancy Renfro, *Puppetry in Early Childhood* (Austin, Tex.: Nancy Renfro Studios, 1982), p. 24.

Probably the most extensive use made of puppets as a teaching tool is in the area of the language arts. According to John Warren Stewig, "Children generate more verbal language during dramatic play than in any other situation."[2] In both creative drama and puppetry, extemporaneous speaking is involved; use of the puppet has the added advantage of shielding the speaker who is shy or weak in verbal skills, thus enabling him or her to communicate through the puppet. A skillful teacher makes use of the opportunity afforded by this communication to open up new areas of learning and tune into a student's thinking. Telling stories with puppets not only is fun, but also is a valuable activity on all levels. The move from storytelling to story dramatization is a natural next step, involving dialogue, character study, play structure, and growth in language competency. The use of puppets in the teaching of poetry has also proved successful in promoting the appreciation and composition of this form of literature.

Some teachers have found puppets to be invaluable aids in the study of elementary science and the environment; the writing of original skits on these subjects, later to be enacted by puppets, is strong motivation in two areas that are difficult for many children. Social studies provide a wealth of puppetry opportunities for the study of other people, other countries, historical events, and current events. "Famous People Puppets"[3] is suggested as an activity for classes in the intermediate grades. Puppets provide exercise in bilingual education also; this can be done by way of dramatic sketches or directly by a familiar mascot puppet. The mascot, incidentally, is often able to hold the attention of the most restless group, a phenomenon observed by anyone who has ever used puppetry with children. In short, there is no area of the curriculum that cannot be enhanced by these appealing little creatures who come alive in the most inexperienced hands, teaching and entertaining simultaneously. Their popularity with all kinds and ages of groups practically ensures success.

PUPPETS AS THERAPEUTIC TOOLS

Puppets have been used effectively as both diagnostic and therapeutic instruments. It is understood that neither the classroom teacher nor the creative-drama specialist is a therapist; nevertheless, puppet theatre offers insights often undiscernible in other situations, and the sensitive teacher will take note of them. The puppet becomes a nonthreatening

[2] John Warren Stewig, *Teaching Language Arts in Early Childhood* (New York: Holt, Rinehart and Winston, 1980), p. 123.

[3] Bojabi Treehouse, *Puppetry—a Tool for Teaching* (New Haven, Conn.: New Haven Public Schools, 1973).

A child making a puppet to express emotion becomes happy in the process. (Courtesy of Mary Freericks)

little friend in whom a child can confide, entrusting his most private thoughts and feelings without fear of censure. This friend has access to the child's world and is able to speak to the outer world as an intermediary.

Puppetry provides socially accepted avenues for the discovery, expression, and release of emotions and attitudes. Therapists do not aim at well-rehearsed, finished performances; rather, they use puppets to encourage and help motivate patients and students in clinical and educational settings. Some professional puppeteers have engaged in special ongoing programs. George Latshaw, a well-known puppeteer, worked with a group sponsored by the National Committee, Arts for the Handicapped, using puppets with severely handicapped children. Latshaw's puppets played and interacted with children in classrooms, often eliciting response from those who had until then been detached from others or lacked verbal skills.[4] In their use of puppetry, the classroom teacher and the therapist share a similar goal. Thus the teacher will find puppetry an exceptionally effective way of drawing out children who are reluctant to participate in creative drama. Here are a few exercises to stimulate expression of strong feelings.

1. Try to find ways of showing that the puppet feels:
    angry   shy   happy   scared
    excited   tired   curious   hungry

2. Next, see if you can put actions with a feeling:
    a. curious   and looks into a box
    b. angry   and hits someone
    c. happy   and claps its hands for joy
    d. thoughtful   and comes up with an idea

3. Most of us get into trouble at one time or another. Do you remember a particular time when you got into trouble? Was it your fault? Did you think you were punished unfairly? How did you feel about it? Let your glove puppet be the other person in this story, and the finger puppet be you. Act it out.

4. Imagine that your puppet cannot speak English. Try to make it understand you.

5. Imagine that your puppet's feelings are hurt. Can you say or do anything to make it feel better?

6. Try out the following verse as you look into your own inner world. Some children are amazingly perceptive in comparing their inner and outer selves.

I HAVE TWO SELVES[5]
TAMARA HUNT

I have two Selves or so I'm told,
    My Outside and my In.
And if I take a thoughtful look
    I'll see myself within.

Although I know my Outside Self,
    I see it every day,
My inside self seems hidden,
    So neatly tucked away.

---

[4] *Puppets—Art and Entertainment* (Washington, D.C.: Puppeteers of America, 1980), p. 9.

[5] Tamara Hunt, "I Have Two Selves," in Hunt and Renfro, *Puppetry in Early Childhood*, p. 123.

It seems so strange I cannot touch
  Or taste or hear or see. . . .
I only *feel* all those things
  That are inside of me.

Both my Selves are special.
  That's what I'm about.
Feeling on the *Inside*,
  Showing on the *Out*.

MASKS

Closely related to the art of puppetry is the art of mask making. Masks can be either part of a puppet project or an extension of creative drama. Interesting experimental work with mixed media is being done in which the human actor, often masked, and the puppet are used in the same production. I recall one imaginative production given by a small professional group; actors playing human beings, actors wearing grotesque masks, small puppets, and a larger-than-life cardboard figure were used together. In this way, the company was able to suggest more characters than it had actors to play and to suggest the size differences among adults, children, a giant, and other fantastic characters. The effect was both childlike and smart, suggesting ways in which a teacher might solve problems that otherwise are insoluble.

Many persons link the mask with theatre, even though its functions go far beyond costume and performance. The mask is used in a variety of ways, but its four major functions are:

1. To act as a protective covering for the head or face (ski and fencing masks)
2. To function as a disguise or concealment
3. To describe or identify a character (in a play)
4. To serve as a symbol (in religious and ritualistic rites)

In children's theatre, the mask is commonly used in costuming an animal or a fantastic creature, although stage make-up is preferred by many directors and costumers.

HISTORY OF MASKS

Historically, masks and make-up have enjoyed wide popularity throughout the world. Tribal societies have worn them in performing religious rites and rituals. Primitive peoples thought that by putting on the face of another, a person gained power over the other. For example, a hunter believed that wearing the skin and mask of an animal would bring him a good day of hunting. The masks of primitive tribes were thought to be potent in other ways as well. They could release the wearer's personality by concealing it, and they became symbols of a universal awareness of gods or a creative force in the universe. In time, the mask or facial paint became stylized and more elaborate, as it was embellished by generations of wearers.

In the ancient Greek theatre, the mask served the practical purpose of projecting the actor's features and amplifying his voice. The mask was larger than the human face and was made with protruding lips that created resonance. Thus the masks of comedy and tragedy gave the actor in the huge amphitheatres, where performances took place, an objective reality larger than life.

In the oriental theatre, the mask was part of an elaborate costume, designed primarily for its aesthetic appeal rather than its practical use. Japanese masks, familiar to audiences today, are colorful, decorative, and smaller than the human face. While it is true that they suggest the characters in a play, they make no attempt at realistic representation.

In the commedia dell'arte, the Italian traveling theatre of the sixteenth and seventeenth centuries, the mask was an essential part of the actor's costume. Special masks represented stock characters and were always associated with them. A character's actions and appearance thus were closely connected; in fact, the covering of the face seemed to have an effect on the actor's body, making it more free and more expressive. An example of this connection may be found in Punch, the descendant of a commedia character, whose flesh-colored face, with its great red nose and bulging eyes, is as familiar to us as his outrageous behavior. His face and his actions go together in more ways than one.

Clowns, who prefer grease paint to the mask, observe a unique tradition relating to the mask. Each clown creates his or her own face and is careful never to copy that of another. A clown's face is, therefore, an individual creation to be respected as long as he or she lives.

Most children are fascinated with these various uses of masks and attitudes toward them and enjoy inventing masks of their own. One of the most creative projects I have ever seen involved puppets and children wearing paper-bag masks, both puppets and masks made by a class studying North American Indians. Because the mask has been used by so many people at so many different periods in history, it is a valuable resource for the teacher and a magic prop for the child who makes and wears it.

TYPES AND VALUES OF MASKS

The mask may cover the entire head, the face, or the upper part of the face only, leaving the lower part exposed. The simple half-mask, worn on Hallowe'en or at masked balls, is a well-known example. The obvious advantage of the half-mask is its comfort. It is cooler than the mask that covers the entire face, and it makes speaking easier. Speaking through the mouth of a mask is difficult and distracting for the inexperienced performer.

Masks may be simple or elaborate, beautiful or grotesque; but except for the representation of animals, they are rarely realistic. The values of mask making are many and are implicit in this brief discussion. Masks provide an extension of the drama lesson; they reveal aspects of a culture in which the mask is an important artifact; and they release the wearer from inhibitions. Many children feel freer when they are shielded from view by even a partial face covering. They project feelings and ideas through the mask, while they remain hidden. The mask serves the same purpose as the puppet in this respect.

Teachers would be wise to avoid using the commercial masks sold in stores around Hallowe'en. One of the values of including the mask in the classroom is the opportunity it offers for imaginative construction and design. This is particularly valuable for a child who is shy about acting, but who has interest and ability in arts and crafts. In using the commercial mask or puppet, the teacher misses a rich opportunity for teaching.

MAKING MASKS

Like puppets, masks can be made of a variety of materials.

Paper-Bag and Cardboard Masks.   The paper-bag mask is by far the easiest and cheapest to make; it is also the most satisfying because it can be completed in a single class period. The brown paper bag from the grocery store slips comfortably over the head, and holes can be cut in it for the eyes and mouth. Strips of colored paper can be pasted on the bags for hair, mustaches, and even eyelashes. Paint, chalk, and crayons can be used to color them. Older children, studying a particular culture or tribal society, may paste or sew on feathers, cloth, jewelry, buttons, and the like.

Cardboard boxes can be used effectively to suggest robots and stylized characters. They are more difficult to work on than bags, and it often is hard to find boxes of the right size and shape. Because both bags and boxes cover the entire head, they muffle speech and limit freedom of movement.

As a follow-up activity, after a class has worked on material dramatically, masks have value in extending the learnings. When they are incorporated into a project that is further developed for an audience, they offer an added dimension for the observers.

Paper-Plate Mask.   Masks made of plain, white paper plates 9 to 10 inches in diameter are recommended for the middle grades because of their shape, toughness, and availability. To make the mask appear three-dimensional, cut slits (one on each side of the plate) slightly below center. These should be about 2 inches long. Overlap the sides adjacent to each slit and staple them together. This makes the flat plate more nearly fit the child's face. As with the paper-bag mask, holes for eyes, mouth, and nose must be cut in the appropriate places. A nose that protrudes from the face can be made of construction paper and pasted on the plate. From here on, experimentation with other materials is fun and will make each mask unique.

Papier-Mâché Mask.   Papier-mâché is made of pulped paper or paper strips moistened with thin wheat paste (wallpaper paste). The paper used may be newspaper, tissues, napkins, or toweling. Wheat paste can be secured from a hardware store (follow the directions on the package).

You will need a form or mold to work on. This can be made of modeling clay, or you can use a wig form or a large round balloon as a foundation. Be sure that the mold is lightly greased with oil or cold cream. Then cover it with strips of *torn* paper (approximately 1 inch by 10 inches) dipped in the wheat paste. Apply the strips diagonally, bandage fashion, wherever possible, and overlap them. Two layers of paper usually are enough. Paper pulp (soft paper torn into small pieces, soaked in paste, and squeezed out) may be added to build a nose, eyebrows, lips, and so on. Allow the mask to dry for two to three days before removing it from the form. When dry, it will be firm and brittle. Holes for the eyes, nose, and mouth may be cut with a razor blade, an X-Acto, or a mat knife.

If you use a balloon blown to larger than head size, you can make a

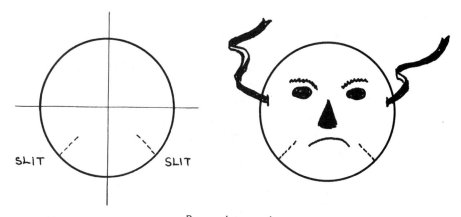

Paper-plate mask.

whole-head mask (for example, an animal). Leave it open at the base, and trim it so that the form will slip over the head and rest on the shoulders. Basic forms for whole-head coverings may be made of chicken wire, covered with cheesecloth. The form is then layered with papier-mâché. This will require tin snips to cut the wire; be careful that all wire ends are bent under and covered with papier-mâché. When dry, the head or face mask may be painted or decorated with cut paper. Feathers, yarn, or paper strips may be added for whatever effect you want. If you spray the mask with a lacquer or plastic finish (Krylon), it will be more durable.

Unless you want to cover the entire head, which is uncomfortable for the wearer, make a face mask and fasten it with elastic across the back of the head. A scarf, hat, or wig will complete the disguise.

Activities for Masks

While masks are fun to make just for themselves, they are even more fun and more satisfying when they serve a purpose—for instance, when they are worn in a play or creative-drama class or when they carry out a theme. Sometimes, however, the masks will suggest an idea to the wearer!

1. *Pandora's box*   Pandora's box contains a variety of evil spirits. Try making masks to represent them. Players who have created movements for the spirits will love adding masks; this is a perfect example of the relationship between mask and movement.

2. *A circus*   A circus calls for clowns, animals, a ringmaster, and any number of sideshow characters. Every person in the class can invent a mask for a circus parade.

3. *Holidays*   Although Hallowe'en comes to mind first as an occasion for mask making, every holiday contains possibilities. Take St. Valentine's Day, the Fourth of July, or St. Patrick's Day. What about your birthday? Every child in the class might try making a mask of himself or herself. It may look like you, or it may be simply your own invention.

SUMMARY

Puppetry and mask making provide an added dimension to creative drama as well as being arts in their own rights. Although it has been stated repeatedly throughout the chapter that the types of puppets and masks described are simple, requiring no previous experience or special course work in puppets and mask making, it is always wise to try out an assignment before giving it to a class. In this way, the teacher can foresee any problems that might arise and solve them in advance. Gathering materials and providing enough space for construction is important. As in creative drama, the encouragement of original ideas will help to prevent imitation of familiar television characters.

The teacher who includes puppets and masks in the curriculum will find them a rich resource. Regardless of the reasons for including them, the possibilities they offer are limitless. The major values may be summarized as follows:

1. Puppets and masks provide opportunities for developing motor skills. Tools and materials must be handled with care in order to construct puppets and masks that are sturdy and functional.
2. Dressing and decorating puppets requires imagination. Each puppet must become a character, first through its costume, and then in the way in which it is decorated and painted.
3. Puppets require control. It takes controlled fingers to manipulate a puppet so that it can perform as the operator wishes.
4. Puppets and masks offer an avenue of expression. Through them, the puppeteer or wearer expresses the thoughts and feelings of characters.
5. Both puppets and masks have therapeutic power. Through them, timid or withdrawn children can find release, whereas aggressive children learn to subordinate themselves to the personality of the characters they are presenting.
6. Puppetry demands cooperation. Children learn to take turns and work together for a successful performance.
7. Puppetry and mask making are inexpensive. Delightful results may be obtained within the most limited budget. If there is no stage, a box will do until the teacher is able to construct something more permanent.
8. Puppets and masks may be ends in themselves or the means by which other ends are reached.

Given half a chance, the puppet engages the child as performer, playmate, teacher, and alter ego. The mask, although less versatile, is closely related, serving many of the same purposes.

ACTIVITY 9.1
_____

STORY WITH LIMITED MOVEMENT

"Darby and Joan" appeals to both boys and girls and is easy to play on a puppet stage. There are only three characters, but the story is so short that, unless a group is large, every boy and girl may have a chance to try one of the parts.

Objective: To tell a story with puppets that children have made

Suggestions for the Teacher

First plan scenery (a little house with two doors, a table and chairs). Discuss how best to handle the story. The characters make this little story particularly appropriate for puppetry as well as relatively easy, with the three characters and limited movement. Let all the children try it, scene by scene, if playing the entire story is too time consuming. They love the quarrel scenes, which recur.

DARBY AND JOAN

Have you ever seen a little house about the size of a birdhouse, with two doors in front marked "Fair" and "Rain"? And have you ever noticed that a little woman stands in the doorway marked "Fair," and a little man in the doorway marked "Rain"? And, depending on the weather, that one is always out while the other is in? Well, this little man and woman are known as Darby and Joan, and the following story is told of how they came to be there.

Many years ago, Darby and Joan lived happily in a little cottage together. As time went on, however, they began to quarrel. Regardless of how peaceably the day had begun, before long, they were disagreeing and finding fault with each other. And so a spell was put on them: from that day forth, one must be out while the other was in, depending on the weather. Our story begins many years later. The day has been fair, but the weather is beginning to change, and Darby is about to come out, allowing Joan to go inside and finish her housework. As they talk together, not seeing each other, they regret the quarreling that led to their punishment.

"How I wish I could see you, Joan. Do you realize it has been 10 years since we sat down at the table together?"

"I know, Darby. I'm sure if we could be released from this spell, we should never quarrel again."

"Imagine not seeing one's own wife for 10 years. It was too cruel a punishment."

As they are talking together, Darby notices someone approaching the cottage. He calls out, "It's beginning to rain. Won't you stop and rest here for a bit?"

The stranger, who is a Fairy in disguise, comes to the doorway and asks Darby why it is that he is standing out in the rain while his wife stays in the house. He explains and sighs over their misfortune. The Fairy then tells him who she is and offers to release them from their spell, but only on one condition—that they never quarrel again. They agree joyfully, and the Fairy goes off; but not without warning them that if they do quarrel, they will be put under the spell again, and this time it will be forever.

The old couple can scarcely believe their good fortune as they move their arms and legs stiffly and venture outside together. The rain is clearing, and they decide to have supper in front of the cottage. Darby brings out the table and chairs while Joan gets the food. Scarcely have they sat down to eat, however, when Darby criticizes the way Joan slices the bread. Joan replies with annoyance that if he objects, he can cut it himself. Furthermore, she notices that he is wearing his hat at the table. Before they know it, they are quarreling furiously.

Suddenly, the Fairy appears. The old people are stricken. They beg the Fairy for one more chance to try getting along, but she replies, "It is too late. You knew the condition and should have thought of the consequences."

Darby and Joan feel the spell coming on, and slowly move back into their old positions. The Fairy disappears, with the old couple once more back in their doorways marked "Fair" and "Rain."

ACTIVITY 9.2
_____

A REGIONAL LEGEND

Regional legends and tales handed down from one generation to the next make excellent material for puppets and may tie in beautifully with social studies. "Befriended by a Panther" is excellent for presentation by puppets because there are no more than two puppets on stage at one time, and the action is limited.

Objective: To present a puppet play in which a narrator tells the story

Suggestions for the Teacher

Discuss how the class wishes to do the story. It can be read or told by a narrator standing at one side of the stage while the puppets perform in pantomime. It also can be done with Juan de Dios improvising the dialogue. Perhaps the children will want to try it both ways to decide which is more effective.

BEFRIENDED BY A PANTHER*
J. FRANK DOBIE

There are stories of friendly panthers, . . . but they belong mainly to the Spanish countries southward. No one has told them so well as W. H. Hudson in *The Naturalist in La Plata*. Here is one I heard one night in a camp of *sotoleros* in a desert of northern Mexico. Leaves of the yucca-like sotol plant afford an inferior fiber for cords and ropes; the distilled juice makes a fiery liquor; the head when roasted and split open by machete or ax provides nourishment for stock. With absolutely nothing growing on the parched earth for our horses to graze on, my *mozo* Inocencio and I were glad to camp with the sotol-cutters and feed our horses on sotol they had already roasted.

Another growth in that harsh country is the low-growing lechuguilla, every leaf of it a dagger. It is as bitter as green persimmon. "Did anybody ever try it for thirst?" I asked of the chief sotol-cutter, named Juan de Dios.

"I did. One time."

I waited.

"God saved me, not the lechuguilla."

Juan de Dios now with fervid energy began sticking bits of twigs into the ground. Near them he put the backs of his hands against the earth, holding up his gnarled fingers to indicate stubble.

* J. Frank Dobie, *I'll Tell You a Tale* (Austin: University of Texas Press, 1984), pp. 212–215.

"The land up there to the northwest where you are riding," he went on, "is like that—just tables and slopes of lechuguilla daggers. But in the land also grows the guayule. In 1907 I was gathering guayule to be sold to the factory of rubber. We had our camp at a big tank. There was no other water for a long, long distance. Each day we had to go farther and farther out from the tank to find the guayule. I was gathering it by myself. I went out in the morning with my tortillas for dinner, a bottle of water, and an old knife. It was in the time of the *canicula*—the dog days of July and August— and it was so hot that the rattlesnake crawled only at night.

"One day I went afoot because my burro was too lame. I would gather the guayule into piles and later carry it in. I went far out. *Bueno*, by noon I had drunk all the water. The sun in the sky danced up and down like a crackling frying in grease. The thirst came, but I had to keep on gathering guayule in order to buy frijoles and corn for my family. There was no *remedio* for this. I pulled until nearly dark, and then I started back to the tank. The thirst of the body was like that of the ground under a dead broomweed.

"And then—I do not know how, perhaps it was the thirst—I found myself lost. There was no moon. There was no trail. And lechuguilla everywhere. I cut out the heart of one to chew. The bitter juice gave thirst more thirst. I kept on, but I did not know where I was going. Sometimes I would stop to listen, to consider; then I would go on.

"Know you, *señor*," and here the voice of Juan de Dios lowered into that tone of confidence I had already noted in him, "a man who lives all the time out sees some strange things come to pass. *Bueno*, according to the stars it was two hours past midnight when I sat down on top of a hill to rest. I did not know what to do. I am a man of the camps; yet I was confused.

"While I was sitting there, the moon, weak and thin, came up over my shoulder. And then right out in front of me, perhaps twenty feet away, I saw a *león* [panther]. He was just sitting on his haunches, still, his face toward me. I could see the white of his breast.

"I did not wish to fight with this animal. I arose and started away from him. At once he made some jumps and galloped around in front of me. There he sat again, silent, not moving, just gazing."

Juan de Dios slunk his shoulders and held the palms of his hands outward in front of his body to simulate the posture of the panther.

"And now fear made thirst die. I gave a shout and leaped away from the *león*. Quickly he gave some jumps and again was in front of me, just sitting there silent as if he were going to say a prayer. *Por Dios*, I could not comprehend this. Then God seemed to give me valor and I stood up straight and I said to myself, 'This animal is not offering to attack me. He is not waving his tail and stretching out his body in preparation to leap. It seems that he is not my enemy. Therefore, he may be my friend.'

"I took one step toward the animal. He arose, but in a gentle manner like a dog. I took another step. He turned and started off. Another step and he was retreating slowly but with his head turned back as if to advise me to follow. I went on, following the adviser. He went this way and that way, twisting through the lechuguilla and the chaparral. Then in about half an hour we entered a trail. I did not know where the trail went to or where it came from. It was well beaten, but I knew not which direction of it to take. I followed the *león*. He went on and on.

"In summer the light comes very early. Not long after the time for the first rooster crow my guide stopped, looked at me, and then stepped out into the chaparral. Now I saw just ahead in an open place a cabin. I advanced. In front of the cabin was a little wagon with two barrels of water in it. They had been hauled from a hole three leagues away. Thus the lion, as a friend of man, saved my life."

New or Unfamiliar Words

Broomweed. Coarse weed, the stems of which are used to make brooms.

Bueno. Good, kind, useful.

Canicula. The dog days of summer.

Chaparral. Any dense thicket (a word used in the West).

Frijoles. Beans.

Guayule. A rubber-yielding plant or the rubber from it.

Lechuguilla. Lettuce.

León. A lion (in this story a panther, although the Spanish word for panther is really *pantera*).

Machete. A large, heavy knife (tool or weapon) used to cut tough plants.

Mozo. A young man or a manservant.

Remedio. Remedy.

Sotol. A plant that grows in the Southwest of the United States and in Mexico; similar to the yucca plant.

Sotoleros. Workers who cut the sotol.

Tortilla. A thin cornbread cake.

Yucca. A desert plant with many leaves, that grows in the Southwest of the United States and in Mexico.

ACTIVITY 9.3

A CANADIAN TALE

This French-Canadian folk tale works better for puppets than for human actors. One of the characters is a ventriloquist, which makes it ideal for the puppet stage.

Objective: To present a puppet play in which one character must use two voices

Suggestions for the Teacher

Have all the children who want to, try using two voices. Ventriloquism fascinates most children and is a challenge to the older player.

This story can be either acted or partly narrated, with only the dialogue spoken. Let the children try it both ways; the narrated version may be easier for less experienced groups.

THE TALKING CAT

Characters

Tante Odette, *an old woman*

Chouchou, *her cat*

Pierre, *a workman*

Georges, *his friend*

There is an old woman, who is fooled into believing that her cat can speak. Tante Odette lives alone on her farm, deep in the Canadian woods. She is careful and thrifty, always keeping a pot of soup on the stove for herself and her old gray cat, Chouchou. She takes good care of her small farm. But as the years go by, she sometimes complains that the work is becoming too much for her. She talks to Chouchou about the chores that have to be done and how she must save her money for later. Often she says to him, "How I wish you could talk, Chouchou. Then I should not be so lonely."

One evening as Tante Odette is sitting by the fire, there is a knock at the door. When she opens it, she sees a man in workman's clothes with a red sash tied around his waist.

"I am looking for work," he says politely. "If you can give me some chores, all I ask is a bowl of soup and a night's sleep in your barn."

"Go away," says Tante Odette. "I do not need anyone to help me. Besides, I have only enough soup for myself."

Just as she is about to close the door in his face, an amazing thing happens. Chouchou speaks! "Wait a minute," he says. "You are getting older, and it would be a good idea to have a strong young man on the place."

Tante Odette can't believe her ears. She looks at the man; then she looks at the cat. "Well, if you think so, Chouchou."

"I certainly do," says the cat. "Ask him to come in and join us in a bowl of soup."

The old woman invites the man in and asks him to supper. "It's only cabbage soup and bread, but we like it."

The man thanks her. When he has finished his supper, he tells her tales of his travels and the different places he has worked. But he says that now he would rather stay in one place, even though he wouldn't make any money. He tells her his name is Pierre. As time goes on, both the old woman and Chouchou become very fond of him.

One day, Chouchou says to Tante Odette, "Why don't you give Pierre meat and cakes? He works hard. I'm sure he gets very hungry."

"But we have no meat," she replies.

"Then let him go to the store in the town and buy some meat. He will not waste your money."

Pierre appears in the doorway. "I heard what your cat said just now. He's very wise. Let me strike a good bargain."

The old woman goes to a chest of drawers and takes out some money. "Mind you, don't waste it," she tells Pierre.

When Pierre has gone, she turns to Chouchou. "How is it that you never spoke in all the years that I've had you, and now you are giving me advice?"

But as always, when they are alone, Chouchou says nothing.

The next day when they finish their dinner of meat and cakes, Pierre is in a very good mood, and Tante Odette says that she has never enjoyed a meal so much! "Why don't you let Pierre move into the house?" asks the cat.

"What?" says the old woman.

"Winter is coming, and it will soon be cold in the barn. We have plenty of room inside."

Pierre says that he would like this very much. And so he moves in.

A few weeks later, when the old woman is alone in the house, there is a knock at the door. She opens it, and to her surprise, she sees a workingman standing there. He is wearing a red sash just like Pierre's.

"Have you seen a workman who calls himself Pierre?" the new-comer asks.

"A man by that name works for me," the old woman says.

"Is he a good worker?"

"A very good worker," she says; and she tells of all the things Pierre can do.

"It certainly sounds like the same man. One more thing, can he throw his voice? Is he a ventriloquist?"

"Throw his voice? Oh, no! I could not stand having anyone around who did that."

"Then it can't be the same person," says the man, as he turns to go.

At this moment, Pierre comes to the door. "Georges!" he shouts. "My old friend!"

"Pierre! I've been searching for you everywhere. I want you to go with me to get furs. You know they pay good money for furs in the city. How about it?"

Pierre thinks for a moment. "If I go with you, I'll make money, but it will be cold. If I stay here, I have a good job, food, and a warm place to sleep. What shall I do, Chouchou? You're a wise cat."

"Stay here," the cat answers. Then the cat turns to the old woman. "Why don't we pay him some wages? You have money in the chest. Surely he's worth a few pieces of gold."

The old woman doesn't know what to do. Finally she says, "Very well. I can give you a small wage, if you'll stay."

"Good!" says Pierre. "Then I'll stay." He says good-bye to his friend and walks with him down the road.

The old woman looks at Chouchou. "I don't believe he throws his voice, do you?"

There was no answer. She stares at Chouchou, who says nothing, as usual.

Just then, Pierre returns. "It will be a much better winter for me here than in the north woods. And I can earn money at the same time, thanks to your cat."

The cat bows and speaks.

"That's all right, Pierre. Fair is fair." Then Chouchou looks at the old woman. "Well, we may as well sit down at the table and celebrate the way it has all worked out."

10

DRAMA AS A
TEACHING TOOL

"Sometimes it seems that the surest way to the human mind lies through the stage door," Richard L. Coe told an audience at the American Theatre Association's 1984 convention in San Francisco. The drama critic emeritus of *The Washington Post* went on to characterize the power of the theatre to teach, to illuminate social issues, and to spark social changes as "the theatrical imperative, a potent force that has operated throughout history."[1]

The use of drama as a teaching tool is not new; historically, both drama and theatre have long been recognized as potent means of education and indoctrination. The ways in which they are used today, however, are new, and they differ in a number of respects from the ways in which they were used in the past. The United States has only recently discovered the relationship between theatre and school. Indeed, the twentieth century was well advanced before the arts began to have any real impact on public education in this country. Private schools often offered opportunities in the arts, but usually as extracurricular activities or as minor subjects, rarely placed on a par with the so-called solids. On the secondary-school level, they were given even less emphasis.

In the minds of many, theatre and dance were even questionable as to their being part of a young person's education. Drama, in fact, followed music, athletics, and the visual arts into the curriculum. Few today would argue against arts education; yet the inclusion, let alone require-

[1] *Theatre News* 17, no. 2 (November–December 1984): 1.

ment, of drama in the elementary-school curriculum is far from widespread.

The first major curricular offerings in child drama and theatre in this country appeared in the 1920s. They were the result of Winifred Ward's pioneering efforts at Northwestern University, which brought the public schools of Evanston and the Evanston Children's Theatre into sharp focus. For the first time in this country, creative dramatics, as Ward called it, had a place in the public-school curriculum; and plays for children were produced and scheduled on a regular, ongoing basis. Ward's own books were among the first to appear on the subject, becoming landmark texts. College courses and textbooks on drama education and children's theatre followed. Since then, there has been a steady increase in the number of colleges and universities offering courses and degrees in the theatre arts and in the teaching of drama and theatre. At the same time, there has been fluctuation in both quantity and quality of drama education in the public schools. Budget cuts and the lack of well-prepared teachers have been the most commonly given reasons for eliminating the arts or curtailing established programs. This is at variance with our recognition of three major areas of a modern curriculum: the *cognitive*, which deals with the recall of knowledge and

Lessons come alive through drama. (Children in South End School, Cedar Grove, New Jersey; photograph by Lois Koenig)

development of intellectual abilities and skills; the *affective*, which includes attitudes and values, and the development of appreciation; and the *psychomotor*, or motor-skill. Drama embraces all three, and hence is valuable as both means and end in education.

DRAMA AS A LEARNING MEDIUM

When drama is taught as an art form, the goals are both *aesthetic* and *intrinsic*: aesthetic, because product is emphasized; intrinsic, because the child is a major concern. When drama is employed as a specific teaching technique, it differs from its role as an art form primarily in intent. Many of the same procedures may be followed, but in using drama as a learning medium, the teacher is exploiting these procedures to reach certain *extrinsic* goals: to gain knowledge, solve problems, and change attitudes. Through the process of studying a conflict and the persons involved in it, material is illuminated and interpreted, just as it is in the preparation of a play. Occasionally, an original play with interesting content and good dramatic structure results; this is more likely to happen when drama is used in teaching the language arts than in other curricular areas. The play, however, is not the goal and is not an expected culmination of the study.

INTEGRATED PROJECTS

It is true that the arts have been included in the curriculum in some interesting and effective ways. Projects integrating drama, music, dance, creative writing, and the visual arts with social studies and literature have been popular since the early days of the progressive-education movement. Even the most traditional schools have found integrated projects to be an effective way of teaching and learning. Arts educators have generally endorsed such projects because they placed the arts at the core of the curriculum rather than on the periphery. Accorded an importance equal to the academic subjects, the arts thus became a basic part of the educational system rather than a frill or something of fringe interest. Integrated projects continue to find popularity in schools where staff members are able and willing to work closely together. This is often more easily accomplished in small private schools, where the schedule allows for flexibility and where there is concern for student interest.

The integrated project usually starts in the social-studies or English class. With the topic as a base, various aspects of it are explored. Take, for instance, the topic of a foreign country such as Egypt. In the exploration of Egypt, history, geography, climate, religion, homes, clothing, food, occupations, myths and legends, and arts and crafts would be included; from this study, a project evolves. When the King Tut exhibition was presented at the Metropolitan Museum of Art in New York, one fifth-grade class became so fascinated with the subject that the children made shadow puppets and presented them in a program of short plays based on their favorite Egyptian legends. The project lasted for several weeks and involved the art, music, and social-studies teachers; the results showed both interest and understanding.

A project might also start with a question on a more specific topic, such as the calendar, time, strip mining, or peace. If the children's interest seems sufficiently strong, this could be a beginning of a class project. The teacher then brings in books, newspapers, and visual aids, thus keeping the study within one class or area, rather than integrating it with other subjects in the curriculum.

THE LANGUAGE ARTS

Speech is the most obvious area of the language arts to be taught through creative drama. Improved speech is a shared objective of modern educators and teachers of drama. When children feel the need to communicate orally, they will seek the appropriate words and try to pronounce and articulate them clearly. Many exercises and speech-related activities may be carried on in conjunction with creative drama and may act as an incentive for improving oral expression.

Speech depends on words. The more words we have at our command, the richer and more precise our communication. Children love words and enjoy learning new ones, given half a chance and some encouragement. Vocabulary building, moreover, is a never-ending process. Reading good literature is one of the best ways to learn new words, and the improvisation of dialogue offers an opportunity to put the words into practice. In assuming roles, players learn as much as they can about the characters they are playing: age, education, occupation, likes and dislikes, strengths and weaknesses, and other personal qualities. This knowledge of a character helps determine the vocabulary used as well as the way the words are said.

CREATIVE DRAMA AND PLAYMAKING

Young or inexperienced players will not be able to delineate characters at the outset, but will slowly develop awareness of the speech appropriate to a character and in time will be able to handle dialogue that conveys more than rudimentary information. Particularly effective in pointing out individual differences in speech and the possibilities of enriching them is the discussion held after the first and second playings. The teacher may ask the player some questions about the character: Would the character talk that way? use those words? use slang? Suggest his or her occupation by words or actions. Then the leader may proceed to some general questions about characters: How would a father speak? a storekeeper? a general? a television newscaster? Would a child say the same thing in the same words and phrases? Children are quick to discern discrepancies. Moreover, they enjoy finding just the right words for a particular character and delight in using long words. Proof of this can be seen in the way in which very young children memorize repeated phrases and words from favorite stories: any deviation from the text on the part of a reader, in an effort at simplification, will bring an immediate correction from the listening child, who knows and loves the original.

As to clarity and audibility, no activity better points up the necessity of being heard and understood than does taking part in a play. The teacher need not—indeed, should not—stress such failings as indistinct and inaudible speech, but the other players will be aware of them. A far more effective way of telling a player that his or her voice is too soft is to raise such questions as: Would an angry man sound like that? What kind of voice do you think a giant would have? How do we know that the boy is calling to someone from a distance?

Too much attention to vocal projection and articulation frequently leads to an artificial manner of delivery, but attention to the reasons for a louder voice or clearer speech will accomplish the desired goals, although admittedly this approach takes longer. Observers are quick to comment when they cannot hear or understand a player. Peer criticism is a far more effective way of improving a player's speech than is constant nagging by the teacher. If players really want to be understood, they will make the necessary effort. Again, they will not accomplish everything in the beginning, but with practice and encouragement as well as criticism will show improvement in time. Creative drama offers a unique opportunity to enlarge the vocabulary, promote more audible speech, and improve articulation.

In recent years, there has been a conscious effort to improve the self-image of the speaker whose verbal skills are poor or whose native language is not English. In order to accomplish this, voice and diction have been deempha-sized; in other words, *what* is said is considered to be of greater importance than *how* it is said. The objectives—encouragement of the speaker and the building of pride in a cultural heritage—have been given priority. While no one would quarrel with this as the first step in language improvement, it is to be hoped that once a degree of self-confidence has been acquired, the student should be helped to move on to better habits of speech. Clarity, audibility, and a constantly improving vocabulary are still the goals for citizens in a democratic society. Freedom of speech is of little value without the ability to express oneself clearly and effectively. Today that ability affects almost every facet of life and most jobs. Therefore, the speech arts are more important than ever before, and in the opinion of the author, it is condescending to demand anything less than the best of students in this area as well as in others. The teacher's acceptance of a substandard level of English does the speaker a disservice both now and later. Poor speech, like poor writing, is a handicap. What better place than the public-school classroom to learn to communicate effectively?

STORYTELLING

Classroom activities other than improvisation provide work on oral communication. One of the oldest and best of these is storytelling, a favorite pastime in itself as well as a primary step in the preparation of a dramatization.

Storytelling is an ancient art that continues to be loved in spite of, or perhaps because of, our technical advances in communication. Television brings a vast array of entertainment into the home, but it can no more replace the living storyteller than can film replace theatre. The reader–audience relationship depends on the rapport between the one telling and the others listening to the story—the listeners' involvement in the material and the way it is presented to them, which varies with each telling. But the most important factor in storytelling is always the storyteller. Fortunate the boys and girls who are exposed to a good storyteller; fortunate, also, the one who possesses the skill to choose just the right story for the occasion and make it live again for the listeners.

Traditionally, stories were told for three purposes: to entertain, to teach, and to transmit the culture. These purposes have not changed essentially, although in an era of mass education, the storyteller primarily provides entertainment and aesthetic pleasure. Folk tales, myths, legends, fables, biography, and history offer a wealth of storytelling material. Since curricula for the middle grades generally include study of early America, explorers, and other countries of the world, storytelling ties in beautifully with social studies as well as the language arts.

ORAL READING

Reading aloud is another enjoyable way of sharing literature with others. One form of literature that is rarely used in the classroom is the radio play. Among the values of the radio play are practice in oral reading, vocabulary building, and communication with listeners without the added demands of theatre production. "The Tinker of Toledo," a Spanish folk tale, appeals to youngsters in the fifth and sixth grades; it is not too difficult for them and brings the class an amusing and "spooky" tale from another culture (Activity 10.1).

Speech Problems

In every class, there are children with speech problems. For severe problems such as stuttering, lisping, lateral emission, cleft palate, and nasality, the school may have a speech therapist with whom the children can work. The majority of problems, however, result from learning English as a second language or from slovenliness of articulation. Children with problems sometimes are sent to therapy, but more often, they are not. For the classroom teacher, who does not have a background in speech correction or improvement, there are a number of good books available with which to work. The trouble is that daily drill is boring and, depending on the way in which it is presented, may discourage a child from speaking at all. The more the exercises can be integrated into the curriculum for general class participation, the better. In this way, the teacher avoids singling out children whose speech is substandard and who may be sensitive about it. Serious problems must be recognized and dealt with, of course, but that is the job of the specialist with whom the classroom teacher works.

Amusing little verses and tongue twisters are fun to practice and can be handled like choral speaking for the entire class. Activity 10.2 offers a few examples of drill in verse for some of the more troublesome sounds.

Written Communication

Another advantage of creative drama that has only recently been discovered, and enthusiastically incorporated into the curricula of some schools, is its power to teach writing. Many children have difficulty expressing themselves on paper, but when stimulated by the improvisation of dialogue, they find inhibitions released and an unexpected ability to write. The immediacy of drama gives it an appeal that ordinary expository writing lacks. Discussing a situation or story with the class first and then playing it creatively stimulates the desire to write a play, either individually or in small groups.

Some teachers have found this tool for themselves. But two writing programs have been highly publicized in the past few years: The Young Playwrights' Project, sponsored by the Dramatists' Guild and directed by Gerald Chapman; and Aurand Harris's work with teachers in the classroom. Chapman is a young Englishman whose success in helping children to write brought him to the United States to initiate a similar project. The Young Playwrights' Project is a nationwide program open to children ages 8 to 18 (but still in high school). English teachers do the original screening of plays written by their students; the best plays are then sent to the Dramatists' Guild in New York, where a play-reading committee, acting as jury, selects a dozen or so for production by professional casts. The results have been highly successful and, moreover, have revealed an amazing amount of young talent.

Less sweeping in its scope but equally successful in its results is the work of Harris, who teaches creative writing through creative drama in the classroom. In this way, he also demonstrates techniques that teachers can use themselves. Both men, as well as many classroom teachers, have found drama and theatre to be an effective tool in teaching written communication.

SOCIAL STUDIES

Implicit throughout this discussion are the many ways in which creative drama can be used to teach social studies. Dorothy Heathcote, foremost proponent of drama as a learning medium, states that there is no subject that cannot be taught through drama. By finding the "dramatic moment" in a situation, children are encouraged to dramatize it. Rather than having the lesson culminate in a play, however, the teacher brings in relevant material and visual aids, making the drama a dynamic way of learning. Because children are involved, they are thinking and seeking answers to questions posed by the teacher, who stops the action periodically to discuss it. Current events, history, and peoples of other lands are particularly rich topics for teaching through drama. A play may result, but generally it does not because the intent is to learn rather than to perform. Heathcote rarely uses literature in her work, preferring to have children work through situations in their own ways under her guidance.

Values, ethics, and morals are also imbedded in drama. Any study of the life and customs of a particular ethnic or racial group shows not only *how* life is lived in that society, but also *why* the group behaves as it does. Humane education (Activity 10.3) and environmental studies come alive when children can see and be the world and animals around them. Political issues are often taught through drama—a controversial use, to be sure, but one that is utilized because of its effectiveness.

ARTISTS-IN-THE-SCHOOLS PROGRAM

Another approach to drama and theatre education is the artists-in-the-schools program, which brings performers into the classroom for a morning, a day, a week, or sometimes a much longer period of time. Actors perform, demonstrate, or work directly with the children. This provides an opportunity for the teacher to learn new techniques that help her to continue on her own after the actors have gone. It also exposes children to the creative artist, whom they otherwise would probably never meet. Throughout the United States, actors, dancers, musicians, painters, puppeteers, and poets have been brought into schools through funded programs. Information on available artists (both groups and individuals) is available through state arts councils and state departments of education. Although not every school has made use of either the program or the concept, many have, and children have had their education enriched as a result.

One further comment regarding drama as a teaching tool. In helping children overcome prejudice and reject stereotypes based on race, religion, sex, ethnic background, age, and handicapping conditions, *classroom practice* is as potent a force as subject matter. The way that teachers handle groups and challenge condescending attitudes is also a form of teaching. While the material we use is unquestionably important, the way in which we deal with students makes a lasting impression. Children tend to treat others as they have been treated; thus a fair and sensitive leader is a role model, affecting social attitudes and values. By our own behavior, we are able to creat a climate of acceptance, with respect for all regardless of individual difference.

SUMMARY

The number of activities that can be incorporated into a curriculum to improve speech and teach the language arts is as limitless as the number of areas that can be included. Reading, writing, storytelling, group discussion, improvisation, and play production are among the former; social studies, ethics, and humane education are among the latter. The produced play, once considered the logical outcome of a unit on drama, is now only one of numerous possibilities. What is more, the loosening of rules that previously governed form makes possible the invention of interesting and exciting new uses and structures of plays.

The controversy regarding drama as means or end is not settled, and perhaps never will be. Compelling arguments on both sides press for a curriculum in which there is a place for both functions. Leading educators have declared drama and speech to be central to a language curriculum. They believe that study of the arts gives form and expression to human feeling and that attending the theatre as a spectator is a rich experience not found in film and television viewing. In the foreword to a publication released by the State University of New York in 1978, a strong stand is taken regarding the place of the arts in education:

The arts are a means of expressing and interpreting human experience. Quality education of individuals is complete only if the arts are an integral part of the daily teaching and learning process. The integration of the arts in the elementary, secondary and continuing education curriculum is a key to the humanistic development of students.[2]

[2] *The Arts as Perception (A Way of Learning)*, Project Search, The University of the State of New York (Albany, N.Y.: The State Department, Division of Humanities and Arts Education, 1978), p. iii.

ACTIVITY 10.1

A RADIO PLAY

Objective: To read dialogue interestingly and clearly, giving interpretation of characters and creating mood

Suggestions for the Teacher

The lesson can begin either with a discussion of the radio play as a form or with the tale. In either case, after introducing the play, suggest that the class improvise the story.

When they know the story well and are familiar with the names of the characters, have the children read the play aloud. It is a good idea to change casts periodically in order to give as many children as possible a chance at the first reading.

Sound effects are important to this script, so one or two children will be needed to handle them.

If the children like the play very much, an extension of the experience could be the use of Spanish folk songs, photographs and pictures of the country, and a tape or recording of Spanish music as background and bridge from one scene to another. This much work on it will probably suggest performing for another class or for parents. If so, do it in the classroom rather than in the auditorium or gym. Voices will be attuned to the space, and work on it will have been done there.

THE TINKER OF TOLEDO
Dramatized by Nellie McCaslin

Characters

Narrator

Pedro, *a merry tinker*

Miranda
Maria
Blanca   } *women of Toledo*
Costa

Riccardo }
Estaban } *men of Toledo*

The Ghost

Sound-effects person

The time is long ago, and the action takes place in the Spanish town of Toledo.

SOUND: *Winds and low moans, which fade as the narrator begins.*

NARRATOR: For many years, the people of Toledo pointed out a great stone castle which stood just beyond the city and which was said to be haunted. Although no one had actually seen the ghost himself, many had heard the low moans that came from the chimney top and the strange light that flared in the windows on moonless nights. Tales were told of adventurers who, scorning the legend, went to the castle to find out what caused the disturbance. But none of them was ever seen afterward; and since the townsfolk refused to go beyond the courtyard, no one could tell what their fates had been.

One day there came to Toledo a little tinker, Pedro, who drove his donkey through the streets, mending all the pots and pans as he went. Now, he was inclined to be talkative, and as he stopped at first one door and then another, he soon heard the tales of the haunted castle. Pedro was a brave little fellow and merry, and he could not bear to think of a mystery forever unsolved. So finally he could stand it no longer; he declared he would spend that night in the castle and find out who the ghost really was. Of course, the folk in the marketplace tried to dissuade him, but he was determined to carry out his plan.

SOUND: *Voices in the marketplace, all talking excitedly together. Above them is the hammering on copper as the tinker works.*

MIRANDA: (*over the babble of voices*) But this is Allhallows Eve. You do not know what may happen.

MARIA: No one who's ventured inside those gates has been heard of since.

BLANCA: You had better keep on mending pots and pans, Tinker; leave the ghosts to themselves.

COSTA: Well, my grandmother once saw—

MIRANDA: (*interrupting rudely*) We have heard it before, Costa.

BLANCA: Many times!

COSTA: But the Tinker has not. Wait, let me tell you.

PEDRO: (*laughing heartily*) I know what you will say. But whatever has happened before, I am not afraid.

MARIA: (*in awe*) He is not afraid.

BLANCA: (*scornfully*) So he says.

PEDRO: (*boldly*) I fear neither man nor beast. So why should I fear a ghost whom no one has seen or touched?

MIRANDA: Those who have disappeared in the castle have seen it. Yes, and touched it too, no doubt.

PEDRO: Well, I am willing to risk my neck. Here, Señorita, is your pan. Now, have I finished them all?

MIRANDA: Thank you, Tinker. That is all I have. Here.

SOUND: *Sound of a coin being dropped.*

MIRANDA: Does anyone else have a pot or pan to be fixed?

COSTA: I have. This handle's come off. Can you mend it?

PEDRO: In two shakes of a donkey's tail. Hand it over.

SOUND: *Hammering on copper as the tinker works.*

BLANCA: How quickly he works.

COSTA: That is good, for it's high time I was home getting supper.

MARIA: Riccardo will be coming along the road any minute. And the beans are not even started.

BLANCA: We have spent the whole day here in the marketplace with the Tinker.

PEDRO: To good advantage, Señora. For I have had more business today than in the past month. And who knows, tonight I may have an adventure worth telling.

RICCARDO: (*fading in*) Hello there! What are you doing in the marketplace at this time of day?

MARIA: Riccardo, you are early!

RICCARDO: (*coming into the scene*) Not so very. Ah-ha! The Tinker is here. And so all the pots and pans in Toledo will be shining again.

ESTABAN: (*fading in*) I thought he must be here from the sound of things. And I'll warrant more gossiping has been done this day than mending.

BLANCA: Oh, no, Estaban. But what do you think? We have been telling the Tinker about the ghost in the castle, and he is determined to sleep there tonight.

ESTABAN: What? He is teasing you.

PEDRO: No, Señor Estaban. I am not. These good wives have but whetted my appetite with their stories. And I wish to see this ghost for myself.

RICCARDO: If you do, it will be the last thing you ever lay eyes on.

ESTABAN: Better that you drive your donkey out of Toledo tonight than end your days in the castle. Why, the last man who boasted he would learn the truth was found dead at the gate the next morning.

MARIA: He was twice the size of you, Tinker.

RICCARDO: And he carried a sword and a club. But he was found in the courtyard with his own weapons by his side.

PEDRO: (*airily*) Then I shall go unarmed. Perhaps this ghost prefers a battle of wits.

BLANCA: Do not go, Tinker. Believe what they tell you.

MIRANDA: Forget your boast.

MARIA: Do not add your story to these others.

COSTA: Yes, Tinker, take your donkey and leave Toledo tonight.

PEDRO: No, my good women; my mind is made up. And when my mind's made up, there's no changing it!

ESTABAN: Very well, fellow, since you insist. Though I must say you don't look as stupid as you are.

RICCARDO: To venture inside on just any night would be foolhardy enough, but on Allhallows Eve—

PEDRO: (*brightly*) All the better. I should be disappointed if your ghost did not put on his best show. Therefore, I must be going at once. Here, Señora, is your pan.

SOUND: *Sound of coins being dropped.*

PEDRO: I think I shall have my supper there as well as my night's sleep. I'll take these coins you have put in my pocket and buy some bread and a slice of bacon.

SOUND: *All talk at once, excitedly. Finally above it comes Miranda's voice.*

MIRANDA: Well, at least let us provide his last meal. I have here a fresh loaf.

BLANCA: And my house is yonder. Let me go get a crock of milk and some bacon.

COSTA: Wait for me, too, Tinker. There will be fresh eggs from our hen.

SOUND: *Footsteps going off as the two women leave.*

PEDRO: So! This is a day of good luck. I find more trade in your city than in all Spain and am given my supper in the bargain.

RICCARDO: Make that boast while you can. For if you can say the same thing tomorrow, you are a man of rare fortune.

ESTABAN: I tell you what we will do. We'll go with you as far as the castle gate. But there we will leave you. Tomorrow morning let us return to see how the Tinker has fared.

ALL: (*ad lib*) Yes, let us do that. Yes! Yes!

PEDRO: You are more than kind. I hope I shall have a tale worth telling.

SOUND: *Footsteps as Blanca and Costa return.*

BLANCA: (*fading in*) Here is the milk and bacon.

COSTA: (*fading in*) And eggs from our hens. Here you are, Tinker.

PEDRO: Thank you, thank you! I shall enjoy this supper.

RICCARDO: (*raising his voice*) Then let us be getting along. For the Tinker is packed up, and we, too, are hungry.

SOUND: *Ad lib. Conversation and footsteps as they go from the marketplace together. Noise and talking fade as the narrator resumes the tale.*

NARRATOR: So Pedro, accompanied by the little band of villagers, went to the castle gate. There they left him to eat his supper and solve the mystery of the ghost.

SOUND: *Ad lib. Good-bye, good luck, see you in the morning, etc. The voices fade away, and the narrator continues.*

NARRATOR: (*His voice takes on a ghostly quality.*) Pedro made his way into the great hall of the castle. It was dark and musty; bats fluttered about his face. Cobwebs clung to his fingers, and the wind moaned through the empty rooms.

SOUND: *Wind moaning in the distance. It continues through the narrator's next speech.*

NARRATOR: Pedro shivered as the dampness settled in. Then, as his eyes grew more accustomed to the darkness, he made out a pile of faggots on the floor by the great stone fireplace. He lost no time in lighting them; and soon bright red and yellow flames were leaping high on the hearth. Somehow, in the warmth and firelight, Pedro's uneasiness began to disappear.

SOUND: *Flames crackling. The wind dies down.*

PEDRO: Well, I may as well get my supper. A fire is a good cure for one's fears. Let me see, in this basket the good wives packed the bacon and eggs. And in this is the bread. A fresh loaf, I'll be bound! And a crock of rich milk. I could not have fared better at the finest inn in Toledo. And all because I am willing to spend the night with their ghost!

SOUND: *Something falling in the distance. The wind begins to moan again softly and mysteriously.*

PEDRO: What ho! Have I company already? (*There is a pause, and no answer but the moaning of the wind.*) Very well, then. I shall proceed with my supper. First to fry the bacon and eggs in my skillet.

SOUND: *Sound of eggs being broken in the pan and then the sound of frying. The wind dies.*

PEDRO: How good it smells! But I must have a swallow of milk.

(*raising his voice boldly*) Here's to you, my friend, whoever you are. I drink the richest milk in all Spain in your honor.

SOUND: *A thump, as something falls heavily on the hearth.*

GHOST: (*off mike*) Oh—my! Oh, my! Oh, my, oh, my! Oh—!

PEDRO: That's not a very jolly welcome, I must say. But hardly frightening to a man who owns a donkey that brays. (*There is a pause, then he continues bravely.*) The bacon is browning nicely. How good it will taste. I'll just dip this piece of bread in the egg as it cooks. (*He smacks his lips audibly.*) Good wives of Toledo, I thank you!

GHOST: (*nearer and louder*) Dear me! Dear me! Oh, dear me!

PEDRO: You sound mighty sad, my friend. What is it?

GHOST: I'm coming down the chimney. Look out!

SOUND: *A thump, as something falls heavily on the hearth.*

PEDRO: (*startled*) What is this? A man's leg? Well, if that's all there is to your ghost—

GHOST: Look out below! I'm coming!

PEDRO: (*assuming bravery*) What, again?

SOUND: *Another thump, as something falls.*

PEDRO: Another leg? Well, you may just lie there until I finish my supper. Rude of you to interrupt, I must say.

GHOST: (*louder this time*) Here I come! I'm falling!

PEDRO: (*pretending great annoyance*) You know, this is getting tiresome. Why not come down all at once instead of a piece at a time?

SOUND: *A heavy thud.*

PEDRO: (*a bit shaken*) So you have a body as well as legs? H'm . . . A good coat and vest, though a bit out of fashion.

SOUND: *Two small thumps.*

PEDRO: Ah-ha! Two arms! I thought they would be coming along. (*sighs*) Well, there is nothing left but the head. I must admit I am rather curious to see what sort of a head you do have.

GHOST: (*loud now and much closer*) Here I come! All clear below? I'm falling!

SOUND: *A final thump.*

PEDRO: (*critically*) Well, you are not so bad-looking. Black hair and beard. But I do wish you'd stop rolling your eyes.

SOUND: *Sound of a person scrambling up from the floor.*

PEDRO: (*greatly startled*) Hold on, there! What are you doing, eh? Well, since you now seem to be in one piece, will you join me at supper?

GHOST: (*in a sad voice, now on mike*) No, I am a ghost and can take no food. Not that I wouldn't like to. But you *can* do me a favor.

PEDRO: Do *you* a favor? How?

GHOST: (*going on hopefully*) You are the only man who has waited until I could put myself together. All the others either ran away or died of fright before both my legs had come down.

PEDRO: Perhaps if they had built a fire and kept their minds on a skillet—

GHOST: Perhaps. But now that you're here—and you look as if you'd stay—I'll tell you what you can do. Out there in the courtyard are three bags of coins. One copper, one silver, one gold. You see, I stole them from some thieves many, many years ago.

PEDRO: I see.

GHOST: (*going on confidentially*) I brought them here to my castle and buried them out in the yard. But no sooner were they safe underground than the thieves caught up with me and killed me. (*He sobs as he recalls it.*) They cut me in pieces, but they did not find the bags. All these years I've been waiting to get myself put together again. But not until some brave soul would stay here with me could it be done.

PEDRO: Well, now that you're a whole ghost, so to speak, what more can I do?

GHOST: (*eagerly*) Come with me to the courtyard. There we shall dig up the coins. The copper, you must take to the church. The silver, you must give to the poor. And the gold, you may keep for your trouble. When this is done, I shall have paid for my sins in full, and I may leave this wretched castle forever.

PEDRO: Very well. (*fading out*) Let us go to the courtyard at once.

SOUND: *Footsteps as they go out.*

GHOST: (*fading in*) Stop here! Beneath this cypress tree the treasure is buried. You will even find the spade I used under that rock.

PEDRO: So it is. Let us begin.

SOUND: *Soft thuds as the earth is turned up.*

PEDRO: This has been here a long time!

GHOST: A hundred years I have been waiting for someone brave enough to help me.

PEDRO: Ho! This looks like something! One more spadeful and— The first bag of coins!

GHOST: Yes, I knew they would be here. This is the copper.

SOUND: *Sound of a heavy bag being dragged on the ground.*

PEDRO: Now, just a little deeper . . . and . . . we come to the second. Here it is, my friend! Pull it up.

GHOST: This will be the silver.

SOUND: *Sound of another heavy bag being dragged.*

PEDRO: And the third—right underneath.

GHOST: Just where I put it. Look out, Tinker, here it comes!

SOUND: *Sound of the third bag being dragged.*

PEDRO: (*whistles*) Copper . . . silver . . . gold! I will do as you ask in the morning.

GHOST: One thing more, now that my task is done. I wish to go off and never come back. So will you take my coattails in your two hands and pull?

PEDRO: (*puzzled*) Of course. But what will that do?

GHOST: Just hold on. You will see. Good-bye, Pedro! You may tell the good folk of Toledo that their castle is haunted no more. Now then, pull! Pull!

SOUND: *A great whirring sound as the ghost disappears.*

PEDRO: (*in astonishment*) Up in smoke he goes! With me holding onto his coat. I'd say I'd dreamed the whole thing if it weren't for these three bags of coins. Well, there's no use hanging on to some empty clothes. So— (*He yawns loudly.*) I may as well get me some sleep. This has been a big day!

NARRATOR: So the little Tinker went back into the castle and stretched out in front of the fire. He fell into a deep sleep almost at once, and it was not until the morning sunshine filled the room that he opened his eyes. When he realized that the folk of Toledo would probably already be at the gate, he hurried outside. There they were, just where he had left them! And all talking at once!

ESTABAN: (*excitedly*) Not a sign of him. It's too bad. He was a brave little fellow.

COSTA: I told him this would come to no good.

BLANCA: We shall never know what did happen. Do you suppose he was spirited away?

RICCARDO: Look! Look! Here he comes now!

MIRANDA: So he does! And swinging along as bold as you please. Or do you suppose it's his ghost?

ESTABAN: Well, we shall soon find out. (*raising his voice*) Tinker, oh, Tinker! Come here!

ALL: Tinker! Tinker, here we are! Come here!

PEDRO: Well, upon my word, you *are* out early!

MARIA: Tell us what happened.

PEDRO: (*fading in*) What happened?

MIRANDA: How did you sleep?

PEDRO: Sleep? Never better. Of course, the floor was *hard* but so peaceful. No noise, no—

ESTABAN: (*cutting in*) Come now, Tinker, don't tell us nothing happened. On Allhallows Eve yon ghost was not quiet.

ALL: (*demanding*) Yes! Tell us, Tinker! What happened?

PEDRO: (*finally giving in*) Very well. I did see your ghost. (*There is a gasp from his listeners.*) But he was a friendly fellow. Quite nice, in fact, once he pulled himself together. And we reached an understanding in no time at all. He left me these three bags of coins to dispose of. The copper must go to the church. The silver, to the poor. And the gold I may keep for myself. You can see where we dug them.

ALL: (*ad-lib exclamations of surprise*)

PEDRO: His duties on earth are now done, so I promise you he will not return.

ALL: (*ad-lib their thank you's*)

ESTABAN: Tinker, the folk of Toledo owe you much. Will you not settle down here with your fortune?

PEDRO: Settle down here? In Toledo?

RICCARDO: Why not? You have wealth. You no longer must mend pots and pans for a living. And besides, you will have a good name in our city.

MIRANDA: Yes, why not, Tinker?

ALL: Yes, Tinker, why not?

PEDRO: Perhaps I shall. But first I must do your ghost's bidding. Will you help me carry these bags? Just think—the ghost story is ended!

Production Notes

Sound Effects

Wind

Hammering on copper

Coins dropped on pavement

Footsteps

Crackling of fire

Thuds (some soft, some loud)

Breaking of eggs

Eggs frying

Person scrambling from floor

Heavy bags being dragged

Whirring noise

ACTIVITY 10.2

TONGUE TWISTERS*

Objective: To work on sounds that children find difficult or pronounce carelessly

Suggestions for the Teacher

Before working on any sounds, identify which ones are most difficult for the children. These will vary in different parts of the country as well as among individual children.

Then introduce verses and tongue twisters that require work on those sounds. If there is a speech therapist in the school or the school system, seek help before attempting any of them. He or she may be able to start the work for you.

Next, have the children work on the sound(s) together. Do not single out individuals at first; later on, you may do it, but be sure that the child will not be embarrassed when you do.

After work on verses such as the following, find others or make them up. Children will enjoy making up tongue twisters.

You may want to demonstrate your work on oral communication, but this is not the aim and should come, if at all, only when real progress has been made, and you have something to show to parents or younger classes.

THE PICNIC (p)

A pig, a poodle, and a parrot
   Upon a pony gay,
With a pickle, a pepper, and a parsnip,
   On a picnic rode away.

A piper passed the party
   Piping a playtime dance;
The poodle fell into the puddle,
   When the pony began to prance.

The pig rode alone to the picnic;
   In the park he seemed peaked and pale.
He'd eaten the pickle and pepper,
   And this is the end of the tale.

BABY BUNNY BOBTAIL (b)

Baby Bunny Bobtail,
   The black and brown rabbit,
Had formed, it was feared,
   One very bad habit.

* Alice L. Wood, *The Jingle Book for Speech Improvement and Speech Correction* (New York: Dutton, 1968), pp. 31, 35, 51, 58, 63, 64, 114, 115.

Before a meal was ready,
He would bounce on the table
And grab and nibble
As fast as he was able.

'Till once he ate some popcorn
As fast as he could grab it.
Burned his paws and tongue and nose,
A wiser bunny rabbit.

THUMPITY THUMP (*th*)

Thump! Thump! Thump!
Thumpity, thumpity, thump!
Thin Thelma Thayer fell down the stairs,
Thumpity, thumpity, thump!

BIRDS OF A FEATHER (voiced *th*)

Said the Bat to the Owl,
"Here I am without a feather.
If you'll give me one of yours,
We'll both be birds together."

TIPTOE TOWN (*t*)

Tiny Tim went to Tiptoe Town,
To Tiptoe Town he went,
He couldn't talk and he couldn't turn
And he lived in a tucked-in tent.

LITTLE NETTIE (medial-position *t*)

Little Nettie threw confetti
And it settled on her hat.
What a pity in the city
To have such poor aim as that.

FOUR J'S (*j*)

John and Jim, Jack and Joe—
Four "J's" jogged out to Burney.
But they joked too much, this jolly band,
For they never came home from their journey.

WITS

An old sage named Benjamin
Once lived beside the bridge.
When asked his age, he flew in a rage,
As mad as any hatter.
"It isn't years that count," said he,
"But only wits that matter."

ACTIVITY 10.3

BLIND WALK*

Objective: To help children understand the relationship between a guide dog and its blind owner

Suggestions for the Teacher

Discuss the problems confronting the blind person, and ask the children about the guide dog.

1. How many of you have seen guide dogs?
2. What did you notice about them?
3. Have you ever wondered why certain breeds are trained for this work?

Bring in materials on training both the dog and the person who will own it.

The exercise "Blind Walk" simulates the interaction between a guide dog and its blind owner. It is designed to induce trust and a sense of what responsibility and dependency really mean. Divide the students into pairs, with one student serving as the guide and the other student wearing a blindfold. Have the guides escort their "blind" partners around the schoolyard or down a path of your choosing. You can even devise some sort of obstacle course, with minor hazards that might make the "blind" partners stumble (but not fall!). Then have the students in each pair switch roles and repeat the activity. Afterward, discuss:

1. How did it feel to be blind? to be a guide for a blind person?
2. How do guide dogs serve their blind owner?
3. What feelings characterize the relationship between a guide dog and its blind owner?

* Information available from Guiding Eyes for the Blind, Yorktown Heights, N.Y. 10598

11

CREATIVE DRAMA FOR
THE SPECIAL CHILD

Let each become all that he was created capable of being;
expand, if possible, to his full growth; and show himself at
length in his own shape and stature, be these what they may.

THOMAS CARLYLE

This chapter considers creative drama in one of the newer areas of education: special education, or the education of the exceptional child or the child with special needs. *Special education* may be defined as any program of teaching techniques designed to meet the needs of children whose abilities deviate markedly from those of the majority of boys and girls of their age. Included in this group are the intellectually gifted as well as the mentally retarded, the physically handicapped, the emotionally disturbed, the culturally and economically disadvantaged, the non-native speaker of English, and the under-achiever, whose problems may not have been identified.

Until recently, very little was done to help these children, whose basic needs are the same as those of so-called normal children but whose individual needs require special educational services. A difference of opinion still exists as to how much or when these children should be integrated into regular class-rooms; but there is recognition that their special needs must be met and that they should be helped to take their places with their peers in as many areas as possible and as soon as they are able to do so. One of the greatest obstacles to this goal has

219

been the widespread notion that such children are "different" from normal children. Modern educators and psychologists have pointed out the values of getting these boys and girls into regular classrooms while they are receiving additional enrichments, remedial help, or therapy. The remediation should be an aid to their instruction, rather than a separate program of instruction.

MAINSTREAMING

Mainstreaming is the term used to define the integration of exceptional children with the so-called normal. The major objective is social: to assist both groups in working and living together. To this end, many practices may be followed.

Speech therapy, remedial reading, language classes for non-English-speaking children, psychological counseling, and special classes for the partially sighted or deaf may be included in the school day without removing a child from the group for more than a period or two at a time. Most schools do not have such extensive programs of special services, but many schools have set up some programs to meet the more urgent needs of the school or community. In some instances, special activities have been added as enrichment for the culturally disadvantaged as well as for the gifted. In all these programs, there is an opportunity to use creative drama as a therapeutic process. As used here, the term *therapeutic* does not imply psychodrama or sociodrama, but points to an aspect of an art form in which children find pleasure, emotional release, mental stimulation, personal satisfaction through success, and, most of all, a chance to use and stretch their imaginations.

SPECIAL CHILDREN

THE GIFTED CHILD

One group of children that has received very little attention, perhaps because they are able to move ahead on their own, is the intellectually gifted. Only recently have educators and parents taken constructive steps to enrich the curriculum so that these gifted boys and girls may receive the stimulation they need by participating in extra classes and following individual interests. One of the areas that has been used most successfully for enrichment is the arts. This is not to imply that *all* children should not have wide and continued exposure to the arts, but because this is an area with endless possibilities, it has been selected often for use with the gifted. Arts programs have been designed both as after-school activities and as additional classes during school time. Some programs include field trips to museums, theatres, and concerts, although funds given for this purpose are generally allocated for the use of all children rather than for one specially selected group. Classes in drama, dance, music, and the visual arts offer gifted children a chance to use their abilities in putting on plays—often written by the children themselves—and in designing and making costumes and scenery.

Gifted children have the ability to think of many things at a time; therefore, drama, with its wide range of responsibilities, is an ideal choice. When dealing with gifted children, the leader must always present a challenge. Drama, by its very nature, does this.

THE MENTALLY RETARDED CHILD

Mental retardation describes a condition rather than a disease. Although any degree of retarded mental development may be involved, the classifications most commonly used are the following: the educable mentally retarded, the trainable mentally retarded, and the dependent mentally retarded. This discussion of creative drama in the education of the mentally retarded child centers on the first category. It is with this group that play can be most rewarding as both a teaching tool and a pleasure. Inasmuch as play constitutes an important role in the all-around development of the child, it has a special significance for the mentally retarded.

According to a survey taken in the early 1960s,[1] the major objectives of teachers using creative drama in the education of the mentally retarded child are to stimulate language and to promote social development. The nature of drama makes it a versatile tool in working with these handicapped youngsters. Rhythms, dramatic play, and pantomime are activities that are widely used by many teachers of the educable and trainable mentally retarded. Adaptations of the techniques used with normal children and developed over a longer period of time can bring both immediate satisfaction and lasting benefit. According to one teacher who has used creative drama successfully with mentally retarded groups, some of the best material comes from the very social situations that cause the retarded child to be stared at and shunned: entering a restaurant; ordering food and eating it; going on a bus, train, or plane trip; and dressing—simple daily activities that the average child easily masters.

---

[1] Geraldine Brain Siks, *Children's Theatre and Creative Dramatics* (Seattle: University of Washington Press, 1961), chap. 17.

Like all children, the retarded want to be members of a group, to contribute to it, and to have their contributions accepted. Drama offers this opportunity. One characteristic of the retarded child is slowness to use the imagination or to deal with abstract ideas. Some teachers believe that the retarded child becomes more imaginative when placed in a class with normal children. Whether in a regular class or a special class, however, the pace is slow. Recognizing this handicap, the teacher can guide retarded children's dramatic play and stimulate their responses. Frequently, the leader errs in expecting too much too soon. Retarded children need more help and encouragement than do other children; they have to repeat experiences more often; and, finally, they must learn self-confidence and feel the satisfaction of having their contributions, however small, accepted. The game of pretending can help such children learn to use their imagination, to prepare for new experiences, and to lay a firmer foundation for oral communication. Experienced teachers state that dramatic activities help to develop the skills of listening and looking. In this way, attention is engaged.

Rhythms and movement games are excellent beginning exercises. They aid the development of large muscles while they motivate use of imagination. The acting out of simple stories comes much later. At first, retarded children will be more comfortable participating in a group than working individually. They probably have experienced frustration and the sense of being different; their need for praise and encouragement, therefore, will be greater than that of a normal child. When they show an interest in moving out of the group to become specific characters—someone other than themselves—they are ready for the next step. Now, instead of general group activities, individual roles may be undertaken. The teacher not only needs to provide stimulation at this stage, but also must give clear and simple direction: Who is the character? How does he walk? What is he doing? How does he do it? What does he say?

If social ease and a sense of security are the first consideration, oral expression is the second. Guided dramatic play is a way of introducing oral vocabulary and developing concepts that prepare the child for reading. A variety of experiences will help to provide a better understanding of the world, and acting out words that describe this world will give them meaning. Action words such as *jump, run, skip, skate,* and *throw* teach by doing. Nouns such as *farmer, mailman, mother,* and *grocer* can become the basis for dramatic play and pantomime. Mentally retarded children who have been guided carefully and slowly through dramatic play will eventually be ready to dramatize simple stories. By this time, they will have achieved some personal freedom and mastered a functional reading vocabulary. The procedure of planning, playing, and evaluating is the same as that followed in the normal classroom, except that with these children, the task and the process must be simpler and will take longer.

One particularly important point to remember is that adjustments in all activities for the retarded should be made on the basis of their interests and needs. Stories selected for dramatization should, in addition to being clear and simple, reflect the interests that give meaning to the children's lives. As their interests widen, a greater variety of stories may be introduced, with new words to express and describe them.

Not only literature but other subjects as well can be taught through the medium of improvisation. For example, one teacher had the children in her arithmetic class be plus and minus signs and pieces of fruit; through acting out simple problems of subtraction and addition, the children were able to see the correct answers. So-called creative walks, on which children became trees, flowers, stones, birds, and animals, helped them to observe and recall what they had seen after they returned to the classroom. Such use of creative drama is not generally sanctioned; with retarded children, however, communication and social development are the primary goals; art is secondary. The potential in drama for motivating children and achieving these primary goals validates its use.

Participation by the retarded child in a formal play is to be discouraged. A continuing program of creative drama, in contrast, offers an opportunity for social growth, emotional release, and a way of learning. As one teacher put it after using creative-drama techniques successfully for many years: "These children need to be crawled with first—then they can walk." When they have reached the walking stage, they often astonish us with what they have learned.

The Emotionally Disturbed Child

It is with emotionally disturbed children that the classroom teacher must exercise the greatest caution. We know so little about these children and the causes of their problems that the possibility of doing harm is greater than with any other group. Indeed, it is often difficult to distinguish between the emotionally disturbed child and the mentally retarded child because of the frequent similarity of behavior. Frequently repeated testing must be done in order to determine the nature of the condition. What might be a rewarding activity for the retarded child might not be good enough for the child who is disturbed. Psychodrama and play therapy are accepted techniques in the treatment of emotionally disturbed children, but they can be damaging in the hands of the lay person, regardless of his or her background and skill as a teacher of creative drama. The seriously disturbed child probably will not be found in the regular classroom, but will be enrolled in a special class or special school, in which services—which may or may not include psychiatric help and play therapy—are provided. Children in special schools often are referred to outside clinics or therapists, and drama may be part of the treatment.

Remedial Drama.   *Remedial drama* is an umbrella term used here to cover several specific techniques. As was stated earlier, drama/theatre has historically been an essential part of human development. In preventive and therapeutic work, drama is primarily concerned with communication and therefore with helping individuals and groups develop and build better relationships. According to Sue Jennings, "[It] does not differ in content or technique from other types of drama, although great care must be taken in selecting and applying drama techniques to remedial work."[2] Her emphasis is on experience; and the goals of drama, used in this way, are *socialization, creativity*, and *insight*.

Eleanor Irwin, well-known drama therapist, draws a distinction between a therapeutic experience and therapy as a treatment. She says that "any experience which helps an individual to feel a greater sense of competence and well-being may be thought of as therapeutic."[3] This is the sense in which the word *therapy* is used by many persons and in which it would be most accurately applied to the work of most classroom teachers using drama with the children on a regular basis.

Drama therapy, role playing, psychodrama, and *sociodrama* are the terms most frequently heard with reference to remedial drama. They differ both as to technique and as to thrust. David Johnson of Yale University, a leader in this new field, defines drama therapy as "the intentional use of creative drama toward the psychotherapeutic goals of symptom relief, emotional and physical integration, and personal growth."[4] Drama therapy, like the other arts therapies, applies a creative medium and establishes an understanding or contract between the client and the therapist. Thus it is differentiated from creative drama in an educational setting.

Sociodrama, as the name implies, deals with the group and with group problems or conflicts. A class in creative drama may become a sociodramatic experience when a real-life situation is employed, leading to discussion and subsequent benefits for all the participants. Classroom teachers sometimes use sociodrama in a limited way to help solve problems that arise and persist, with a damaging effect on the group.

---

[2] Sue Jennings, *Remedial Drama* (New York: Theatre Arts Books, 1974), p. 4.

[3] Eleanor Irwin, "Drama Therapy with the Handicapped," in *Drama/Theatre and the Handicapped*, ed. Ann Shaw and Cj Stevens (Washington, D.C.: American Theatre Association, 1979), p. 23.

[4] David Johnson, mimeographed material, 1978.

Although individuals are involved, it is the group and the group relationships that are the primary concerns.

There is a difference of opinion as to the desirability of drama for the emotionally disturbed child. Some teachers believe that role playing is beneficial; others, that the child's problems present difficulties that may make this form of expression less desirable than participation in the other arts. Seriously disturbed children need to make sense out of their own environment before they can enter another; moreover, until they know who they are, they will have difficulty being someone else.

There is general agreement that dance, rhythms, and ritual movement are excellent for disturbed children. Physical activity gives them a sense of the body; the large movements, such as skipping, galloping, stretching, and moving the arms, are wonderful exercises for those who are poorly coordinated. "Reaching for the sky or pushing away the clouds," "feeling big," "growing tall"—all are movements that contain an element of drama. The Dance Therapy Center in New York City works for release through the improvisational method, whereby the student is made conscious of new insights through bodily action. The philosophy of this unusual center is based on the "restoration of spontaneous movement to break the tenacity of the neurotic hold of body memory and on the experience of new psychophysical action as health is regained."[5] This is a relatively new field, and it is interesting that it recognizes movement as a specific therapeutic technique in dealing with emotional problems.

Many teachers have reported that nonverbal children can develop the ability to express feelings and knowledge through the use of movement and panto-mime. In movement, they find a means of communication, and from movement, may find motivation for speech. The teacher may also discover capabilities and awareness that remain hidden in the usual classroom situation.

Activity 11.1 suggests exercises that may be done with emotionally disturbed children.

Both finger puppets and glove puppets have been found to work successfully with children who are too inhibited to assume roles themselves. Such children usually have a poor self-image; thus it takes longer to build interest and ego strength to the point where they are able to move out of the group to assume roles and sustain them through improvised situations. Again, we are speaking of children with knowledge of themselves and their reality. When they reach the point where they can enter into dramatic situations with relative ease, these emotionally disturbed children will begin to derive some of the same benefits gained by other children. In terms of objectives, interaction with the group,

[5] Dance Therapy Center brochure (New York, 1972–73).

ability to concentrate, ability to express themselves orally, and ability to take the part of another come first on the list. After these objectives have been met, these children should be able to work with joy, accomplishing as much as, and sometimes more than, the others in the group. Their sensitivity, if properly guided, can be an asset to their understanding of a character and their creation of a characterization. Drama, because of its total involvement—physical, mental, emotional, and social—offers a wealth of activities, all of which have therapeutic value, if properly handled.

Circus Skills. Some of the newest and most effective techniques being used in the field of special education are basic circus skills. First introduced as an after-school activity for children, circus skills were discovered to have diagnostic and therapeutic benefits as well. The educated clown/teacher has become a popular phenomenon, whose contribution goes far beyond slapstick entertainment. Circus skills have been found useful in identifying learning disabilities, improving vision, strengthening concentration, and developing self-confidence. Children who have failed in ordinary subject areas and lack interest or talent in the arts have learned to juggle as many as three balls at once, to walk on stilts, and to ride a unicycle. Acrobatics appeal to children who reject dance and drama. Sleight-of-hand and rope tricks are difficult skills that, once mastered, bring praise and admiration from peers. Because the demands of circus skills are different from those associated with school, and because the mystique of the circus has such a strong appeal for children of middle and upper grades, these new techniques seem to work.

They have been used to advantage not only with emotionally disturbed children but also with mentally retarded, physically handicapped, and economically disadvantaged children. A recommended text for persons interested in using the techniques is *A Suitcase Circus* by Reg Bolton.[6] The author is a certified teacher and professional clown, who wrote the book out of his own experience teaching and performing for children.

THE PHYSICALLY HANDICAPPED CHILD

In many ways, physically handicapped children present fewer difficulties to the classroom teacher than do the emotionally disturbed or the mentally retarded. Their handicaps are visible, and their limitations, obvious. Problems are easier to identify, and, depending on the seriousness of the disability, decisions have already been made as to

[6] Reg Bolton, *A Suitcase Circus* (Rowayton, Conn.: New Plays, 1983).

whether they can function in a regular classroom. As with all exceptional children, the physically handicapped are thought to be better off integrated into a normal classroom rather than segregated; if the disability is so severe that special services are required, however, they may have to be enrolled, at least for a time, in a special school or in a hospital.

For our purposes, we shall consider the physically handicapped to include the deaf child, the partially sighted or blind child, and the child unable to function normally because of some other physical disability. Frequently, children with physical problems have emotional problems as well; to overcome both these handicaps, they need all the support and encouragement that the teacher can give as they struggle to reach their goals. Because of the conspicuousness of the handicaps, however, they are generally treated with more compassion and understanding than are their classmates with emotional problems whose behavior is inappropriate or immature. Persons whose psychological problems cause them to behave in a socially unacceptable manner are often criticized or ridiculed, prompting the comment, "Why must they act that way?" Persons on crutches never evoke this reaction, for we know that they are walking as well as they can. In spite of, or perhaps because of, their physical limitations, children who cannot hear, see, or speak

Children performing in "Hands, Hands." (Courtesy of Milton Polsky; photograph by Ann Rachel)

clearly or who lack physical coordination or cannot walk need an opportunity to escape the walls of their prison on the wings of the imagination. Creative drama offers this opportunity, although admittedly the goals must be modified for physically handicapped children.

The Little Theatre of the Deaf, which achieved national prominence at the end of the 1960s, is a shining example of what can be done by actors for children who cannot hear. Because oral communication is emphasized in early education, deaf children are at a disadvantage when attending theatrical performances, just as they are in ordinary classroom situations. Pantomime is the obvious means of reaching the hard-of-hearing, and it is in this form that The Little Theatre of the Deaf has succeeded so brilliantly. A cue can be taken from this experiment: pantomime is an area of drama that the child with hearing loss can participate in as well as enjoy as a spectator. Incidentally, we have recently become accustomed to seeing interpreters using sign language on television to bring important programs to nonhearing viewers.

Again, movement is an ideal way to begin activities. Large physical movements come first, and then rhythms and dance. Small-muscle movements follow. Sensitive to the deaf child's keen visual perception, the leader can move from dance into pantomime. There is motivation for speech in drama, but the easiest communication is through pantomime, in which the deaf child can achieve success. Stories may be told in this medium, giving pleasure to both player and observer. My observation of creative-drama classes in a school for the deaf revealed remarkable possibilities for learning and emotional release.

Blind or partially sighted children face different problems. They are at home with speech, so storytelling is an excellent beginning activity. Choral speaking, like music, is also an art in which they can excel and at the same time find pleasure. Original poetry composed by the group offers a chance to express feelings and personal responses. Free movement is more difficult for the blind child than for the sighted child, but it is not impossible. Carefully guided improvisation may be attempted, although the formal play, in which movement is predetermined and is not changed in rehearsal, is by its nature easier. One director who has had great success with a blind drama group stresses the fact that she never moves scenery or props once the placement has been established. A knowledge of where things are enables the players to move freely and easily about the stage. For the blind or partially sighted player, formal drama offers greater security than does improvisation.

Children with physical problems that prevent them from running, walking, or even using their arms or legs easily have also found drama to be within the range of their capabilities. Participation of the children while they are seated is an excellent way of involving everyone in pantomime, choral speech, and puppetry. In preparing a dramatization, the

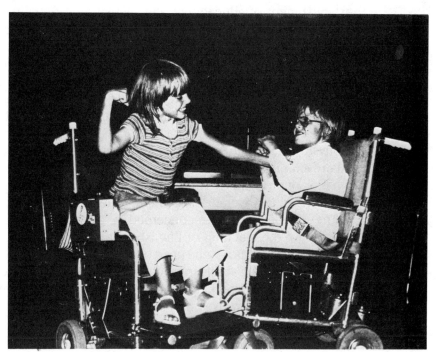

Members of the Rainbow Company enjoy creative drama. (Courtesy of Jody Johnston, Las Vegas)

roles of narrator and storyteller are highly regarded and can be handled by a child who may not be able to engage in more active participation. The imaginative teacher can find a place for the disabled child in which he or she is able to add to the group endeavor, thus enhancing the self-image and giving a sense of achievement. The philosophy of all therapeutic recreation includes this sense of pride in a job well done and the joy of creative accomplishment.

Physically handicapped persons are able to do and enjoy a much wider range of dramatic activities than was formerly thought possible. Most obvious but little used in the past is puppetry. The puppeteer in a wheelchair is able to run, jump, dance, fly—in short, to perform every physical activity through the puppet. And, in most cases, such a puppeteer is at no disadvantage.

The Culturally and Economically Disadvantaged Child

Since the advent of the Head Start program, we have been hearing much about the culturally disadvantaged child, or the child in the disadvantaged urban area. This is not a new problem in our society but one that, for a variety of reasons, is now attracting wide attention, with government and private-foundation funds having been allocated for the establishment of educational and recreational programs. The arts, including dramatic play and creative drama, are emphasized in many of these programs. The values cited in Chapter 1 have tremendous implications for these children, who were born into an environment lacking books, playing space, supervision, the arts—and, in many cases, language itself. According to one group of leaders at a conference on the subject of creative drama in special education, the problems of these children are manifold. For example, poverty may preclude treatment of a physical handicap; the handicap causes feelings of inadequacy; and this results in emotional disturbance. Hence, the child suffers a combination of problems requiring understanding and skill beyond the qualifications of the average well-prepared teacher.

The schools have been concerned in recent years with bilingual education and the teaching of English as a second language. Particularly in large urban areas has the need been felt for teachers with a knowledge of Spanish and the ability to teach English in the early grades to children who enter school speaking a foreign language. One technique used and discussed today involves movement and pantomime.

For over a century, body movement has been recognized as bearing a relationship to the acquisition of a second language. Indeed, several methods making use of mime, rhythm, and sign language have been devised for teaching foreign languages. Movement is, therefore, not a new technique; rather, it is now recognized as an integral part of the learning process. Movement plus oral activities offer a great variety of opportunities for learning on any level.

The child who is learning a second language is faced with a problem not unlike those faced by disabled children. It is therefore suggested that the procedures be much the same. Dance is recommended as a beginning because it forces more concentration than does pure verbal exercise. Folk dances involve a physical response to oral commands. Pantomime makes the spectator guess what the performer is doing and thereby ties the word to the act. Choral speech has great value because it offers practice in talking, pronunciation, and interpretation. It is, in addition, an enjoyable exercise that does not single out the less able speaker.

Creative drama with bilingual children does not differ from creative drama with other groups except in the matter of vocabulary. The most common error in dealing with these children is underestimating their ability and overestimating their verbal skill. If given very short but interesting activities, they can be successful and thus improve their self-image.

One gifted young drama teacher, whose work with a bilingual sixth grade I observed recently, used television commercials as assignments.

Each child wrote and performed a commercial for a well-known product. These skits were clear, brief, and, in some cases, humorous; in every instance, they were within the capabilities of the youngsters, who enjoyed creating and improvising them.

THE PROBLEM GROUP

Occasionally, a teacher has a group composed of hyperactive or simply tense, overstimulated children, who can pose a problem for the leader. These children may not be termed special, but they are difficult for the inexperienced teacher or the teacher who is used to an average class. What to do when your usual procedures do not work? when the group cannot be assembled? when the children lose interest quickly or cannot handle the freedom of creative drama? I am convinced that the best methods come through "trial and error," which varies with the individual. But here are a few suggestions that I have found to work successfully with problem groups.

1. Find out all you can about the children. If the group numbers more than 12, see if it can be split into two groups, each meeting for half the allotted time. Sometimes the art or physical-education teacher is glad to help in this way.

2. Establish clear-cut boundaries of space and freedom. If you are meeting the class in a large or all-purpose room, set up boundary lines with chairs. These chairs are not to be moved.

3. Give children the magic command "Freeze!" whenever you want them to stop moving and talking and to listen. This works well with most groups, provided the word is not overused.

4. Keep your directions clear and to a minimum. Too much talk on your part will turn them off.

5. Have definite plans for the day, with alternative plans ready in case the first fail to capture the interest.

Now you are ready to start, and Activity 11.2 suggests a few methods to focus the children's attention.

SUMMARY

This chapter has dealt with the subject of the special, or exceptional, child in the most cursory way, and it is hoped that teachers of any handicapped group or of a class in which there is a child with a handicapping condition will avail themselves of the growing literature in the field. Each condition cited merits a book in itself. The purpose of discussing them here is to:

1. Raise the consciousness of the teacher in order to make him or her become more aware of the needs of the disabled or special person in the group
2. Offer encouragement to try creative drama and puppetry with disabled persons
3. Give an introduction to some of the materials in the field

A practical starting place for the beginner is with assessment—of oneself, of existing programs, and of the facilities that are available.

The exceptional child, regardless of the condition that sets him or her apart, suffers isolation and unhappiness. The exceptional child merits individual attention, and each teacher knows the capabilities as well as the disabilities of the various children in the group. We are not here discussing the special-services school; we are, rather, concerned with the exceptional child in the regular classroom and the ways in which creative-drama techniques can be utilized to meet his or her needs and potential. Although unable to do everything that the normal child does, the exceptional child can do some things well, and from this experience can move forward, thus gaining pleasure and a sense of accomplishment. One successful teacher stresses *listening* as the first and most important element of the teaching process. What is the child trying to tell us about his or her desires or frustrations? What is unspoken and why? Important cues are there to be picked up by a sensitive ear.

The classroom teacher does not presume to be a therapist, but by knowing the exceptional children in the class—their problems and needs—the teacher may apply the techniques of drama to effect growth, strengthen abilities, and build more positive self-concepts. Moreover, the teacher can work with the therapist to their mutual benefit. These are our goals.

ACTIVITY 11.1

_____

<u>BEGINNING EXERCISES IN MOVEMENT</u>

Objective: To develop concentration and group work through mime

Suggestions for the Teacher

The following is a good exercise for any group of children but is particularly good for the disturbed. One child begins a pantomime. This might be a man shoveling snow. Another child, who knows what the first child is doing, steps up and joins, either shoveling snow or doing something that relates to it. The pantomime is kept up until all the members of the group have entered into the activity, one at a time. This is an excellent means of focusing attention and assisting each child to "join" the group in a natural and logical way. If the class is large, two small groups can be formed, each taking a turn at the same exercise.

Another suggestion is a variation on the old game "Statues." One person goes to the center of the room and strikes a pose. He or she freezes as another person joins in. Each one stays in a pose until the entire group has come together, forming a large sculpture. This exercise is not drama therapy but is pantomime with possible therapeutic benefits, inasmuch as it encourages both observation of others and movement that relates to them.

Although it is suggested that all groups benefit from starting a session with movement, it is essential for children with problems. Through ritual, they find security; through warm-ups, use of the body; through moving as a group, a lessening of self-consciousness. It is further suggested that dance involving physical touch is often helpful, and patterned dance— with its structure—is a better starting place for some children than are freer dance forms. Under any circumstances, rhythms that involve the whole body, clapping the hands, and making sounds to a drumbeat are good ways of getting and holding attention. Sue Jennings warns against imposing "end of session" discussions on children with problems. "Let them happen," she advises. The first job is to establish trust and security. Verbalization may be slow, and any analytical discussion should be a future goal.

_____

ACTIVITY 11.2

PREPARING FOR GROUP WORK

Objective: To help children function as a group so that they can work on a project together

Suggestions for the Teacher

Find out what most interests the children. Is it art? music? gym? This will help you in your selection of material.

Find a strategy to get and hold their attention. Until you do, you probably will not be able to conduct a lesson of any kind.

Start the session with movement—big, vigorous movement to stretch tense muscles. Then move quickly to another activity. If you play a guitar and sing, you can get the group to sing songs that they know and like; or, if a new song, something they will respond to and find easy to learn.

Some leaders start with a game: Simon says, blindman's buff, say a word and pass it on. When you sense the children's readiness to do something more serious, tell them a story. Again, be sure that it is a simple story, such as "The Three Little Pigs," that they know and like.

If the activity holds their interest, suggest that they might want to make paper-bag masks of various characters. For "The Three Little Pigs," get large cardboard cartons from the custodian for the houses. They can be painted to look like straw, wood, and brick, or they can be used just as they are.

Varied activities are better than is a complicated story for children whose attention span is short. Above all, remember that these children need structure. Unless there are serious problems, in time they will develop the self-discipline needed for creative work. Then you can push back the boundary lines and expect more of the group. For the present, however, start where the children are. Your objective right now is to help them achieve a focus and work cooperatively on a project to its completion.

12

SHARING WORK
WITH AN AUDIENCE

The formal play, in contrast to creative drama, is primarily audience centered and has, from the beginning, public performance as its goal. A script is either written or selected in advance and is memorized by the players. It does not matter whether the lines were written by a playwright or by the teacher, or were composed by the children themselves. The use of a script distinguishes the formal play from creative drama.

It would be unwise to attempt to cover both informal and formal dramatic techniques in one book, whatever its length. It is hoped that teachers of young children will confine their efforts to creative drama exclusively. But for teachers of older children who may wish to share their work with others, a few elementary suggestions are offered as to the smoothest way to move the play from the classroom to the stage.

This transition should come easily and naturally to the group that has spent many hours in improvisation. For boys and girls who have played together informally over a period of time, the desire is more likely to be one of "sharing" than of "showing," and to this end, the teacher should be able to help the players achieve their goal—successful communication with an audience. Public performances, regardless of their popularity, should be infrequent, however, and then planned only for other classes or for parents. This chapter has been included to help the teacher move, if necessary, from informal classroom drama to the sharing of an experience with others or to the experiencing of performance as the natural outcome of creative playing.

Unless the teacher has had some theatre training, directing the formal play can be a difficult undertaking. That is the reason for emphasizing simplicity; a long script, requiring elaborate scenery and costumes, poses problems for the most seasoned director. The average teacher does not have the background, time, or facilities to cope with such problems, but he or she can support and help enthusiastic young players prepare and demonstrate their work. In guiding beginners of any age, the most important single element is the approach of the leader. Enthusiasm and guidance help young players to cross the bridge between self-expression and successful communication.

Creativity is less dependent on training and past experience than on a special way of feeling, thinking, and responding. It is, therefore, quite possible for the teacher to be a highly creative person in theatre arts without having specialized in any of the arts. Nevertheless, the formal play does make technical demands whenever an audience is involved.

THE SCRIPT

It is to be hoped that the play presented by children will be one that they have written. When the script comes as the result of enthusiasm over a good story or as the culmination of their study of a subject, it is much more likely to have meaning for the class. If, for example, a class has been studying another culture (the American Indian, life in the United States a century ago, China, the Middle Ages) and has dramatized material relating to it, the play emerges from this background as a natural result. The children may decide to dramatize one of the stories or legends they have read. After playing it creatively a number of times, they will be ready to write, or have the teacher write, the dialogue as they suggest it. The results will be childlike and crude, but the story itself has stood the test of time and, therefore, serves as a good scenario.

Sometimes a group wants to try an original plot. This is infinitely more difficult than is reinterpreting a legend. Again, if the desire comes as the result of great interest in a subject that the class has been studying, the children will know something of the background (time, place, occupations of the people, beliefs, superstitions, education, food, housing, and folk or tribal customs). Their very enthusiasm is the primary requisite. Beyond that, they will need the guidance of the teacher in planning a story and developing characters who motivate the action. Inexperienced playwrights of any age cannot be expected to turn out well-made plays. What they *can* do is demonstrate their understanding of the subject matter about which they are writing and show believable characters involved in the story. The play that comes as the result of integrating drama with social studies, music, literature, dance, or art will have its greatest value to the players. Another class will enjoy seeing their work and perhaps will be stimulated to try a play of its own. These are sufficient reasons for deciding to share the project, but unless the children are older and the teacher has had considerable experience in drama, it probably should not go beyond the school-assembly audience.

Occasionally, however, a class of sixth or seventh graders will want to do a play that is not related to classwork. When this request comes, the problem is somewhat different. There is the question of finding a good script that will offer as many opportunities as possible, without featuring three or four talented players. There is a scarcity of such material, although some good short plays have been written with the class or drama-club group specifically in mind. The values cited in Chapter 6 should be considered when making the decision. Is it worthwhile material? Are the characters believable? Does the dialogue offer enrichment? Is the play interesting to the players? Has it substance? Beyond that, we must ask if it has enough parts to involve the whole group in some way.

The text, by whomever it is written, should be a literate entity. Language should help to create character, provoke action, further plot, and offer color and credibility. The construction of the play is of equal importance, for content and form should work together. A good play offers opportunity for young people to interpret not only its literary content, but also its production requirements—scenery, costumes, lighting effects. Finally, a good play generates interest beyond itself—beyond its subject matter, ideas, or characters. It should move and stimulate thought in both performers and audience. This is a big order, and not all plays meet these demands equally; but material that is worth working on must contain some of them. Students work best when challenged and tire or become bored when too quickly satisfied.

Within the past few years, a number of good collections of plays for children have appeared on the market. Teachers should consult the catalogs of publishers who specialize in this area of dramatic literature and visit bookstores that carry their material. If resources of this kind are not available in the community, teachers should write away for scripts; most publishers are helpful in supplying information and books for examination through the mail.

There are also some short plays by major dramatists that are suitable and challenging for junior- and senior-high-school students. These plays are seldom considered, but they make excellent material on which to work. Moreover, one of these plays will hold the attention of an audience of peers if the cast can project its meaning and dramatic value. The choice of play is important because it is the foundation of the production. A play of good quality is worth all the time, effort, and study that will be required in the weeks that follow.

A play written expressly for classroom use often has several major characters and groups of townsfolk or a chorus. This structure gives everyone a chance to participate, makes double casting possible, and may even offer an opportunity to add music or dance. Production problems are another consideration. What are the staging facilities? Or will the play be performed in the classroom? If so, will it be in the round or in proscenium style? Are scenery and costumes essential, or can the script be simply performed with the tables and chairs that are available?

Sometimes the teacher will find a play based on a favorite story. Other times, the children will want to work on a particular kind of play—for example, a mystery. Whatever the choice, it should be a short script, requiring as little time as possible for rehearsals; long periods spent in rehearsing difficult scenes rarely make for a lively experience. ("The Rich Man," in Activity 12.1, is a good example.) If the group does a play for an audience, the choice of a script is the first important consideration.

Occasionally, a sixth- or seventh-grade class will want to do a Shakespeare play. This is a challenge to the teacher as well as to the class, but it can be done intelligently and effectively, if approached in the right way. Of course, the play will be far too long as it stands. If the teacher familiarizes the class with the story, has the students improvise scenes from the play, and then cuts the play to a manageable length, the project will be realistic. Rather than cutting within the play, it is better to select key scenes on which to work. In this way, there is no dilution of the literature; what is performed has been carefully selected to be performed as written.

A Shakespeare play requires more time to prepare than does a modern play because of the language and the necessary orientation. But children who can experience Shakespeare's work as *theatre* rather than as a textbook assignment are amazingly quick to grasp meanings and see its humor. *A Midsummer Night's Dream, Twelfth Night, As You Like It, Julius Caesar*, and *The Merchant of Venice* are among the plays I have seen or have done with sixth and seventh graders; and they have all been successful.

Not only Shakespeare, but Molière, Goldoni, and Rostand as well, have appeal for children. Again, only scenes should be performed, rather than the full-length play; however, the actors must have knowledge of the entire work. An advantage of working on classics is that scenery is rarely important. Two or three chairs, a bench, a table, perhaps some sturdy boxes, a screen—these are pieces of furniture and props that schools and community centers have on hand. The classics are certainly not for beginners or for the very young. Still, for children who have had previous work in creative drama, they provide a real challenge and can establish a lifelong love for some of the world's greatest dramatic literature.

THE DIRECTOR

The teacher moves from being guide to being director during the rehearsal periods. Some directors are permissive and allow much opportunity for individual interpretation. Others plan action carefully in advance and supervise every detail. The director of inexperienced casts often finds the greatest success in an approach that is somewhere between the two extremes: he or she gives enough direction to make the cast feel secure but provides enough leeway for individual interpretation and inventiveness. Regardless of method, however, the use of a script and the anticipation of an audience automatically place the emphasis on product rather than process.

Production also implies scenery and costumes; hence, time and effort must be given to their design and construction. They need not be elaborate; indeed, they seldom are, in school or club productions, but the mounting is an important aspect of the formal play. When children assume some responsibility for scenery, costumes, and properties, they gain additional learning experiences as well as the opportunity for integrating arts and crafts with drama. Cooperation between the players and the backstage crew is essential to success and is certainly one of the greatest satisfactions that a group can experience.

It is suggested that before any work on the play is begun, the director have the group play the story creatively. Improvisation helps the players become familiar with the plot, get acquainted with the characters, and remain free in their movement. When the cast is thoroughly acquainted with the story, it is ready to rehearse more formally.

THE FLOOR PLAN

The director should make a floor plan or diagram of the playing space in advance. On this, he will sketch in the essential pieces of scenery or furniture and indicate the entrances. This is not a picture of the set, but a careful diagram of the floor area, which indicates where each piece of scenery will be placed, its relative size, and the space left on the stage for easy movement. The director should be careful to put

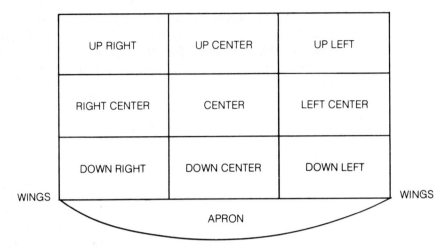

UP RIGHT	UP CENTER	UP LEFT
RIGHT CENTER	CENTER	LEFT CENTER
DOWN RIGHT	DOWN CENTER	DOWN LEFT

WINGS ⌐ ⌐ WINGS

APRON

The areas of the stage. Left and right always refer to the actor's left and right.

entrances where the actors can use them most comfortably and effectively. Although the scenery probably will not be available much before final rehearsals, the director should try to find pieces of comparable size so that the cast becomes used to the plan and will have as little trouble as possible adjusting to the setting when it appears.

The director also should list all pieces of scenery in order to check them off as they are collected or made. The beginner will find that the simpler the setting, the fewer the problems and, incidentally, the more effective the stage will probably be. Children can be involved in all the details of the production; they will enjoy it and learn from the experience.

THE STAGE

The term *arena stage* is used to describe a central playing space. Some smaller theatres are built with the playing space in the center and the seats on all four sides; others, often called *thrust stages*, have seats on only three sides. In either case, a different style of acting is demanded from that required by the proscenium stage, but it is one that is often easier for the less experienced player than for the professional adult actor, accustomed to the techniques of the proscenium stage.

In schools with an all-purpose room, plays are frequently given in the round. Although such areas lack proper lighting and good acoustics, they have the advantage of being familiar territory to the students, and they require little in the way of scenery. What scenery there is should be simple and low, so that it does not block the view, and so lightweight

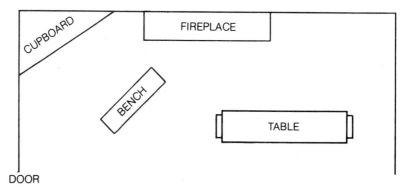

An example of a simple floor plan.

that it can be carried on- and offstage in front of the audience. Entrances may be indicated by putting masking tape on the floor. The audience must be told when it is seated that the taped-off areas will be used by the actors and must therefore be kept open. If the play calls for audience participation, it is much easier to handle in the round than on an elevated proscenium platform.

Whatever the space, it should be small, with as good acoustics as possible. This not only will put the actors at ease, but also will help to prevent the constant reminders to "speak up" or "louder, please!" These admonitions all too often lead to a stilted, unnatural performance, with children talking to the audience rather than to the other characters in

ARENA STYLE

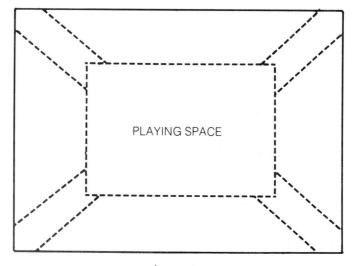

Arena stage.

the play. Large high-school auditoriums are probably the worst possible places for children to perform. A small room, in contrast, deemphasizes the lack of performance skills and puts the attention where it should be—on the play.

THE STAGE MANAGER

The stage manager's is an important job, and one that a responsible girl or boy can do and enjoy. The stage manager should be appointed at the same time that the cast is selected. He or she attends all scheduled rehearsals and keeps a record of all cuts, action, and business. During the performance, it is a good idea for the stage manager to sit at one side of the stage where it is easy to see and hear and to call the actors for their entrances.

Under most circumstances, the stage manager will pull the curtains and handle or give cues for the lights. The stage manager has a chance to grow in the job and learns, by doing, the meaning of the word *responsibility*.

THE CAST

The preliminary work done, the director is now ready to attend to casting the play. In creative drama, the cast changes with every playing. In the formal production, however, one cast rehearses each scene a number of times in preparation for the performance. The matter of casting is, therefore, important. The director tries to get the best possible cast together and usually does it by means of tryouts. A certain amount of typecasting is inevitable. For example, a giant must be played by a very large child; a dwarf or an elf, by a small child; other characters who may have certain specified physical characteristics, by children with similar characteristics. To cast for any other reason than theatrical effectiveness is a questionable practice.

The audience must believe in the reality of the characters, and if they are too obviously different from the description or implications in the script, an audience cannot find them acceptable. Likewise, older players will feel uncomfortable if they realize that they are not believable, and so the good that the experience may do them is negated by their own feelings of inadequacy. This, of course, is one of the strong arguments against public performance by children. An actor cannot grow when constantly cast in the same type of role.

Casting should be done carefully, for a mistake made in the beginning may be fatal later. Some directors like to have two casts. This is a good idea, provided there is sufficient time for a double set of rehearsals. It is a precaution against illness and accidents and gives the entire group a feeling of security. Double casting also provides twice as many opportunities for participation and should work out well if there is time enough to rehearse both groups equally. It goes without saying that both casts must be given a chance to perform.

STAGE MOVEMENT

Stage movement is the movement of actors about the stage. The director who plots it in advance will find that valuable time in rehearsal is saved. Writing notations in her script, or even making diagrams, helps the director to see at a glance where the various characters are. Although most published scripts have action included, it seldom works, for the simple reason that no two stages are alike. For example, an important entrance, which the script indicates should be from the right, may have to be reversed if the wing space in the school auditorium cannot accommodate it.

If the movement is memorized along with the lines and is not changed, it is an advantage. Once the general movement is set, the cast is free to develop appropriate business (action) and work on characterization. Early memorization of lines also helps the group move ahead, giving attention to the rhythm of the play, the building of climaxes, the projection of voice, and general polishing. Perfection is never the aim when working with children, but their satisfaction is certainly greater when they feel well prepared, comfortable, and able to enter into the performance with a sense of security. Encouragement, plus necessary constructive criticism, help to make the rehearsal period one of pleasure and learning.

SCENERY

Scenery is the large pieces that suggest the locale of the play. There is always controversy over the difference between scenery and properties, or "props." Scenery is background, whereas properties are those items used by the actors.

The trend today (and a fortunate trend it is for inexperienced and young groups) is toward curtains rather than box sets and toward suggested rather than realistic settings. For example, a bench, a table, chairs, stools, and perhaps a fireplace or a hutch—if available—will suggest a peasant's cottage, without the necessity of building flats, putting in doors, or painting an elaborate representational background.

Platforms and steps are useful in creating different levels, thus adding variety in appearance and making for interesting movement. A bright tablecloth, a few large artificial flowers, and two or three benches or stools can provide an attractive setting. Children have wonderfully imaginative ideas for suggesting scenery; what they do need is practical help in constructing it and in supporting the pieces. If the director works closely with the art department of the school, most backstage problems can easily be solved. And, best of all, the stage crew or scenery committee wil have an ideal opportunity to learn techniques of painting and handling materials.

Scenery is usually not needed until the final rehearsals. If it can be ready a week in advance of the first dress rehearsal, the players will have a chance to get used to it and will not have to add that adjustment to costumes and other last-minute details. A few *dos* and *don'ts* may be helpful:

1. Scenery should enhance, not distract.
2. Scenery should be firm, not flimsy.
3. Scenery should unify the production.
4. Scenery should be in keeping with the mood of the play.
5. Scenery should suggest the time and place of the story, and the circumstances of the characters.
6. Scenery and costumes should be planned together.
7. Scenery should help the players, not get in their way.

PROPERTIES

Very little needs to be said about properties. They are all the objects (usually small) used by the players. If the school has a property closet, many commonly used items can be kept and brought out when needed. Baskets, canes, wooden bowls, china, swords, and the like are basic equipment. Some things must be borrowed, some made. It is a challenge to the ingenuity of the property committee when, for example, such things as a "golden goose," a "snowman," a "roast chicken," or a "birthday cake" are called for. Papier-mâché and Styrofoam are excellent materials for the unusual item, but, again, the young or inexperienced committee needs help in constructing props.

One other word regarding props: the property committee learns through its assignment what responsibility is all about, for objects often are needed at particular moments in the play, and their absence can ruin an otherwise excellent scene. Properties should be checked before and after every rehearsal and performance, and if damaged or missing, they must be replaced. It is a good idea to begin gathering the properties as soon as the play goes into rehearsal so as to give the actors ample time to get used to handling them.

COSTUMES

Costumes, like scenery, can be a source of worry and frustration to the teacher whose group is too young or inexperienced to assume responsibility for them. Sometimes parents take a hand with the costumes, and sometimes the art department offers assistance. The help of parents may be a satisfactory arrangement, but all too often, it builds what should have been a simple performance into a major production. Too much emphasis is put on the appearance, and the public performance with adult contributions takes precedence over the learning. The second arrangement—assistance from the art department—is decidedly preferable, since it keeps the play within the framework of the school and may give the class an opportunity to help design or even make some part of the costumes. If neither type of cooperation is available, the teacher should try to solve the matter of clothing by merely suggesting it or by adapting easily obtainable garments to the play.

Aprons, hats, vests, capes, boots, and shawls are easily acquired and go a long way toward suggesting various kinds of characters. Children accept simple suggestions and do not demand complete or authentic outfits. Blue jeans, tights, and colored T-shirts are in the wardrobes of most children, regardless of economic circumstances. If these are chosen with a color scheme in mind, they can be used as costumes for many folk tales or for plays with historical backgrounds.

Paper should be avoided. It tears easily and so is hazardous. It is suggested that all good costumes, whether made for a particular occasion or given to the school, be saved and kept in good repair. The collection of basic garments should be a continuing project; as time goes on, it will provide many, sometimes all, of the costumes needed for future school productions.

Here a few suggestions are offered as to the function of costumes:

1. Costumes should suggest the personalities, ages, occupations, and financial circumstances of the characters.
2. Costumes should belong to the period and setting of the play.
3. Costumes should be appropriate to the season of the year, as suggested by the story.

4. Costumes should help to unify the production.
5. Costumes should be planned with the scenery in mind; they should carry out the color scheme and look well against the background.
6. Costumes should not distract by their brightness, richness, or design, unless, of course, there is a reason for it.
7. Costumes should fit the wearers and be clean and well pressed.
8. Costumes should be secure, neither carelessly made nor too fragile to be safe.
9. Costumes should make the wearers feel appropriately dressed and comfortable, not self-conscious.

REHEARSALS

In the beginning, the director will have many decisions to make and many details to organize. Once the play is cast, the floor plan is designed, and arrangements for settings and costumes are made, the director can get down to the serious business of rehearsing. As stated earlier, time spent on improvisation will be time well spent: the cast will become thoroughly acquainted with the characters and the plot. Better yet is the play that evolves from a comprehensive unit of study. When children have been deeply immersed in a situation, a period, or a place for a long time, the play they build will have much greater meaning for them and for the audience.

The director is now ready to set up a rehearsal schedule. It is hoped that, for the teacher or director of children, this will be an informal procedure. Even though a performance date has been set and the work planned, the anxiety and boredom that mar rehearsals of so many non-professional productions must be avoided. For this reason, rehearsals should be frequent but short. Scenes, rather than the entire play, should be rehearsed first; complete run-throughs come later.

Early memorization of lines is advocated, since it frees the players to move and develop pertinent business or individual action in keeping with the character. People memorize at different rates of speed, but the sooner it is done, the more productive the rehearsal periods will become. Most important is interpretation. Discussions along the way help the actors to learn who the characters are and why they behave as they do. First of all, there should be an oral reading of the whole play. Then such questions as these should be answered.

1. How would you describe the character you are playing?
2. What does the character have to say about him- or herself?
3. What do others have to say about him or her?

4. What are the character's relationships to other persons in the play?
5. What are the character's aims? motivations?
6. What are the character's individual qualities? details that help in understanding him or her (personality, temperament, age, occupation, background, likes, dislikes, education, beliefs)?
7. What are the main events of the play? How does each character fit into them?

One word of caution: the dramatist's intention must be respected in interpreting the play. Altering the meaning is dangerous and disrespectful. If the group does not like the play as written, better give it up and select something else. Changing mood or meaning will throw the play out of focus. Leave out the "spoofs"; this is a questionable practice at best and is not for young players.

Blocking the scenes comes next. If the director plans the movement in advance, he or she will be able to approach a rehearsal knowing when characters enter and leave, by what door, and where they sit or stand. It is a good idea to note all movements on a master script. Often, when a few days have passed between rehearsals, there is disagreement about what was done before. A careful record will answer the questions so that the rehearsal can proceed.

Business, or action, is developed next. For example, knitting, sweeping, eating, and so on add to the reality of the characters and give young players something definite to do. The more times that business is repeated, the more natural it becomes. As was mentioned earlier, if properties are available at the beginning of the rehearsal period, the players grow used to them and can handle them with ease and naturalness.

Composition, or "stage picture," is another thing for the director to bear in mind. Even an experienced actor cannot see the grouping on the stage when he or she is a part of it; hence the director, who is watching closely from the front, must be aware of the composition. Are the players hiding one another? Can important business be seen? Are entrances blocked? If there are several players together, do they make a pleasing picture? Does one composition flow into another? All this pertains primarily to the play designed for an outside audience; yet even under the most informal circumstances, it is important that the players be clearly seen and heard.

If dances or songs are included, they should be rehearsed and integrated into the play as early as possible. It is always a temptation to let them go, but the director will find that this makes for a weak spot or a slow transition. Such business should appear to spring from the play and belong to it; it should not be imposed for the purpose of adding more people or relieving monotony.

As with scenery, cooperation among the drama, classroom, and music teachers is an advantage. The more a staff can work together on a project, the better the learning and the better the production. If a player is absent, the stage manager or another person should step into the part. When the director reads the lines from out front, the cast is at a disadvantage; although the lines are delivered, the space is empty, and the scene very often breaks down. Incidentally, this is another good reason for double casting. It ensures each group of a substitute at a moment's notice.

As the rehearsal period proceeds, the play should grow in feeling, understanding, and unity. Smoothness will come as the lines are learned, the business is perfected, and the actors develop rapport with one another. Rough spots should be ironed out in the beginning, rather than left to the end for polishing. And, finally, if the director can maintain a spirit of fun, the rehearsal period will be a source of pleasure as the cast shares the satisfaction of building something.

As in creative drama, the director occasionally finds a show-off, or clown, in the cast. One does not want to inhibit inventiveness, but by-play disrupts the rehearsal and takes the attention away from the script. Clowning must be stopped at once, for it can jeopardize the entire performance. Most children and young people, if approached constructively, will see that practical and private joking are out of order and that, for the good of the production, their energy must be used to build, not break up, a scene.

Teamwork is both a necessity to a good performance and a source of deep satisfaction to the players. There is probably no experience comparable with the camaraderie that develops during rehearsals. A special feeling binds a group together when it shares the hard work, the creative effort, the interdependence, and the fun of rehearsing and presenting a play.

The Dress Rehearsal

The dress rehearsal can be either a day of confusion or a satisfying culmination of weeks of work. When details have been well planned and the scenery and costumes are ready, there is no reason why it should not be the high point of the rehearsal period. The old adage that "a poor dress rehearsal makes a good show" is fallacious. It is true to a degree only when the dress rehearsal is so bad that the cast makes one last mighty effort to prevent the play from being a disaster. This always involves work that should have been done weeks before; with this work completed, the cast is ready to add the final details with a sense of security.

Two, or even three, dress rehearsals are desirable and should be planned from the beginning. At the first one, the scenery should be finished and in place. At the second and third, costumes should be worn, so that by the time the play goes on, the cast and backstage crew have mastered all the problems. After each dress rehearsal and performance, costumes should be hung up carefully and properties should be checked. This not only helps to keep things in good order, but also instills a sense of responsibility in the players. Even in the most informal of plays, the actors should remain backstage and not mingle with the audience. Food and other refreshments have no place onstage or backstage. They are a risk to the costumes and distract the players.

If make-up is used (and with children, it is almost always unnecessary), it should be tried out first for effectiveness. Make-up only extends or enhances a character; it does not create one.

If there is a curtain call, it should be rehearsed so that the players are ready to come out and take a bow to the audience. One curtain call is sufficient for the audience to show its appreciation. Although there is some difference of opinion about the advisability of a curtain call, it is a convention of the formal theatre, and an audience should be given a chance to learn about it.

THE PERFORMANCE

Once again, let it be stated that a performance by beginners or children should be simple and informal. The director has the greatest responsibility here, for an attitude of calm encouragement will be contagious. If he or she regards the play as a good piece of work that the cast and crew take pleasure in sharing, they will view it in much the same way. They will look forward to the performance with anticipation rather than with anxiety. Both excessive criticism and excessive praise are as harmful at this stage as at any other. The most satisfying response a group can be accorded is the appreciation of the audience. The players will know that they have succeeded in achieving their goal: successful communication.

One performance of a play is recommended for younger children, for they plan and anticipate it as a special event. Repeating the experience rarely recaptures the fun; the play lacks the original spontaneity, and the players become bored with what was once a lively involvement. Older students, however, can gain a great deal from the experience of giving a play a second time.

In any children's production, the director supplies the necessary showmanship. This does not mean dictating the way lines should be read or imposing a style that is unnatural to young players. It means being sensitive to their ideas and helping them express those ideas most effectively. It means checking costumes and props and making sure that the players look and are comfortable in their clothes and that the clothes they wear add to the individual and overall effect. Attention to cleanliness, color, design, and fit need not take up much time; but it is worth every minute spent and will avoid the amateur look of the old-fashioned school play.

THE AUDITORIUM

One aspect of producing a play that is frequently overlooked is that of the auditorium seating area. Ushers may be members of the class who have worked on play committees and so are free when the dress rehearsals are over. Ushering is an excellent way for them to perform a necessary function. If there are programs, they may hand them out, although in an informal situation, a narrator is a preferred way of imparting necessary information to the audience.

Attendance should be by invitation only, rather than by ticket. Publicity, also, should be restricted to posters made by the group. The greater the participation of the class in every aspect of the production and the fewer the contributions from outside, the more positive values the experience will have.

SUMMARY

The presentation of a play for an audience should be done only when older children are involved, and then infrequently. Informality and simplicity should be stressed if the basic values of communication and sharing are to be realized. There is a difference of opinion as to whether children should ever appear before an audience, for fear of destroying their spontaneity and naturalness. This is a valid argument, but my contention is that performance will do no harm if it is done without pressure, thus avoiding drudgery.

In a school play, the educational and social values come first. The product will hold interest for the viewers if they are properly oriented and their appreciation is the natural consequence of a successful attempt at communication. If these emphases are preserved, the leader and group will find producing a play to be a rewarding experience. There is probably nothing that binds a group together more closely than the production of a play, and no joy more lasting than the memory of a play in which all the contributions of all the participants have dovetailed so well that each has had a share in its success. This can and should happen, when exploitation does not enter the picture. If teacher and class work together on a play from the beginning, discussion of costumes, set, and style will expand the learnings. Although the director (teacher) is the final authority when important decisions are made, showing the cast pictures and photographs; relating costume to period, place, and role; and helping the players visualize the scene will provide further opportunities for learning.

Finally, theatre is a performing art. The suspicions that have surrounded the theatre in our country from the beginning are still here, if masked. When we cut the arts from the budget in times of depression and deemphasize *acting* in favor of the word *learning*, we are giving tacit acceptance to an old prejudice. If a demonstration of classwork in creative drama is given in lieu of a play, the fun of performing for others is preserved, but the expectations of the audience are different. Both offer an opportunity to see children working creatively, which, after all, is what interests parents and administrators the most.

ACTIVITY 12.1

STORY THEATRE

The following script, written in story-theatre form, is short, simple, and fun for children in the middle grades to perform. Before children attempt a longer play with many characters and many lines to memorize, short pieces like *The Rich Man* make excellent material. Sixth-grade children may even want to try writing some of their own plays in this form. A program of three or four of the more finished scripts could be performed for a school assembly or given as a demonstration for parents. Incidentally, a demonstration of work in progress is generally far more interesting than is a full-fledged production; it gives parents and teachers a chance to see what a class has been working on without the pressure of rehearsing children for a finished performance.

Objective: To perform a scripted play

Suggestions for the Teacher

1. Explain what a story theatre is.
2. Have the class take turns improvising scenes from "The Rich Man."
3. When they are familiar with the dialogue, have them read it aloud and try out the sound effects.
4. Next, let different combinations of children enact the play.
5. Suggest they try writing story plays of their own.
6. If the children are interested, use this as an occasion for inviting a primary class or two in to be the audience. This completes the experience of a play performed for others.

THE RICH MAN*
SHIRLEY PUGH

(Stage is dark. There is sudden noise of drum, cymbals, and what-have-you. Lights up. The tinsmith is at one side of stage, pounding out a pan [mime], and the blacksmith is at the other side, forging a horseshoe [mime]. The Rich Man steps front and center to speak. He waits. There is a lull.)

RICH MAN: Once there was—
            (Noise resumes. He waits. A lull)
            Once there was a very—

* Shirley Pugh, *In One Basket*, 2d ed. (New Orleans: Anchorage Press, 1982), pp. 5–7.

(*Noise resumes. He waits. A lull*)

Once there was a very rich man who lived in a grand mansion. He ate well and drank well and slept on a bed of softest down. His life would have been perfect, except for two things.

(*Noise. A lull*)

TINSMITH: At one end of the rich man's street there lived a tinsmith who spent all his days fashioning pots and pans for the good wives of the town.

(*Noise, as he works on a pot. Lull*)

This will be a sturdy kettle to cook many a tasty stew!

BLACKSMITH: At the other end of the rich man's street there lived a blacksmith who forged shoes of iron for the horses of the town.

(*He forges shoe. Noise. Lull*)

There's a shoe that will travel many a rough road without breaking!

(*Noise resumes. A lull*)

RICH MAN: With the tinsmith at one end of this street and the blacksmith at the other, I can hardly hear myself—

(*Noise. A lull*)

—I can hardly hear myself think. If the two of them would move out of their houses, this would be a quiet neighborhood.

(*Noise. Lull*)

I can bear it no longer! So he went to see the tinsmith.

(*Much noise as he approaches tinsmith. Rich Man tries to shout over noise*)

Tinsmith! Tinsmith, I say.

(*Lull. Rich Man shouts louder than ever*)

Tinsmith!

(*Quietly*)

I beg your pardon, tinsmith. I have come to make you an offer.

TINSMITH: You wish to buy a skillet or a soup pot, sir?

RICH MAN: No, no. I wish to pay you a large sum of money— if you will leave this house—move somewhere else—

TINSMITH: But I've always lived in this street, sir.

RICH MAN: I know that, believe me! But if I pay you very well, would you agree to move to another house?

TINSMITH: I think I would do that, sir.

RICH MAN: Then here is a handsome sum in pieces of gold—

and I will expect you to be gone from here by the day after tomorrow.

(*Noise. Rich Man goes to blacksmith. He tries to shout over noise*)

Blacksmith! Blacksmith!

(*He taps blacksmith on shoulder. Lull*)

BLACKSMITH: Yes, sir. You have a horse that needs a shoe?

RICH MAN: No, no. I have two ears that need—

BLACKSMITH: Shoes for your ears?

RICH MAN: No! I have two ears that need a rest! I have come to make you an offer.

BLACKSMITH: What sort of offer, sir?

RICH MAN: I wish to pay you a large sum of money—if you will leave this house—move somewhere else—

BLACKSMITH: But this is where I work, sir.

RICH MAN: Heaven knows I am aware of it! But, look. If I pay you very well, would you agree to move to another house?

BLACKSMITH: Another house might suit me, sir.

RICH MAN: Then here is a handsome sum in pieces of gold— and I will expect you to be gone from here by the day after tomorrow.

(*Noise. Rich Man goes home. Lull*)

What a peaceful place this will be when both of them have moved!

TINSMITH: (*Hurrying to the middle of the street*) Wait till I tell my friend the blacksmith of this good fortune!

(*They meet on the street*)

Blacksmith! You will never guess what has happened!

BLACKSMITH: Just a minute, Tinsmith. I have news for you, too. The rich man has paid me to move from my house.

TINSMITH: No! And he has paid me to move from mine! When must you be gone?

BLACKSMITH: The day after tomorrow. And you?

TINSMITH: The same. The day after tomorrow.

BLACKSMITH: Where will you go?

TINSMITH: I don't know that yet. Where will *you* go?

BLACKSMITH: I don't know either.

BOTH TOGETHER: Listen, I have a good idea—

They whisper together and gesture toward each other's houses. They each run home and stack up tools, pans, iron scraps—noise again—[mime] and leave their respective houses. Each wheeling a cart [mime] they meet midway and do an Alphonse and Gaston routine in silence—"you go first," "excuse me," "you go first"—and finally make the double crossing to each other's houses, where each re-establishes himself)

RICH MAN: (*Simultaneously with their crosses*) There is nothing I cannot buy with gold! The tinsmith will leave his house, the blacksmith will leave *his* house, and I will have silence at last.

(*As the Rich Man ends his speech, the Tinsmith and the Blacksmith are settled in again and begin to work. Noise. Rich Man runs to Tinsmith. Shouts over noise*)

No!

(*Runs to Blacksmith. Shouts over noise*)

No!

(*Runs home, puts fingers in his ears and [mimes] a horrified single word*)

NO!

(*Blackout*)

(*Noise continues for a moment in the dark. Lull*)

13

UNDERSTANDING AND
ENJOYING THE THEATRE

Theatre is one of the most enriching experiences a person can have. Not only does it widen one's experience with life but it helps develop skills for coping more effectively with life's real problems. I am certain that human dignity has its roots in the quality of young people's experience.

DR. LEE SALK

"There's going to be a play!"

Probably nothing generates as much excitement as does the announcement of a play for assembly. This can be merely an entertaining hour or a much richer experience, leading to a desire for more information, a deeper understanding, or some creative expression. The last is what is meant by aesthetic education: an integration of the arts into our lives, resulting in a lifelong appreciation.

Although an ancient art form, the theatre both entertains and reflects society's most current ideas and problems. A good play offers the audience not only diversion, but also substance; indeed, to engage our attention, a play must first entertain, but in order to hold our interest, it must have content as well. A play that merely entertains, palls in time; a play that attempts to educate without entertaining, bores. A children's play, even more than a play for adults, must have an interesting story, content worth spending time on, and a performance by a skilled and talented company. Beyond that, it may have scenery, costumes, special lighting effects, and perhaps music and dance. These visual elements enhance a performance, but they are not found in every production, nor are they always necessary. They explain, however, why the theatre is often described as encompassing all the arts and why it has such a universal appeal.

In early societies, all members of the community took part in dramatic celebrations. As time went on, some persons emerged as superior dancers and musicians. This eventually led to a separation between those who performed and those who watched—between actors and audience. Today, except for children's participatory plays, when we attend a performance, we go as spectators; but in order to get the most out of the experience, we need to know something about the play that we are going to see—not every detail or the outcome, of course, but the theme, some idea of the plot, and the style and quality of the production. As adult theatregoers, we read what the critics have to say in advance, or we talk to friends who have already seen a performance.

Children's plays are not, as a rule, professionally reviewed. This may account, in part, for the popularity of the traditional folk and fairy tales with both children and the adults who select their entertainment. The appeal of the familiar is strong, and the announcement of a well-loved story brought to life on the stage has tremendous drawing power. The adult who selects a child's entertainment is also inclined to respond to the known over the unknown title. This is a good reason for encouraging critics for children's theatre, of whom our country has very few. A growing number of playwrights are bringing new stories and modern themes to the theatre, including some of the more troubling problems that young

Children absorbed in a performance. (Courtesy of Periwinkle Productions, Inc., Monticello, N.Y.; photograph by Joe Lippincott)

people face. To help children better understand and enjoy these plays, it is more important than it has been in the past for the teacher to take on the role of reviewer. The orientation that he or she can provide will stimulate interest and prepare a class for a valuable and exciting experience.

There are a number of criteria for evaluating plays for the child audience.[1]

1. Is the story suitable for children in [the middle grades]?
2. Is the story worth telling? Does it have content and meaning?
3. Is it entertaining?
4. Does the play develop along clear, dramatic lines—that is, does it have a beginning, a properly built climax, and a satisfying conclusion?
5. Is the story told without interruption or without the introduction of extraneous action or characters?
6. Is it clearly established to which character the story belongs?
7. Is there an opportunity for identification? Usually a play is stronger if the audience can identify with the character to whom the story belongs.
8. Do characters react to one another naturally?
9. Are character and story developed through interaction?
10. If it is an adaptation, are the essential elements of the source material retained so that the audience will not be offended by the change?

VALUES OF ATTENDING THE THEATRE

There are many values to be gained in attending the theatre, and they are the same for children as for adults. A child's taste is unformed, however, and so adult guidance is needed to help children distinguish among the superior, the poor, and the merely mediocre. Offered the best, they will in time come to prefer it, but with our help, they will understand why and so learn to become selective. In children's theatre, the values may be categorized as *aesthetic, educational*, and *social*, to which the following elements contribute:

1. *A good story.* A good story holds the interest of the audience from beginning to end. Something happens as the result of a conflict or problem, which must be solved. Beyond that, a good story has literary

[1] Adapted from "CTAA Guidelines for Writing Children's Plays." By permission of the Children's Theatre Association of America.

value, vocabulary that enriches, ideas that challenge, and dialogue that strikes our ears as true.

2. *Credible characters.* Credible characters are those in whom the audience can believe, whether or not they are real. In other words, the characters may be witches, giants, ghosts, or elves, but the audience must accept them as real. Children are quick to detect the false or inconsistent, but they will accept the most fantastic characters when they are well developed and consistently played (witness the enormous popularity of the movie *E.T.*).

3. *Well-developed performance skills.* Well-developed performance skills include speech that is clear and audible; music, well played or sung; dances, choreographed and performed by disciplined dancers; and such other skills as juggling, fencing, and acrobatics that may be called for. These must not detract from the story but should be so well integrated that unity as well as a high standard of performance is maintained throughout. Sometimes a director will add songs and dances to enliven a show, but unless they are an integral part of it, they will take away from the production, actually weakening it.

4. *Beautiful visual effects.* While not every play requires elaborate mounting and costumes or special lighting effects, many do, and children respond with delight to them. The word *beautiful* includes color, a sense of proportion, and good composition; therefore, even a slum setting or a simple screen can achieve an aesthetic quality. Likewise, a costumer can use color and design in such a way as to bring beauty to the poorest garments without sacrificing the authenticity of the wardrobe. I shall always remember the inner-city children who attended plays at a college where I once taught. Their response to a beautiful scenic effect was as thrilling to the cast and backstage crew as the set was to the audience. The gasp of appreciation that was heard when the curtains opened was clear proof of the joy that color brought into their lives, contrasting with the drab neighborhoods from which they came.

Many producers today dress their actors in a uniform costume, such as jump suits or leotards. There are reasons for this choice, and in many cases, the uniform is appropriate and effective. The Paper Bag Players, for example, whose aim is to stimulate the imagination of the audience, are always dressed alike, except for color. With their succession of short skits, the actors simply add bits of clothing to save time and suggest different characters. As a general practice, however, the elimination of costumes deprives the audience of one of the theatre's most colorful components and one of its aesthetic values.

5. *Challenging ideas.* Challenging ideas stimulate thinking about attitudes, solutions to problems posed in the play, or social values. Consciousness often can be raised more effectively through theatre than in any other way. Even the folk and fairy tales that have been handed down to us convey valuable lessons, which is one of the reasons for their survival, according to Bruno Bettelheim.[2] Modern plays and theatre-in-education programs present issues more directly, but unless the plays are too didactic, children are affected by them and are concerned with the message. Children want to see justice done, an almost universal reaction reflecting their strong sense of fair play.

6. *Experience as a member of an audience.* Going to a play, unlike reading a book or even watching television, is a social experience. It involves being part of a large group, sharing a common experience. It also provides material for discussion later on, either at home or at school.

7. *Involvement with the players.* This relates to being part of the audience. The living theatre differs from television and film in that the response of the audience affects the performance. Theatre is communication; hence, the rapport between actor and audience is an essential element. Actors are quick to say that no two performances of the same play are ever alike because of the differences in audience response.

8. *The opportunity to learn about other persons and different cultures.* In the theatre, we are able to view other cultures and learn about persons different from ourselves. Characters living in foreign lands or at different times come alive on the stage, often making an indelible impression. This, incidentally, is another reason for truthful and accurate portrayals. Far too many stereotypes have been imposed on children, both in the theatre and on television, for us to ignore misrepresentations. Aware of this, responsible producers are making a conscious effort to show characters as they really are, by treating them with respect as individuals and as members of a social group. This principle, incidentally, should always hold, even in comedy. To be genuinely funny, characters should not be consistently presented in a derogatory light, for it is the exception that amuses us and the unusual situation that makes us laugh.

A stereotype, in which all members of a particular group are presented as identical, reinforces an impression that not only is untrue,

---

[2] Bruno Bettelheim, *The Uses of Enchantment* (New York: Knopf, 1976).

but is difficult to erase. The villain should not always be presented as foreign and dark; the hero, as tall, handsome, clever, and strong; the heroine, as blonde and beautiful. On stage, as in life, human beings come in a wide assortment of colors, ages, and backgrounds, each one possessing individual strengths and weaknesses. An honest portrayal helps children to distinguish between them and, in doing so, to develop the values and insights that are believed to be the characteristics of an educated adult.

9. *A strong emotional response.* Aristotle wrote of the catharsis of theatre. Anyone who has ever been in a children's audience can readily understand what he meant, for their emotional reactions are strong and spontaneous. Children are caught up in the excitement of the drama. They cheer the hero or heroine and may even "boo" the villain, and they often participate vocally by calling out advice to the actors. Unless it gets out of hand (and an experienced cast will see that it does not), this is a natural outlet for emotion. The child has a vicarious experience, one that he probably would never have in real life. He participates in a great adventure; he identifies with the protagonist; and in the end, he wins through just and honorable actions. In some modern plays, the spectator is left with an ethical or a moral question to think about after the final curtain has closed. The emotional reaction has come first, however, and now comes the time to consider alternative solutions and their consequences.

10. *The foundation for an appreciation of the theatre.* Good theatre experiences when young often lead to lifelong pleasure. Few persons pursue the theatre as a profession, but all of us may enjoy it as members of the audience. The opportunity to see even a few fine plays, well produced, under optimum conditions, is the best possible preparation.

The values of theatre can scarcely be overestimated. Granted that not all children's entertainment is of the quality we should like to see offered, but much of it is, and it is improving constantly, thanks to better-educated producers and the numerous funding sources now available. By orienting children to the best at an early age and helping them to extend the experience, we are able to increase these values immeasurably. Let us see how we can best go about it.

While teachers ordinarily do not have an opportunity to preview productions that children will see in school assemblies, their opinion is often sought afterward. This is particularly true when attention has been poor or the audience has appeared to lack interest. The following guidelines were prepared by a committee of the Children's Theatre Association of America as an instrument to use in selecting plays for a show-

A professional company comes to the school. (Courtesy of Henry K. Martin and Sue Martin, The Actor's Trunk, Detroit)

case of children's entertainment. It is offered here for teachers and administrators, who may find it useful in determining what made for success or failure, and why.

Adapted From
EVALUATION FORM FOR CHILDREN'S THEATRE PREVIEWERS
Designed by Region 2, CTAA

Production Title _____

Date Previewed _____   Estimated Number in Audience ____

Name of Auditorium _____   Seating Capacity ____

Producer _____

         (Name)   (Address)   (Tel. No.)

Note to Previewers: The prime criteria we use in children's theatre is a respect of the production for the audience—of the audience for the production. Does the production present an idea worthy of a child's consideration? Does it do so in a manner which honors his intelligence and integrity? Does it evoke his honest responses to quality in the theatre?

Report on this form by applying this rating code:

Excellent	Good	Adequate	Fair	Poor	TOTAL:
5	4	3	2	1	

Using the question as a guide, rate each category by the NUMBERS SHOWN ABOVE. Feel free to comment in answer to any specific question and enlarge on it.

1. DOES THE PRESENTATION RESPECT THE AUDIENCE IN THE PLAYSCRIPT?

☐ *Content:*
Is it worth doing?
Did you feel the children were involved enough to care about the people in the story and what happened to them?

☐ *Dramatic Development:*
Is the story line clear and forward moving?
Is the piece well paced, or does it drag? (Or, is it too hectic?)

☐ *Dialogue:*
Does the vocabulary, which is essential to the comprehension of the plot, come within the range of the audience? Beyond that, does it offer enrichment?
Is the dialogue suitable to the style and mood of the piece?

COMMENT:

2. DOES THE PRESENTATION RESPECT THE AUDIENCE IN THE PRODUCTION?

☐ *Direction:*
Is stage business pertinent to the situation and style? (Or, inserted for its own sake?)
Does the director have a point of view through which he unifies the elements of the play?
Is the physical movement in keeping with character and style?
Does the director achieve an ensemble performance?

☐ *Mounting:* (Costumes—Scenery—Lighting—Music)
Are settings and costumes expressive of the style, the characters, the locale, and the period?
If there is available equipment, is the lighting also consistent?
Are settings and costumes fresh looking and attractively executed?

☐ *Acting:*
Do you believe the actor in his character? In relation to the style of the piece? (Or, does he ever step out of character?)

Is there a sense of joy in the performance? (Or, is it flat?)
Is dialogue well spoken (Voice? Diction? Interpretation?)
Are songs and dances well performed?
COMMENT:

Question: *DID YOU ENJOY IT?* _____

PREPARING CHILDREN FOR THE OCCASION

By the time children are in the fourth or fifth grade, the chances are that they have attended several plays and are looking forward to seeing others. It is equally possible, however, that some children have attended only informal performances in an all-purpose room or gymnasium and so have never been to a community or university theatre or seen a play produced formally in an auditorium. In that case, the subject of theatre etiquette and conventions should be part of the orientation. This should not be presented as a disciplinary measure; rather, it should be explained as courteous and expected behavior.

ORIENTATION

By the time children have reached the middle grades, they are ready for substantial background material that will spark interest and enrich the performance. Many producers send packets of teaching material to the school in advance; these materials are well worth using, since they provide additional information for the class before seeing the play. Producers often list books they have found useful in doing their own research on the subject. These books are usually available and may even be in the school library. Sometimes, when a company tours a region on a regular basis, it will develop a program for a particular grade-level curriculum. In this case, it is easy to relate the play to the unit of study. The class already may be familiar with the major character, in which case the children will be eager to see him or her brought to life on the stage.

In contrast, the protagonist may be a well-known figure in real life. I am reminded of a production I saw recently based on the career of Jackie Robinson. He was a hero to the audience as a result of television sports news, so the story of his boyhood and struggle as he rose to fame had a strong attraction. The background the children brought with them made the play twice as meaningful as it would have been, had it involved the struggle of an unknown protagonist.

Assuming that the class does not know what the play is about and that the title is also unfamiliar, the teacher will want first to introduce the theme and then, if it is important to their understanding, to give the class an idea of the plot. In the Bicentennial year, many children's-theatre companies wrote their own plays based on historical events or, if they toured a particular area extensively, on a topic of regional interest. Since the children might not have been familiar with the material, some study of it in advance was necessary. Schools were appreciative of the cooperation that these companies offered, for it enriched and extended the learning.

Preliminary study has the same effect as knowing a story and then seeing it dramatized. It is the time to bring in relevant background material—historical, biographical, cultural—so that the class may gain a better idea of where and how the characters lived or live. If the play takes place at a former time or in another place, not only will the clothing be different from ours, but so will the furnishings of the homes, the occupations, the props, and the lives of the people. Social attitudes may differ also; therefore, the class will get more from the play if it understands why the characters behave as they do. Speech patterns may be strange, so that some knowledge of the dialect used makes for appreciation rather than amusement. The extent of the orientation that teachers give varies, of course, depending on the play and the amount of time they have at their disposal. I believe that some information about the prospective assembly program or excursion is always desirable in order for the audience to derive maximum pleasure and benefit.

Play structure was treated in Chapter 6. By the middle and upper grades, children should have some knowledge of dramatic form. They know the difference between comedy and tragedy and are familiar with a few of the more common theatrical terms. Opportunities for attending plays as well as creating and writing them help young people gain a deeper understanding of an art form that involves the work of many artists, yet does not live until it is shared with an audience.

AUDIENCE PARTICIPATION

Some theatre companies, both commercial and educational, perform what is called participatory drama. This means that instead of acting on a stage, they perform in the round in an all-purpose room or a gymnasium, with the audience seated on three or four sides, where it can become actively involved in the performance. The actors request help from the children from time to time, in response to their questions or to a request to come into the playing space as fellow actors. Occasionally, a company will invite suggestions as to what course of action to take, and the responses may alter the outcome of the story. An experienced cast is able to handle audience participation skillfully, thus giving children a dual experience: that of spectator and that of participant.

Before a participatory play is given, actors usually go into the classrooms of the children who are going to attend. They discuss the play and may rehearse the scenes in which the class will be taking part. This can be a richly rewarding experience, when it is carefully planned and rehearsed. Participatory theatre is most effective with younger children; beyond the fifth or sixth grades, there is an inherent risk involved in asking the audience to take part, unless the techniques are sophisticated and the children are used to participation. The majority of companies that offer plays for middle and upper grades perform on a proscenium stage in a traditional manner. While this does not require the same kind of preparation as does the participatory play, it does warrant some pointers on theatre conventions and etiquette. Everyone will enjoy the performance more when these simple ground rules are observed.

Theatre Etiquette

One aspect of theatregoing that must be treated is etiquette. Accustomed to television, with its frequent breaks for commercials, children must be told that the theatre makes certain demands on the audience so that all may see and hear well. A good audience:

1. *Does not talk aloud or annoy others.* Once seated, the members of the audience should refrain from whispering, standing up, or leaving without permission.

2. *Does not bring food into the auditorium.* Candy, gum, potato chips, and other easily accessible foods interfere with attention in addition to causing clutter on the floor. The practice of eating while watching television has cultivated a habit that should be discouraged in the theatre. Eating should take place before or after the performance, but never during the play.

3. *Does not run around the auditorium during the intermission.* An intermission need not be a trying period for teachers and ushers, if its purpose is explained. It is a time to move and stretch, to go out for a drink, or to use the rest rooms while scenery is being changed. Some producers are afraid of intermissions, but I have never seen one misused when the play held the interest of the audience.

4. *Does not destroy printed programs.* Some companies provide printed programs. This is a theatre convention that children should understand. Programs are not to be made into airplanes or balls and

thrown around the auditorium. They are to be read. In addition to information about the play, they often include activities for children to try at home or in class afterward.

5. *Waits for applause and curtain calls.* Applause and curtain calls are theatre conventions. Applause is our way of thanking the actors for the good time they have given us, and curtain calls let us see the actors as people instead of as characters in the play.

6. *Leaves the auditorium in an orderly manner.* Putting on coats, getting up before the curtain is closed, slamming seats, and running noisily up the aisles are bad manners. If children realize this, the majority of them will wait till the lights in the auditorium are turned on, and it is time for the audience to go.

7. *Meets the cast afterward, if invited.* Some casts make a practice of meeting the children in the lobby on their way out, and many youngsters enjoy it. I have mixed feelings about this practice, for it removes the mystique that the cast has taken pains to establish. But some older boys and girls have questions about the play or technical effects that they want to ask, and this is an ideal way to have them answered.

THE PERFORMANCE

The day of the play has finally come. The class has been well prepared and should be in the auditorium and in their seats 5 or 10 minutes before the curtain is opened. If the play is presented in the school auditorium, the teacher can easily gauge the time it will take to go from the classroom to the reserved section of seats. If it takes place in a community theatre or the auditorium of another school, then more planning is involved to be sure that the group arrives on time, neither late nor too early. If school buses are employed, this may present problems, but it is important to arrange the arrival in plenty of time to hang up wraps, or at least to remove them, and to be comfortably seated before the performance begins. I have often seen classes come into a darkened auditorium 15 or 20 minutes late, which is a shame because they can never catch up on what happened before they arrived, not to mention the disturbance they caused for others who were absorbed in the story.

By the time children have reached the third or fourth grade and have attended a number of programs and plays, they are accustomed to listening carefully to the dialogue and to refraining from whispering or annoying their neighbors. Indeed, when children can see and hear well, this rarely happens. Only when plays are given in huge auditoriums with

Peter the Postman *by Torben Jetsmark, translated by Stephen Gilmour. (Courtesy of Kenneth Graham, University of Minnesota)*

poor acoustics and poor sightlines is the audience restless and uninvolved. Some companies stipulate the size of audience they will play for, refusing to perform for more than 200 or 300 spectators. This is ideal, but it is not always possible to arrange; nevertheless, it is a safe bet that children who can see and hear everything that happens on the stage not only will be a better audience, but also will get far more out of the play than if they had missed lines or had trouble seeing the actors.

Should the audience be restless under ideal conditions, there is obviously something wrong. It may be that the script is geared to a younger age level than is present or is over the heads of the audience. Most children are willing to reach up to the latter, but they are bored by anything they consider "babyish." It also may be a poor production. This is another matter altogether, which should have been discovered before the contract was signed. There are so many excellent university theatre departments sending out student groups and so many good professional touring companies available that there is little excuse for engaging a mediocre company. It can happen, however, and when it does, it is a problem for the faculty and administration. Good companies are expensive, but one good show is worth far more than half a dozen poor ones. When university troupes are available, they are an ideal resource. Not only are they less expensive, but their standards tend to be consistently high, their choice of material usually is excellent, and the student actors are sensitive to the interests and needs of children.

Although carrying on conversations during the performance has been termed inconsiderate, it does not mean that an audience should observe total silence. Indeed, it is a pity when children are made to think they cannot utter a sound. There is nothing wrong with laughter, cheers, even calling out spontaneously to the actors when the comments are appropriate; an experienced cast can handle such responses, and most actors enjoy having this rapport with the audience.

EXTENDING THE EXPERIENCE

Although a good performance of a fine play will certainly stand by itself, it can be enriched by a follow-up period afterward. As adults, we like to discuss a play or film we have seen, and children react in much the same way. They will discuss the play on their own, but with proper guidance, the discussion can be made richer and more lasting. There are many ways of starting. Least likely to lead to discussion is the question "Did you like it?" But questions relating to the underlying theme or the characters and their solutions to problems will usually generate a lively discussion. Depending on when and where the action took place, the way of life, or the social attitudes of the characters, questions will be raised, offering an ideal opportunity for further exploration. While it is true that children find many programs diverting, they are capable of remarkable insights, when guided toward a more discriminating point of view.

As in all teaching, we are most successful when we begin where the children's interests lie, following their lead before making suggestions. The following are some of the successful ways in which teachers have followed up a performance.

A traditional but still worthwhile activity is writing letters to the cast. This should not be imposed on children as a tedious assignment, but when it represents an honest expression of appreciation, it is an outlet for feelings, a courteous act, and a valid exercise in writing. Actors, incidentally, love the letters children write and often keep them in their scrapbooks.

Painting or drawing pictures of the play is another favorite activity. The Paper Bag Players of New York, aware of the effect that their performances have on young children, put up yards of brown wrapping paper on the walls of the lobby, where space permits, so that audiences can draw pictures during the intermission and after the production.

Some teachers' packets include folk songs and dances that children can learn. Many folk tales, particularly those of the Indians and Eskimos, suggest tools and artifacts that children can make. Masks, jewelry, woven fabrics, pictures of the clothes the Indians and Eskimos wear, and photographs of the land are always fascinating, especially to children in urban areas. I have seen many excellent exhibits of art work stimulated by a performance of Joanna Kraus's *Ice Wolf*, a serious drama that invariably arouses discussion. Stories of the American Indians never fail to stimulate interest in learning their dances and making totem poles and masks.

Many children are eager to enact scenes from the play. While this is a sure sign of interest, it is also a way to encourage further improvisation. New scenes, action that might have taken place, different endings—these can begin with such questions as "How else?" or "What if?" Creative drama and the scripted play are different, but the one often leads to the other. Seeing a play may stimulate creative drama, whereas creative drama may result in an original play.

Some teachers find that other forms of writing come more easily as well. The release of emotion into verse is not uncommon. The theatre reaches us on many levels, and because it embodies all the arts, it makes for various verbal, visual, and physical responses. Older children are often led to further study of a culture and will share their findings in oral or written reports. Whatever form the expression takes, the ramifications of theatre go far beyond the enjoyment of the performance, when time and opportunity are offered.

A word of caution. While there is no doubt that preparation and follow-up enhance the experience, the teacher must never give the impression that she is testing for right or wrong answers. A child who thinks that he is expected to reply in a certain way is robbed of spontaneous, honest reaction. Response to a work of art is an individual matter. Adults do not agree about what they have seen, and we should not expect it of children. Appreciation of any art form is difficult to assess, if, indeed, it is even possible. Sometimes it takes days, weeks, or years to integrate what one has thought and felt. This does not mean that everything a child sees should embody a lesson or aim to teach. There is a time for serious study, but there is also a time for fun. Children love humor, and a good comedy has many values, not the least of them laughter. In her book *Understanding Your Child's Entertainment*,[3] Muriel Broadman discusses concerns we all share, but implicit and explicit throughout is a plea for quality, whatever the material may be. Integrity, performance skills, and respect for the young audience—in her opinion, these are of equal importance. While her text is addressed to parents, the points she makes are valid for anyone responsible for selecting children's programs or guiding young people in the development of aesthetic awareness, critical judgment, and appreciation of the living theatre.

SUMMARY

Theatregoing can be one of the richest experiences of a child's life. With its aesthetic, educational, and social potential, a good play, well produced, can lead to appreciation of a great art form and add to knowledge and deeper understanding of humankind. Orientation to the event prepares children by familiarizing them with the theme, the style of the production, and any other aspects that will enhance their enjoyment. In the case of a traditional story, less preparation is needed. But for the majority of children, who have grown up watching television, some orientation to live performers is necessary. For many, the school assembly program may be the first exposure to theatre they have.

Theatre etiquette, simple as it sounds, is also necessary, if we are going to teach consideration for the right of others to enjoy the play. The theatre makes demands, not only on our hearts and minds, but also on our social awareness, for the living theatre, unlike television, is shared enjoyment.

Follow-up activities in the classroom offer a further opportunity for enrichment. Most children enjoy reliving a performance; hence giving them the time and place in which to do it is a welcome extension. Theatre can be a one-time hour of entertainment, but it can be much more than that, as teachers and producers have discovered.

---

[3] Muriel Broadman, *Understanding Your Child's Entertainment* (New York: Harper & Row, 1977).

14

PUTTING IT
ALL TOGETHER

Although there are suggested activities in most chapters, no step-by-step lesson plans are included. This chapter suggests ways in which teachers might approach and guide creative-drama sessions until they develop techniques and strategies of their own. Also included are possible extensions of lessons, should the subject matter be relevant to children's interests or to other curricular areas. This is a good way to approach social problems and issues, although it is neither necessary nor always desirable. Teachers will soon sense how far to carry a creative-drama lesson and when the end becomes a means.

LESSON PLAN FOR MOVEMENT TO MIME (CHAPTERS 3 AND 4)

1. Begin with physical warm-ups, with children standing in a circle. If the class is too large for the children to move freely, divide it into two groups, alternating turns so that all have equal opportunity for participation. Exercises might include:
   a. Stretching, bending, swaying, and using large movements
   b. Shaking the arms and then the hands; shaking one foot and then the other to loosen tight muscles
   c. Walking very slowly in a circle, then moving faster, next running, and finally stopping on "Freeze!"
   d. Moving as different animals and birds: bears, tigers, monkeys, squirrels, giraffes, horses, gulls, cranes, hawks, chickens, and road runners

   e. Discuss the different kinds of movements made by animals and birds because of their physical structure and size.
 2. Tell the class the Indian story "The Bat's Choice" (Activity 14.1).
   a. What does the story mean to them? Discuss it before playing it.
   b. If music is available, play appropriate music for the war scenes.
   c. Try the story in movement. Then add pantomime. Play it several times, each time adding to it.

LESSON PLAN FOR THE IMPROVISATION OF A STORY (CHAPTER 7)

 1. Begin with physical warm-ups, with all children standing in a circle.
   a. Stretching, bending, and swaying the body, using large movements
   b. Shaking arms, then hands, and then feet (one foot at a time) to loosen muscles
   c. Walking briskly in a circle, then slowly, next very slowly, and finally stopping
   d. Walking as persons who are young and strong, then as persons who are tired, and finally as old persons at the end of a day's work
 2. Read or tell the story "The Wise Old Woman" (Activity 14.2).
 3. Discuss the story: the characters, the plot, the most important scenes. This will take time because the action moves from one place to another, and the class will have to discuss how to handle it. It may take several sessions to plan and play the entire story.
 4. Class discussion will involve important issues that will be raised as the story is studied in more depth. This story is one of the most effective in raising children's consciousness of a social problem in our country. Through *being* older persons, they can be guided past the stereotype to a compassionate understanding of human beings in a period of life that all of us will experience someday.
   a. How are older people treated in *our* society today?
   b. Where do they live?
   c. How did older people live a century ago?
   d. What do we know about the old in other countries?
 5. Bring in material on the subject: pictures, magazine and newspaper articles.
   a. Talk about retirement homes, retirement villages, nursing homes, activities for senior citizens, and extended families.
   b. Think of some of the problems and interests of older people in the United States.
 6. Older children may want to work on improvisations based on some of the contributions that have been made.

LESSON PLAN FOR STORY THEATRE (CHAPTERS 7 AND 12)

1. Begin with physical warm-ups. Again, have the children get in a large circle for free movement.
   a. Stretching, bending, and swaying, using large movements
   b. Shaking arms, hands, one foot, and then the other; rolling the head to right, back, left, and front—several times
   c. Running in the circle and then running "in place"
   d. Walking "in place" around the room; running "in place" around the room—always moving a little so as to appear to be covering long distances
2. Seat the class while you tell them "The Saga of Bukolla" (Activity 14.3).
3. Show pictures of Iceland. Bring in any craft objects that are available. Travel agents have excellent brochures and posters of the country and the people that they are usually glad to provide.
4. Discuss story theatre.
5. Then, reading the Narrator's part, have the children play the story. Try this several times until all have had a chance to act the various parts, and the children indicate more understanding of the story than mere recall of action.
6. Work on the Son's journey and "running in place."
7. After three or four sessions, the class will have played the whole story. Since this is a complicated and little-known tale, it might be fun to share it with another class. Done in the round in an all-purpose or other large room, "The Saga of Bukolla" can be a satisfying culmination of classwork in creative drama.

LESSON PLAN FOR PRESENTING A PLAY FOR AN AUDIENCE (CHAPTER 12)

1. For children in the intermediate grades, it is generally better to share plays that have been developed through class work in creative drama than to begin with a script and an audience in view. To be sure, not every project will be appropriate or interesting to outsiders, but when one is, it has a depth and richness that is rarely achieved when "showing" is the primary motivation.

   Assuming that a dramatization of either a good story or an original play is developed to the point that an outside audience will also enjoy it, plans must be made. The following steps are necessary whether the production is simple or more elaborate.
   a. Who will be cast in the various parts? Decisions are best made democratically through discussion and class vote.

b. Consider and list all the other jobs involved, making them just as important as that of the actors.

c. Plan what, if any, costumes will be worn. What are the garments in the classroom costume box, and what should be brought from home?

d. What scenery and properties are needed? Form a scene committee.

e. Posters, announcements, or invitations can be the job of another committee. Every member of the class should have a part in the project, and each child should feel a responsibility for it.

f. Plan a particular date and time for the play and schedule rehearsals in class time. This is the most difficult aspect of a production because several areas are involved. Some children may be able to work on scenery or posters while the cast rehearses, but it is hard to supervise both groups unless there is a student teacher in the room or unless the art teacher shares the responsibility. There is no one way to handle it, but working cooperatively with the art, music, and dance teachers (provided there are specialists in the school) is ideal. The less help available, the less elaborate the production should be.

2. The excitement will be high on the day of the play, but if the work has been well done in advance and the class is prepared, the performance should go off without tension or self-consciousness. Ideally, the audience will be composed of other classes and/or parents, who will come with a friendly and sympathetic understanding.

3. When the performance is over and the audience has left, props and costumes should be put away and the room restored to its normal condition. "Clean-up" is a part of every school project, and children should learn to take that responsibility along with the more exciting preparation and performance. Putting on a play can be a wonderful experience, providing a unique opportunity for children to work cooperatively with others and to learn basic theatre techniques. It will also provide good background for theatre appreciation when the class attends a play presented by skilled adult actors.

LESSON PLAN FOR A CHARACTER STUDY

1. There are dozens of men and women from whom to choose, but a well-known historical character taken from the language arts or social studies is always a good choice. For the sake of illustration, let us take George Washington Carver. Most children in the intermediate grades will be acquainted with his name and work and will be curious

LESSON PLAN FOR A CHARACTER STUDY **277**

about how he became interested in botany and chemistry and how he achieved success at a time when both education and employment were difficult for blacks to achieve.

a. Once the selection of a character has been made, be ready to supply books, stories, and articles about him or her.

b. Share the biography with the class (in this case, George Washington Carver). Encourage discussion and questions:

How did he get the name of George Washington?

Was he interested in plants as a child?

Where did he go to school and college?

Was he a good student?

What caused his interest in peanuts?

c. Put up pictures of Carver on the bulletin board. Find pictures of his home, his home state of Missouri, and his later life.

d. With the children's help, put an outline of his life on the board. This might be divided into three sections:

Part one: Childhood

Place and date of birth (1864)

Family and home life

Schooling

Interests

Part two: Young Manhood

Higher education

Friends and colleagues

Early predictions of success

Part three: Adult Life

Work

Lasting achievements

Death

e. A few books on Carver should be available throughout the study.

Graham, Shirley, and George D. Lipscomb. *Dr. George Washington Carver.* New York: Messner, 1944.

Stevenson, Augusta. *George Carver: Boy Scientist.* Indianapolis: Bobbs-Merrill, 1959.

White, Ann. *George Washington Carver: The Story of a Great Scientist.* New York: Random House, 1953.

2. Have the class select episodes from Carver's life to dramatize.

a. Who is in those episodes?

b. Where do they take place?

3. Improvise the episodes, taking one at a time. Discuss the scenes after playing, and then replay with other students. After several playings, the scenes will become richer and more detailed.

4. This is the kind of study that can easily develop into a play that

another class or other classes will enjoy. At this point, the transition is made from drama (a process) to theatre (a product). "Jelled improvisations" or a script written by the class is necessary, and sixth-grade children will find the latter a challenging exercise in creative writing (Chapter 12).

5. This lesson actually incorporates three: creative drama as a process, drama as a way of learning, and work shared with an audience. *Content* and *form* have become of equal importance, and this is the basis of good theatre.

ACTIVITY 14.1

EXTENDING STORIES

Suggestions for the Teacher

"The Bat's Choice" lends itself equally well to dance, mime, or dramatization. The birds and animals suggest movement, whereas the plot is so simple that it can be easily told without words. There is plenty of action to make it interesting. If the group prefers to use dialogue, however, the story can be improvised. Another way would be to have a narrator tell it, while the group pantomimes the action. In a story of this kind, any number can play. It is included to show the possibilities in a simple tale with a strong conflict and minimal characterization.

The tale should lead to some good discussion. You might ask questions like:

1. Has there ever been a time when you could not make up your mind about which side to be on?
2. Can you think of any people or individuals who have had such a problem? What did they do about it?

These questions can prompt interesting discussions and may lead to the improvisation of scenes, using dialogue. Some sixth graders have brought up political questions; others, the problems that families face after a divorce; others, such potential difficulties as friendships with minority children in a class; and still others, the more everyday conflicts of how to spend an allowance or what clothing to buy when *need* and *desire* are involved. Whatever suggestions are volunteered, they represent serious conflicts to children and therefore are bases for drama. It is at this point that pantomime automatically moves into improvisation.

Divide the class into several groups, each group choosing one of the suggestions. Give them 15 minutes or so to plan how they will handle their improvisations.

After playing each skit, see if there appears to be a desire for further discussion. It is an excellent opportunity to explore concerns of children without seeming to pry into their personal lives.

THE BAT'S CHOICE

In India, they tell why the bat hides by day and comes out only at night. Many, many years ago, there was a war between the birds and the animals. The bat, who had wings like a bird but a body like an animal, watched them fight but could not make up his mind which side to join. Finally, he decided he would go to the winning side. That appeared to be the animals, so he went over to them, declaring his everlasting loyalty.

Then suddenly, things changed. With the help of the eagle, the birds began to overcome the animals. Now the bat wondered whether he had made a mistake; perhaps he would be better off with the birds. Until he could be sure, however, he hid in a tree and watched.

When peace was finally reached, the bat found himself unpopular with both sides. And so it is to this day that he hides in a tree by day and comes out at night, when the birds and most of the animals are asleep.

ACTIVITY 14.2

MORAL QUESTIONS

This version of the Japanese folk tale "The Wise Old Woman" is included for several reasons. First of all, it is a good story. The narrative holds the interest of the players and provides complications that make demands on them. Also, the characters may be interpreted in considerable depth. The situation, though extreme, can be discussed in relation to our attitude toward older people.

Suggestions for the Teacher

It is suggested that the major discussion of "The Wise Old Woman" be held after several playings. By that time, the story will have had an impact on the group, and the players will be ready to discuss the theme and its modern implications. This can lead into an exploration of stereotyping of age, the meaning of wisdom, and the social values in our society.

1. How do we feel about older people?
2. How do we treat them?
3. What value do older people have in our society?
4. What have we to learn from them?
5. Why do you think we react to them as we do?
6. What has caused our attitude?
7. What are the implications in this story for our own old age?

The depth of perception will affect the playing of the story, for as the children discover its meaning, they will find their playing to be enriched and more serious.

THE WISE OLD WOMAN*

Yoshiko Uchida

Many long years ago, there lived an arrogant and cruel young lord who ruled over a small village in the western hills of Japan.

"I have no use for old people in my village," he said haughtily. "They are neither useful nor able to work for a living. I therefore decree that anyone over seventy-one must be banished from the village and left in the mountains to die."

"What a dreadful decree! What a cruel and unreasonable lord we have," the people of the village murmured. But the lord punished anyone who disobeyed him, and so villagers who turned seventy-one were tearfully carried into the mountains, never to return.

* Yochiko Uchida, *"The Sea of Gold" and Other Tales* (New York: Scribner, 1965), pp. 61–71.

Gradually there were fewer and fewer old people in the village and soon they disappeared altogether. Then the young lord was pleased.

"What a fine village of young, healthy and hardworking people I have," he bragged. "Soon it will be the finest village in all of Japan."

Now there lived in this village a kind young farmer and his aged mother. They were poor, but the farmer was good to his mother, and the two of them lived happily together. However, as the years went by, the mother grew older, and before long she reached the terrible age of seventy-one.

"If only I could somehow deceive the cruel lord," the farmer thought. But there were records in the village books and everyone knew that his mother had turned seventy-one.

Each day the son put off telling his mother that he must take her into the mountains to die, but the people of the village began to talk. The farmer knew that if he did not take his mother away soon, the lord would send his soldiers and throw them both into a dark dungeon to die a terrible death.

"Mother—" he would begin, as he tried to tell her what he must do, but he could not go on.

Then one day the mother herself spoke of the lord's dread decree. "Well, my son," she said, "the time has come for you to take me to the mountains. We must hurry before the lord sends his soldiers for you." And she did not seem worried at all that she must go to the mountains to die.

"Forgive me, dear mother, for what I must do," the farmer said sadly, and the next morning he lifted his mother to his shoulders and set off on the steep path toward the mountains. Up and up he climbed, until the trees clustered close and the path was gone. There was no longer even the sound of birds, and they heard only the soft wail of the wind in the trees. The son walked slowly, for he could not bear to think of leaving his old mother in the mountains. On and on he climbed, not wanting to stop and leave her behind. Soon, he heard his mother breaking off small twigs from the trees that they passed.

"Mother, what are you doing?" he asked.

"Do not worry, my son," she answered gently. "I am just marking the way so you will not get lost returning to the village."

The son stopped. "Even now you are thinking of me?" he asked, wonderingly.

The mother nodded. "Of course, my son," she replied. "You will always be in my thoughts. How could it be otherwise?"

At that, the young farmer could bear it no longer. "Mother, I cannot leave you in the mountains to die all alone," he said. "We are going home and no matter what the lord does to punish me, I will never desert you again."

So they waited until the sun had set and a lone star crept into the silent sky. Then in the dark shadows of night, the farmer carried his mother down the hill and they returned quietly to their little house. The farmer dug a deep hole in the floor of his kitchen and made a small room where he could hide his mother. From that day, she spent all her time in the secret room and the farmer carried meals to her there. The rest of the time, he was careful to work in the fields and act as though he lived alone. In this way, for almost two years, he kept his mother safely hidden and no one in the village knew that she was there.

Then one day there was a terrible commotion among the villagers, for Lord Higa of the town beyond the hills threatened to conquer their village and make it his own.

"Only one thing can spare you," Lord Higa announced. "Bring me a box containing one thousand ropes of ash and I will spare your village."

The cruel young lord quickly gathered together all the wise men of his village. "You are men of wisdom," he said. "Surely you can tell me how to meet Lord Higa's demands so our village can be spared."

But the wise men shook their heads. "It is impossible to make even one rope of ash, sire," they answered. "How can we ever make one thousand?"

"Fools!" the lord cried angrily. "What good is your wisdom if you cannot help me now?"

And he posted a notice in the village square offering a great reward of gold to any villager who could help him save their village.

But all the people in the village whispered. "Surely, it is an impossible thing, for ash crumbles at the touch of the finger. How could anyone ever make a rope of ash?" They shook their heads and sighed, "Alas, alas, we must be conquered by yet another cruel lord."

The young farmer, too, supposed that this must be, and he wondered what would happen to his mother if a new lord even more terrible than their own came to rule over them.

When his mother saw the troubled look on his face, she asked, "Why are you so worried, my son?"

So the farmer told her of the impossible demand made by Lord Higa if the village was to be spared, but his mother did not seem troubled at all. Instead she laughed softly and said, "Why, that is not such an impossible task. All one has to do is soak ordinary rope in salt water and dry it well. When it is burned, it will hold its shape and there is your rope of ash! Tell the villagers to hurry and find one thousand pieces of rope."

The farmer shook his head in amazement. "Mother, you are wonderfully wise," he said, and he rushed to tell the young lord what he must do.

"You are wiser than all the wise men of the village," the lord said when he heard the farmer's solution, and he rewarded him with many pieces of gold. The thousand ropes of ash were quickly made and the village was spared.

In a few days, however, there was another great commotion in the village as Lord Higa sent another threat. This time he sent a log with a small hole that curved and bent seven times through its length, and he demanded that a single piece of silk thread be threaded through the hole. "If you cannot perform this task," the lord threatened, "I shall come to conquer your village." The young lord hurried once more to his wise men, but they all shook their heads in bewilderment. "A needle cannot bend its way through such curves," they moaned. "Again we are faced with an impossible demand."

"And again you are stupid fools!" the lord said, stamping his foot impatiently. He then posted a second notice in the village square asking the villagers for their help.

Once more the young farmer hurried with the problem to his mother in her secret room.

"Why, that is not so difficult," his mother said with a quick smile. "Put some sugar at one end of the hole. Then tie an ant to a piece of silk thread and put it in at the other end. He will weave his way in and out of the curves to get to the sugar and he will take the silk thread with him."

"Mother, you are remarkable!" the son cried, and he hurried off to the lord with the solution to the second problem.

Once more the lord commended the young farmer and rewarded him with many pieces of gold. "You are a brilliant man and you have saved our village again," he said gratefully.

But the lord's troubles were not over even then, for a few days later Lord Higa sent still another demand. "This time you will undoubtedly fail and then I shall conquer your village," he threatened. "Bring me a drum that sounds without being beaten."

"But that is not possible," sighed the people of the village. "How can anyone make a drum sound without beating it?"

This time the wise men held their heads in their hands and

moaned, "It is hopeless. It is hopeless. This time Lord Higa will conquer us all."

The young farmer hurried home breathlessly. "Mother, Mother, we must solve another terrible problem or Lord Higa will conquer our village!" And he quickly told his mother about the impossible drum.

His mother, however, smiled and answered, "Why, this is the easiest of them all. Make a drum with sides of paper and put a bumblebee inside. As it tries to escape, it will buzz and beat itself against the paper and you will have a drum that sounds without being beaten."

The young farmer was amazed at his mother's wisdom. "You are far wiser than any of the wise men of the village," he said, and he hurried to tell the young lord how to meet Lord Higa's third demand.

When the lord heard the answer, he was greatly impressed. "Surely a young man like you cannot be wiser than all my wise men," he said. "Tell me honestly, who has helped you solve all these difficult problems?"

The young farmer could not lie. "My lord," he began slowly, "for the past two years I have broken the law of the land. I have kept my aged mother hidden beneath the floor of my house, and it is she who solved each of your problems and saved the village from Lord Higa."

He trembled as he spoke, for he feared the lord's displeasure and rage. Surely now the soldiers would be summoned to throw him into the dark dungeon. But when he glanced fearfully at the lord, he saw that the young ruler was not angry at all. Instead, he was silent and thoughtful, for at last he realized how much wisdom and knowledge old people possess.

"I have been very wrong," he said finally. "And I must ask the forgiveness of your mother and of all my people. Never again will I demand that the old people of our village be sent to the mountains to die. Rather, they will be treated with the respect and honor they deserve and share with us the wisdom of their years."

And so it was. From that day, the villagers were no longer forced to abandon their parents in the mountains, and the village became once more a happy, cheerful place in which to live. The terrible Lord Higa stopped sending his impossible demands and no longer threatened to conquer them, for he too was impressed. "Even in such a small village there is much wisdom," he declared, "and its people should be allowed to live in peace."

And that is exactly what the farmer and his mother and all the people of the village did for all the years thereafter.

ACTIVITY 14.3

STORY THEATRE

"The Saga of Bukolla" is well known to the children of Iceland. For many generations, it belonged to the oral tradition, and the same words were repeated so often that the young listeners eventually learned them by heart. The plot, like those of many folk tales, derived from the physical conditions of the country. At a time when most Icelanders lived on farms, the long, dark days of winter were brightened by storytelling around the fire. It is said that the imagination was fed by the sounds of the wind howling outside the house and by the sight of the lava rocks and cliffs, which in the semidarkness seemed to take the shapes of giants and trolls. Although the majority of Icelanders live in towns today, I am told that there are people who still believe in the old tales. There is probably no country in the world in which one can find more stories about strange creatures with whom human beings communicate. Indeed, it is not unusual for newspapers in Iceland to report stories of monsters, rising up from a lake and then disappearing suddenly into a cliff. Driving through Iceland, one often finds roads winding around rocks, for the countrypeople believed the rocks to be trolls' huts and, rather than move them, built the roads around them, on the vast tundra.

Suggestions for the Teacher

"The Saga of Bukolla" lends itself to dramatization, and I have found that groups love to dramatize it. With the Narrator reading or telling the story, there are very few lines to memorize, so the players can concentrate on the pantomime. It spans a rather wide age range, as younger children love the repetition of words and actions, while older children respond to the challenge of the story-theatre form. "The Saga of Bukolla" can be played in any size room or space and can be enjoyed by spectators, when shared with another class.

Introducing it through a study of the country will help children understand and appreciate the quality and humor of the tale. Knowing something of the geography, history, and way of life of Iceland will make it easier to imagine the harsh landscape and create belief in the situation. Story theatre is a particularly effective way of handling it. A group with which I worked preferred to imagine Bukolla, rather than play her. Trying the story in different ways, however, is the best approach; in doing so, the children become acquainted with the details of the narrative as they decide what form they want it to take.

While costumes are unnecessary in creative drama, a few garments will add to the enjoyment. In "The Saga of Bukolla," for example, the

Farmer might wear a cap; his Wife, a scarf or apron; and the Boy, a pair of suspenders or a vest. The size difference between the Trolls and the Boy can be shown by the way they walk and move as well as by their actual height. Most children enjoy creating these strange characters and making them credible.

THE SAGA OF BUKOLLA

Characters

Narrator

Farmer

Farmer's Wife

Their Son

Big Troll

Small Troll

Bukolla (who may be played or whose presence may be simply suggested by the Boy's pantomime)

NARRATOR: (*walks to the center of the playing space*) Once upon a time in faraway Iceland, there was a Farmer, who lived with his Wife and Son on the side of a mountain. All they possessed in the world were a few poor acres of land and a cow named Bukolla.
(*As the Narrator finishes speaking, the Son appears, leading the cow and stroking her neck affectionately.*)

NARRATOR: Early one morning, when the Farmer's Son went out to milk, Bukolla was nowhere to be seen.
(*The Boy yawns sleepily, picks up a bucket, and walks to an imagined stall. He bends down and prepares to milk, but catches only the air in his hand. Startled, he opens his eyes wide, then runs back to the house, and in great excitement, tells his parents in pantomime what has happened.*)

NARRATOR: Now to lose Bukolla meant disaster. Without a cow, they would have no milk. Without milk, they would have no cheese, and without cheese, they would have nothing to trade for the things they needed. The Farmer and his Wife were very sad.
(*She wipes her eyes with her apron while the Farmer takes his pipe from his mouth and looks down at the ground. Finally he turns to his son.*)

NARRATOR: Boy, you must go look for Bukolla. And do not return without her.

(*The Farmer's Wife goes into the house and puts some food in a cloth, which she ties to the end of a stick. She puts a scarf around the Boy's neck and gives him a new pair of boots, which he pulls on. Ready for the journey, he walks off and waves good-bye.*)

NARRATOR: So the Farmer's Son started off. He walked and walked for a long time. He crossed rivers. He climbed mountains. He made his way over rocks, and he looked everywhere. But there was no sign of Bukolla. At last, feeling tired, he sat down and pulled a piece of bread from the package of lunch his mother had fixed for him and ate it slowly.

(*The Boy walks while the Narrator is speaking. [The distance may be suggested by walking in circles or around the room, depending on its size and shape.] He goes uphill, and he goes downhill. He suggests crossing streams and climbing over rocks. Then, tired of walking, he finds a place to sit down and eat his lunch.*)

NARRATOR: Rested and satisfied with some food in his stomach, the Boy called out.

BOY: Bukolla! If you are here, let me know, please!

NARRATOR: Then, from far away, he heard a strange sound. It was a low murmur. He jumped to his feet and began walking again. He walked and walked until his feet were sore, but he found no sign of Bukolla. So he called out once more.

BOY: Bukolla! Bukolla! If you are alive and somewhere near, please let me know!

NARRATOR: This time, the sound came from close by. As the Boy looked around, he saw the entrance to a cave. He stepped inside, and there was Bukolla tied to a rock. The sound had been her mooing. He ran to her and embraced her.

BOY: Bukolla, Bukolla! How did you get here?

NARRATOR: Suddenly, he realized that he was in the house of Trolls. He must take Bukolla out quickly before they returned. He untied the rope and led the cow outside to begin their long journey home. It was none too soon, for they had not gone far when the two Trolls who lived in the cave returned. As they reached the doorway they stopped, sniffed the air, looked about, and spoke.

BIG TROLL: I can smell men!

SMALL TROLL: And the cow has been stolen!

BIG TROLL: The thief cannot have gone far. Come, brother, follow me.

(The Trolls stamp out of the cave and spy the Boy and the cow in the distance. The Boy looks back and sees them; then all run in place. [Running in place is a good way of suggesting a chase without actually racing. Children enjoy the device, and an audience accepts it. When the story is told and played in a classroom, it is the only satisfactory way of handling a continuing chase.])

NARRATOR: Before long, the Trolls saw Bukolla and the Farmer's Son running ahead of them. Finally, the Boy stopped to catch his breath.

BOY: They are coming after us! What shall we do, Bukolla?

NARRATOR: The cow answered, "Take a hair from my tail and put it on the ground." (*The Boy does so.*) "May this hair turn into a lake so wide that no one can cross it except a flying bird." As she spoke, a lake appeared. And it was so wide that no one could cross it but a flying bird.

(The Boy sees the lake and, with a smile, bends down and washes his face. Then he stands up and continues walking. The Trolls come to the edge of the lake and stamp their feet in anger.)

BIG TROLL: This lake will not stop us! Go home and get our father's ox. He will drink the water until the lake is gone, and then we can go forward.

NARRATOR: The Small Troll did as he was told. The ox drank and drank and drank and did not lift his head until he had swallowed the last drop of water. Meanwhile, the Boy and Bukolla went on. But now that the ox had drunk all the water in the lake, the Trolls could follow them again.

(Again the Trolls and the Boy run in place, faster and harder than before. Finally, the Boy stops for breath, and all freeze. The Boy turns to the cow.)

BOY: What now, Bukolla?

NARRATOR: Again the cow answered, "Take a hair from my tail and put it on the ground. May this hair turn into a fire so high that no one can get over it except a flying bird." At this, a raging fire appeared. The flames leaped so high that no one but a flying bird could get over it. When the Trolls saw the fire, they stamped their feet in fury.

(The Boy shows in mime the heat of the fire; then, taking Bukolla's rope, he turns again toward home.)

BIG TROLL: This fire will not stop us. Go get our father's pitcher with the magic power. It will pour water until the fire is put out.

NARRATOR: The Small Troll did as he was told. With the magic pitcher, he poured and poured and poured, until the fire was completely out. All that remained were the wet coals on the ground. The two Trolls stepped over them and went on.

(Once more, the Trolls and the Boy run in place, all the time seeming to get closer together. Finally, the Boy stops and looks back, and all freeze.)

BOY: What next, Bukolla?

NARRATOR: Once more the cow spoke. "Take a hair from my tail and place it on the ground. May this hair turn into a mountain so great that no one can cross it except a flying bird." At this, a mountain suddenly appeared. And it was so high that no one could cross it but a flying bird. When the trolls came to the mountain and looked up, they stamped their feet in rage.

BIG TROLL: This mountain will not stop us! Go home and get our father's drill. We will make a tunnel in the mountain. Then we can go through it.

NARRATOR: The Small Troll did as he was told. When he returned, the two began drilling. They drilled and they drilled and they drilled. Finally, the Small Troll turned to his brother in great excitement.

SMALL TROLL: The mountain has split! I can see the sky. Now we can go through to the other side.

BIG TROLL: I'm going first. Let me get by.

(With that, the Big Troll pushes the Small Troll aside and tries to go through the tunnel, but he is too large. They push and pull, but the more they work at it, the more thoroughly stuck they become.)

NARRATOR: But the tunnel was too small for the Big Troll. He got stuck and could move neither forward nor backward. In fact, the harder he tried, the worse it was. The Small Troll pushed from behind, but the Big Troll was caught on a rock and could not budge. They were pushing and pulling so hard they didn't notice that their greatest enemy, the Sun, had come up! Before they knew it, the Sun had turned them to stone. By this time, the Boy and the cow had reached home. His Father and Mother were overjoyed to see him, safely leading the cow up the road to the barn. And they say today, when you walk on that side of the mountain, you can see two big stones in the shape of Trolls.

New Words:

Saga Tale, story of adventure or heroic deeds; Medieval Scandinavian story narrated in prose.

Story theatre An oral story told by actors, often with a narrator. When there is no narrator, actors may speak in the third person. Minimal scenery is used, leaving description of the locale to the narrator or actors.

Troll Any of a race of supernatural beings found in Scandinavian folklore; conceived of as giants or dwarfs living underground or in caves.

Tundra Vast, treeless plains of the Arctic regions.

15

PUPIL EVALUATION

DEVELOPMENTAL CHARACTERISTICS OF CHILDREN IN THE INTERMEDIATE GRADES

In order to evaluate children's work in any area it is necessary to know the *characteristics*, *abilities*, *needs*, and *interests* of the particular age level. Not that these are present to the same degree in all children but they serve as guidelines for expectations. Human beings grow at different rates of speed, so there can be no arbitrary rules governing growth and development. Experienced teachers of the intermediate grades know what children of these ages are like, but for the inexperienced teacher, or the teacher working with drama for the first time, the following explanations may be helpful.

CHARACTERISTICS OF THE FOURTH GRADER

1. *Physical.* Constantly gaining better control of the body as he or she grows older, taller, and stronger; works and plays hard; is active, spontaneous, eager to try new things and to learn.
2. *Mental.* Becoming more self-motivated; enjoys discussion and group planning periods; likes to solve problems.
3. *Social.* Independent but likes working with others; can share ideas and work cooperatively on scenes and class projects.
4. *Interests.* Adventure, sports, strong heroes and heroines; enjoys new stories and more demanding exercises.

5. *Activities.* 40 to 60 minutes recommended for drama period. Classes may include exercises, stories, poems, suggestions for creating scenes; interest in play structure; can handle more complicated plots and create original plays; able to work for longer periods and study subjects in greater depth.

CHARACTERISTICS OF THE FIFTH GRADER

1. *Physical.* Continued improvement of physical skills, including tumbling, acrobatics, circus acts, and clowning.
2. *Mental.* Growing ability to solve problems and create well-rounded characters; motivation for characters' behavior becomes important; likes words and can create dialogue appropriate to characters and situations or periods in which the story is laid; accepts constructive suggestions from the teacher or leader.
3. *Social.* Able to analyze feelings; continues to work well in a team; fair play important; still needs help in commenting on the work of others so as not to hurt feelings.
4. *Interests.* Similar to the fourth grader but with a constantly widening spread of interests; fantasy and fairy tales become less interesting as interest in the lives of real persons and tales of heroic acts grows.
5. *Activities.* 40 minutes to an hour or more can be spent on a variety of activities. Can handle longer and more complicated stories; still childlike in spontaneity but more perceptive and thoughtful; able to sustain interest in one activity for a longer period of time.

CHARACTERISTICS OF THE SIXTH GRADER

1. *Physical.* The pre-adolescent is undergoing change; physical growth is reflected in the finer muscle coordination; often self-conscious because of body change but capable of refined movements, well-developed pantomime, and circus skills.
2. *Mental.* Interested in detail and motivation of characters; talkative and investigative; enjoys discussion, shows more mature reasoning ability; has keener critical judgment; is often surprisingly perceptive.
3. *Social.* Interested in the opposite sex; sensitive and aware; has had more experiences on which to draw; vocabulary much larger; can be expected to offer well-thought-out ideas and well-expressed criticism.

4. *Interests.* Many and varied interests; romantic interests as well as love of adventure, mystery, and adolescent problems.
5. *Activities.* Can work for an hour to an hour and a half. Likes writing and may enjoy playwriting as well as performing; can integrate learnings and engage in long-range project involving social studies, literature, and the arts; may want to put on a play for an audience.

USING AN EVALUATION CHART

While grading children in the arts is to be avoided, a simple check list may be helpful in evaluating growth and development. The evaluation chart on page 298 was designed to show the major areas of concern and should serve as: (1) a guide to the emphases in teaching creative drama; and (2) an aid to the identification of children's individual needs and progress. It is suggested that children be evaluated three or four times a semester in order to note change and improvement.

We do not look for performance skills in elementary-school children, nor expect the level of achievement possible among high-school students. Involvement, sincerity, imagination, freedom of movement, and cooperation with the group are the basic goals in teaching creative drama. Beyond that, vocal expression, vocabulary, and the ability to plan and to organize material are important, but they come with experience. The criteria applied to adult actors are inappropriate for children and should not be used. These criteria are audience-centered and therefore do not belong to creative drama, in which the participant is central. Even when children's work is shared with others, the goals remain the same, with the audience prepared for the occasion rather than the players drilled for a performance.

It is suggested that instead of giving children letter grades, teachers use the following three numbers to indicate quality of response in the specific category:

1. Shows good response
2. Is adequate
3. Needs special attention and, perhaps, help

THE AREAS OF CONCENTRATION

1. *Listening.* Listening is an important skill for hearing instructions, discussing topics in class, responding to questions, and helping to create a climate in which all children are able to express themselves freely.

2. *Concentration.* The ability to hold an idea long enough to respond thoughtfully or creatively is essential in any discipline. It is particularly important in drama, for a breakdown in concentration on the part of one participant invariably affects the concentration of all. Group work requires the concentrated attention of every member.

3. *Response.* Responses can be varied; the important thing to note is whether or not the child is able to respond physically, verbally, or emotionally to the challenge.

4. *Imagination.* Imagination is the element that distinguishes a response as original, creative, or interesting.

5. *Movement.* Young children tend to be free in the use of their bodies as a primary means of expression. As they grow older, children become more inhibited in their physical responses. Tight, constricted movement suggests self-consciousness or fear. Unlocking the muscles, therefore, helps the performer to express ideas and feelings more openly.

6. *Verbal Ability.* The older the student, the greater verbal ability is to be expected. Increased vocabulary and added experience in speaking should improve oral communication. Creative drama offers a unique opportunity to develop this skill.

7. *Cooperation.* Cooperation includes the ability to offer and accept the ideas of others easily and graciously. It is an important part of successful living in a democracy.

8. *Organization.* Planning, seeing relationships, making choices, and arranging the components of a project require thought, maturity, and patience. As children work together, they develop the ability to organize materials in such a way as to communicate with others.

9. *Attitude.* Attitude is the feeling or disposition toward the work and the other members of the class. A positive attitude not only enhances the quality of the individual student's work, but also contributes to the combined efforts of the group. A negative attitude, on the contrary, detracts and may even be a destructive force. A *good* attitude, therefore, is the most important element for achieving growth and success.

Although there are other important goals in teaching creative drama, those listed above are the most important in assessing the progress of children in the elementary and intermediate grades or, indeed, of beginners on any level. The evaluation sheet was designed for easy duplication. Teachers may also want to keep brief anecdotal records as well as a check list. The space at the right, marked "Comments," provides for such entries. Specific instances of change, "breakthroughs," or problems of individual children can be written here.

"Class Progress" is the overall picture of the group at work. In the adult theatre, this often is referred to as ensemble. Ensemble means the quality of work done as a group rather than by individual actors. It is not developed in a day or a week; after a month or so, a tentative evaluation can be made. This is because individuals develop at different rates of speed, and some have problems that must be resolved before it is possible for them to become absorbed in a group project. An accurate statement of group progress, therefore, cannot often be made until near the end of a semester.

OTHER YARDSTICKS

The best method of evaluating student progress is, of course, personal observation made on a daily basis. These observations lead to the information needed for a check list later on. Because the teacher's attention is on the lesson and the group, however, and because he or she must move on to other lessons, daily rating is impractical and actually undesirable. If there are student teachers in the room, ask them to be responsible for watching response and variations in behavior from day to day. Should there be more than one student teacher assigned to the class, each can be given a group of children to observe over a period of time. This has two advantages: (1) it is a help to the classroom teacher, freeing him or her for teaching the group; and (2) it sharpens the student teacher's ability to discern growth and development. Again, it must be stressed that teaching comes first and that at no time should evaluation become important to the children or take on the appearance of assigning letter grades. When children try to *please* adults, they lose the most important value of the experience.

Another yardstick, possible in some schools but not in most, is videotaping of the class. This is an ideal way to compare work done at different periods in the semester and to take a second look at a performance that one does not clearly remember. The obvious disadvantage of taping is that when children know they are being filmed, they tend to become self-conscious, thus negating two of our principal goals: sincerity and involvement. Therefore, where videotaping is possible, it is suggested that it not be done until halfway through the semester, by which time the class is comfortable and working easily together. This should make it seem a natural way of recording group work and not like filming a show.

Date: _____

Students' names	Listening	Concentration	Response	Imagination	Movement	Verbal ability	Cooperation	Organization	Attitude	Comments
Doe, John	1	2	2	1	3	1	3	1	2	

Teacher's evaluation of class progress:

Evaluation key:
1. Shows good response
2. Is adequate
3. Needs special attention and, perhaps, help

BOOKS ON CHILD DEVELOPMENT

Bruner, Jerome. *The Process of Education.* Cambridge: Harvard University Press, 1960.

Day, B. D. *Early Childhood Education: Creative Learning Activities.* New York: Macmillan, 1983.

Dittman, L. L., and M. E. Ramsey, eds. *Today Is for Children.* Washington, D.C.: ACEI, 1982.

Flavell, J. H. *The Developmental Psychology of Jean Piaget.* Princeton: Van Nostrand, 1963.

Gesell, Arnold, and Frances Ilg. *The Child from Five to Ten.* New York: Harper & Row, 1946.

Hendrick, J. *Total Learning for the Whole Child.* St. Louis: Mosby, 1980.

Maxim, G. *The Very Young Child: Guiding Children from Infancy through the Early Years,* 2d ed. Belmont, CA: Wadsworth, 1985.

Maynard, Olga. *Children and Dance and Music.* New York: Scribner, 1968.

Piaget, Jean, and Barbel Inhelder. *The Child's Conception of Movement and Speed.* New York: Basic Books, 1969.

—— and ——. *The Psychology of the Child.* New York: Basic Books, 1969.

Spodek, B., ed. *Handbook of Research in Early Childhood Education.* New York: Free Press, 1982.

GLOSSARY
OF COMMON
DRAMATIC TERMS

A number of the words listed in the glossary are discussed at greater length in the body of the text. They are repeated here, however, because of their frequent usage in discussing drama and theatre. Many of the terms will obviously not be part of an elementary-school child's vocabulary, but in the event that they come up in class discussion, the teacher will have brief definitions to share at his or her discretion.

Act. To perform or play a role. A division of a drama.

Actor. A person who performs in a play, who assumes the role of a character.

Adaptation. A play based on a story or novel rather than being an original plot.

Aesthetic growth. Development of sensitivity to art and beauty.

Amateur. A person who engages in an art or a sport for love of it, rather than for a livelihood.

Backstage. The area behind the stage, not visible to the audience.

Body awareness. The sense of the body as a means of enjoyment as well as an instrument of communication.

Border lights. Overhead lighting at the front of the stage.

Box office. The office where tickets are sold, located either in or in front of the lobby.

Choreographer. A person who designs and directs a dance.

Choreography. The design for a dance; the written representation of the steps of dancing.

Climax. The highest point of interest, usually near the end of the play.

Comedy. A play that ends satisfactorily for the hero or heroine; it is entertaining and usually lively, as opposed to a tragedy.

Community theatre. Theatre organized and run by persons living in the community; actors generally perform for the enjoyment of the experience rather than as a profession.

Creative drama. An improvisational, nonexhibitional, process-centered form of drama in which participants are guided by a leader to imagine, enact, and reflect upon human experience. Although creative drama traditionally has been thought of in relation to children and young people, the process is appropriate to all ages.

The creative drama process is dynamic. The leader guides the group to explore, develop, express, and communicate ideas, concepts, and feelings through dramatic enactment. In creative drama, the group improvises action and dialogue appropriate to the content it is exploring, using elements of drama to give form and meaning to the experience. The primary purpose of creative drama is to foster personality growth and to facilitate learning of the participants rather than to train actors for the stage. Creative drama may be used to teach the art of drama and/or motivate and extend learning in other content areas. Participation in creative drama has the potential to develop language and communication abilities, problem-solving skills, and creativity; to promote a positive self-concept, social awareness, empathy, a clarification of values and attitudes, and an understanding of the art of theatre.

Built on the human impulse and ability to act out perceptions of the world in order to understand it, creative drama requires both logical and intuitive thinking, personalizes knowledge, and yields aesthetic pleasure. (Definition accepted by the Children's Theatre Association of America in 1977.)

Cue. The signal for an actor to speak or perform an action, usually a line spoken by another actor.

Curtain call. The return of the entire cast to the stage after the end of a performance, when they acknowledge applause.

Denouement. The final unraveling of the plot of a play; the solution or outcome.

Dialogue. The lines of the play spoken by the actors.

Director. The person in charge; the one who gives directions to the actors and assumes ultimate responsibility for the production.

Double cast. To prepare two casts for a play, both of which will play the same number of performances.

Downstage. The front of the stage; the area nearest the audience.

Dramatist. Another name for a playwright.

Dramatization. The creation of a play from a story or poem.

Dress rehearsal. The final rehearsal or rehearsals of a play, when costumes are worn and all stage effects are completed.

Entr'acte. A song, dance, or short performance that takes place between the acts, most often in plays of an earlier period, although occasionally in children's theatre; it is designed to entertain the audience while scenery is being changed.

Epilogue. A short scene or speech at the end of the play; it is not often found in modern plays.

Expressive use of the body. Freedom to move so that the body reflects the player's true feelings.

Expressive use of the voice. The ability to speak audibly, clearly, and with color so as to reflect the speaker's thought and feeling.

Floodlights. Stage lights that throw a broad beam, as opposed to spotlights.

Footlights. The row of lights across the front of the stage, on a level with the actors' feet.

Hero. The central male character in a play; a man distinguished for valor.

Heroine. The central female character in a play.

The house. The auditorium or seating area of a theatre.

Houselights. The auditorium lights, turned off or dimmed when the performance starts.

Imitative movement. Mime or movement that imitates the actions of human beings, animals, or mechanical objects.

Improvisation. A scene created by actors using spontaneous dialogue; the opposite of a performance based on a memorized script.

Intermission. A recess or temporary stopping of action, usually about halfway through a play.

Lines. The dialogue or words spoken by the actors.

Lobby. The foyer or hall at the front of a theatre.

Mounting. The scenery and costumes used to dress the production.

Musical. A theatrical production characterized by music, songs, dances, and often spectacular settings and costumes.

Pantomime. The expression of ideas through action without the use of words.

Performance. A representation before spectators; an entertainment.

Playwright. A person who writes plays.

Plot. The story.

Production. The total theatrical product, including the play, the acting, the direction, scenery, costumes, lighting, and special effects.

Professional theatre. Theatre in which actors and all other employees earn their living.

Prologue. An introduction to a play, usually spoken by one of the actors; it occasionally is employed in plays for children to orient the audience to the piece or engage its attention.

Prompter. The person who watches the script backstage during the performance of a play; he or she gives the lines to the actors, if they should forget.

Props. The properties or small objects used by the actors.

Proscenium stage. A raised platform at one end of an auditorium, with the audience seated in front of it.

Protagonist. The heroine or hero of a play; the actor who plays the chief part.

Puppetry. An art form in which puppets are the performers. While most puppets are small and resemble dolls, they may be made in any size or shape, so long as they can be easily moved and manipulated.

Rehearsal. The practice or repetition of a play in preparation for public performance.

Resident company. A company of actors who play in a home theatre, as opposed to a touring company.

Rhythmic movement. Movement that follows a rhythmic pattern: marching, folk dancing, repeated movements.

Role Playing. A term most often used in connection with therapy and education. It refers to the assumption of a role for the particular value it may have for the participant rather than for the development of an art. The goals of role playing are attitudinal change and greater sensitivity toward the feelings of others through understanding.

Scenario. The outline or story of a play.

Scene. A location or setting. A division within an act of a play.

Scenery. The large pieces (flats, backdrops, furniture, and so on) that are placed on the stage to represent the location.

Script. The manuscript or form in which the play is written; it contains the dialogue, stage directions, and time and place of each act and scene.

Sensory awareness. A recognition and appreciation of our five senses.

Shadow play. Enacting a story or role in silhouette behind a screen or sheet. The play may be performed by human actors or puppets.

Soliloquy. Lines in a play spoken by one character alone on the stage, in which his or her thoughts are revealed.

Spatial perception. A sense of space as related to body movement; something happening or existing in space.

Sponsor. A person or an organization engaging a theatrical company.

Spotlight. A strong beam of light used to illuminate a particular person or area of the stage, as opposed to floodlights.

Stage manager. The person in charge backstage; he or she helps the director during rehearsals and then takes charge backstage when the play is given.

Straight play. A drama without music or dance.

Subplot. A plot subordinate to the principal plot.

Theme. A topic or subject developed in a play; the subject on which the plot is based.

Theme song. A melody used throughout a dramatic presentation; a strain of music that establishes a mood through repetition.

Thrust stage. A stage or platform that extends into the auditorium, with the audience seated on three sides.

Touring company. A company of actors who take their show on the road, as opposed to a resident company.

Tragedy. A play that ends with the defeat or death of the main character; it is based on a serious theme or conflict, as opposed to a comedy.

Understudy. The actor who learns the part of another actor playing a major role; he or she is ready to go onstage in the unexpected absence of the original actor.

Upstage. The rear of the stage; the area farthest from the audience.

Villain. A character who commits a crime; the opponent of the hero or heroine.

Wings. The side areas of the stage, out of view of the audience; the area where the actors wait for their entrances.

BIBLIOGRAPHY

This bibliography is divided into four parts, each of which is divided into categories. Each category of Part One represents a highly selective list of books based on the premise that classroom teachers will want to follow up on some areas but have little time to pursue all of them. Therefore, only the most relevant, recent, and landmark texts are included.

Prose and poetry for creative dramatization are listed in Part Two. This is also a selective list. Stories and poems that I have found particularly successful are included, but there are dozens more that other leaders might choose and that, indeed, I might have included had I not wanted to keep the list to a useful minimum. I have, however, cited a number of collections and anthologies containing a wealth of fine children's literature. Most of them are readily available in both school and public libraries. The folk and fairy tales are found in so many collections that they are listed by title rather than by any suggested source.

Part Three notes films on a number of subjects of interest to creative-drama teachers and students. A list of mood music is included in Part Four for teachers who have access to record players or who play the piano. The music is grouped according to mood.

PART ONE: BOOKS

CREATIVE DRAMA

In 1977, the Children's Theatre Association of America accepted a definition of creative drama: "Creative drama is an improvisational, nonexhibitional, process-centered form of drama in which participants are guided by a leader to imagine, enact, and reflect upon human experiences. Although creative drama traditionally has been thought of in relation to children and young people, the process is appropriate to all ages."[1]

Chambers, Dewey W. *Storytelling and Creative Drama*. Dubuque, Ia.: Brown, 1970.

This is an invaluable little book for the teacher, librarian, or group leader who wants to learn something of the ancient art of storytelling. Clear and succinct, it guides selection of material and offers simple techniques for effective presentation.

Cheifitz, Dan. *Theatre in My Head*. Boston: Little, Brown, 1971.

This book describes an experimental workshop in creative drama conducted by the author in an inner-city New York church. Cheifitz communicates the need to look *into* children, not merely *at* them, as he reports his successes and failures.

Crosscup, Richard. *Children and Dramatics*. New York: Scribner, 1966.

Crosscup's book is an autobiographical account of his 27 years' experience in one school. Of greatest value is the view he gives of a gifted teacher, able to stimulate the creativity of his pupils. Social values are stressed.

Fitzgerald, Burdette, ed. *World Tales for Creative Dramatics and Storytelling*. Englewood Cliffs, N.J.: Prentice-Hall, 1962.

In this book, the author introduces a wide variety of stories not usually found in collections of this sort. She has drawn from the folklore of countries rarely represented in anthologies of children's literature, thus making an interesting contribution to the field.

Heinig, Ruth. *Creative Drama for the Classroom Teacher*. 2d ed. Englewood Cliffs, N.J.: Prentice-Hall, 1981.

Written by an experienced teacher in the field, this text suggests pantomimes, improvisations, songs, and games. They are arranged in order to guide the classroom teacher through simple to more advanced techniques, and each chapter has suggestions and assignments for the college student.

Kraus, Joanna H. *Sound and Motion Stories*. Rowayton, Conn.: New Plays, 1971.

Although not a text, this book shows how sounds and actions can be used to capture the attention and stimulate the imagination of younger children. The reader can learn from the author's inclusions how to handle other material in this way. The techniques are most valuable in classes where space is limited and where children are being introduced to creative drama.

McCaslin, Nellie, ed. *Children and Drama*. 2d ed. Lanham, Md.: University Press of America, 1981.

---

[1] "Terminology of Drama/Theatre with and for Children: A Redefinition." *Children's Theatre Review* 27, no. 1 (1978): 10–11.

This is a collection of essays on creative drama written by 20 experts in the field. A variety of viewpoints is represented, and different methodologies are suggested. It is of greater interest to the experienced teacher than to the beginner.

Nobleman, Roberta. *Using Creative Drama Outside the Classroom*. Rowayton, Conn.: New Plays, 1974.

In this book, the author tells how creative drama may be taught successfully in nontraditional spaces and places. It is as valuable for the teacher as for the leader of community and camp groups.

Schwartz, Dorothy, and Dorothy Aldrich, eds. *Give Them Roots and Wings*. 2d ed. New Orleans: Anchorage Press, 1986.

This is a guide to drama in the elementary school, prepared by leaders in the field and edited by the co-chairwomen of this project for the Children's Theatre Association. Published in workbook form, it offers the classroom teacher goals and dramatic activities with check lists for rating children's development.

Siks, Geraldine Brain. *Drama with Children*. 2d ed. New York: Harper & Row, 1983.

This latest book by a well-known creative-drama leader and author of other texts in the field is of particular interest to the more experienced teacher or graduate student. It is divided into three parts: the philosophy of drama, the teaching of drama, and individual experiences and uses of drama. In this edition, the author expands on what she calls the "process-concept-structure approach," and includes a selected bibliography and a few short plays.

Slade, Peter. *An Introduction to Child Drama*. London and Toronto: Hodder and Stoughton, 1976.

All the fundamental principles of Slade's methods are here. Children, if unhampered by adult imposition, can find self-expression and reach toward full human development. It is simply written, short, and to the point and is highly recommended for the beginner.

Ward, Winifred. *Playmaking with Children*. New York: Appleton-Century-Crofts, 1957.

This landmark text by an American pioneer in the field still presents good basic material 30 years after its original publication.

Way, Brian. *Development through Drama*. New York: Humanities Press, 1972.

The development of the whole child is the thesis of this book, which is directed particularly to teachers of older children. Many practical exercises in improvisational drama are included. It is highly recommended.

CHORAL SPEAKING

Gullan, Marjorie. *The Speech Choir*. New York: Harper & Row, 1937.

One of the earliest but still one of the few good texts on choral speaking, it gives clear directions for use on any level.

Rasmussen, Carrie. *Choral Speaking for Speech Improvement*. Boston: The Expression Company, 1942.

———. *Let's Say Poetry Together and Have Fun*. Minneapolis: Burgess, 1962.

These two books are among the best sources for choral speech in the elementary grades. Written by a teacher at a time when interest in this form of communication was high, they are still relevant and useful.

CLOWNING AND CIRCUS SKILLS

Bolton, Reg. *A Suitcase Circus*. Rowayton, Conn.: New Plays, 1983.

This is the only book published in the United States on circus skills for young people. Written after years of experience by a British professional clown and licensed teacher, it is simply written, amusingly illustrated, and easy to follow.

Crowther, Carol. *Clowns and Clowning*. London: Macdonald Educational Books, 1978.

This publication discusses the teaching of circus skills to young people.

Earle, Edwin, and Edward A. Kennard. *A Portfolio of 28 Plates in Full Color* from the book *Hopi Kachinas*, 2d ed. New York: Museum of the American Indian, 1971.

This attractive publication shows the relationship between the clown and the kachina, the deified ancestral spirits of the Hopi. It is not a text, but is a valuable resource.

Swortzell, Lowell. *Here Come the Clowns*. New York: Viking Press, 1978.

This history of the clown is written for older children and young adults. Presenting interesting material and carefully researched, it is not a "how to," but an excellent resource for background information.

DRAMA AS A WAY OF LEARNING

Concannon, Tom. *Using Media for Creative Teaching*. Rowayton, Conn.: New Plays, 1980.

A text for today's classroom, in which a media specialist explains how skills may be developed through the use of camera, videotape, tape recorders, and then the human body. Methods and specific suggestions for using media in the curriculum areas from kindergarten to grade 8 are given.

Cullum, Albert. *Aesop in the Afternoon*. New York: Citation, 1972.

This is a most usable collection of Aesop's fables, which can be played creatively by children of all ages.

———. *Push Back the Desks*. New York: Citation, 1967.

The author has written an account of some creative projects and techniques he has used in the public-school classroom to enhance learning. History, reading, vocabulary, and math are included units of study.

———. *Shake Hands with Shakespeare*. New York: Citation, 1968.

Eight of Shakespeare's plays are adapted for children. The results are filled with action and are relatively simple to produce. They do require time to prepare but could also be improvised, if desired. The value of using Shakespeare is the richness of the language and is a further recommendation for this text.

Mearns, Hughes. *Creative Power*. 2d rev. ed. New York: Dover, 1958.

This classic text by a gifted educator offers a philosophy of education in the creative arts and techniques with which to implement it. Long out of print, it was republished in paperback at the instigation of the Children's Theatre Association of America, a strong supporter of his views.

Moffett, James, and Betty Jane Wagner. *Student Centered Language Arts and Reading, K–13*. Boston: Houghton Mifflin, 1976.

Written by two well-known educators, this book is an argument for the use of drama in language learning and comprehension.

Piaget, Jean. *Play, Dreams and Imitation in Childhood*. New York: Norton, 1962.

This landmark work is a study of child development in terms of systematic and representative imitation, the structure and symbolism of games and dreams, and the movement from sensorimotor schemas to conceptual schemas.

Stewig, John Warren. *Informal Drama in the Elementary Language Arts Program*. New York: Teachers College Press, 1983.

This text focuses on the value of drama in the development of language skills. The author deals with the various ways in which the classroom teacher can use movement and improvisation and can evaluate sessions in terms of the language arts. Its greatest value is for the generalist or classroom teacher.

———. *Teaching Language Arts in Early Childhood*. New York: Holt, Rinehart and Winston, 1980.

Although this is a text on language arts by a specialist in the field, drama is stressed for its value in English teaching. The author shares his enthusiasm with readers.

MOVEMENT, MUSIC, AND DANCE

Aronoff, Frances Webber. *Music and Young Children*. Rev. ed. New York: Turning Wheel Press, 1984.

A widely used text for music teaching, this book has much to offer both specialist and generalist in drama. Ways in which music can enrich the lives of children are suggested and explained. It is an excellent resource.

Conner, Norma, and Harriet Klebanoff. *And a Time to Dance*. Boston: Beacon Press, 1967.

This is a sensitively illustrated book that explains, encourages, and shows the reader how to involve children in creative dance. Simply written, it also shows what can be done with the mentally retarded child.

Dorian, Margery. *Ethnic Stories for Children to Dance*. San Mateo, Calif.: BBB, 1978.

This book includes stories from around the world with suggestions for rhythmic accompaniment on drums and other instruments. Years of experience as a dancer and as a teacher of dance give the author knowledge and insight. The choice of material is a valuable addition to the resources available to teachers.

King, Nancy. *Giving Form to Feeling*. New York: Drama Book Specialists, 1975.

This is a sound and useful handbook with many exercises and ideas. The author writes that it is a book of beginnings. This is true, but it is not necessarily written for the beginner; the actor, dancer, and teacher on any level will find help in expressing ideas and feelings through movement, rhythm, sounds, and words.

———. *A Movement Approach to Acting*. Englewood Cliffs, N.J.: Prentice-Hall, 1981.

This text goes from breathing and body-awareness exercises to circus skills, staged combat, and nonverbal elements of drama. Written by an experienced teacher, this book is highly recommended.

La Salle, Dorothy. *Rhythms and Dance for Elementary Schools*. Rev. ed. New York: Ronald Press, 1951.

This collection of rhythms and dances should be extremely useful to the teacher of dramatic play and creative drama or to the children's-theatre director. It contains movement fundamentals, singing games, and folk dances—ranging from simple to advanced.

Lowndes, Betty. *Movement and Creative Drama for Children*. Boston: Plays, 1971.

First published in England, this practical and stimulating book should find enthusiastic readers in the United States. The author, an experienced teacher, explains the value and use of improvised movement and follows with chapters on body awareness, locomotion, mime, sensory awareness, and creative movement.

Maynard, Olga. *Children and Dance and Music*. New York: Scribner, 1968.

This book includes material not usually found in texts on creative drama. It is a good supplement to any text.

Ravosa, Carmino. *Songs Children Act Up For*. Rowayton, Conn.: New Plays, 1974.

Twenty-two action songs were collected by an experienced teacher and composer for use with children. This is a good and seldom-used way of stimulating creative drama.

Slade, Peter. *Natural Dance*. London: Hodder and Stoughton, 1977.

This book is particularly recommended for the teacher of creative drama. In it, Slade discusses "natural dance," or dance that is improvised, as opposed to formal dance techniques. It deals with all ages, levels of experience, and levels of ability; the therapeutic aspects of dance are also included.

PUPPETS AND MASKS

Champlin, John, and Connie Brooks. *Puppets and the Mentally Retarded Student*. Austin, Tex.: Nancy Renfro Studios, 1980.

This book discusses the methods of developing literary comprehension with the mentally retarded child. The text shows how to adapt books for telling stories and offers special techniques for utilizing puppets in kindergarten through sixth grade.

Cummings, Richard. *101 Hand Puppets: A Guide for Puppeteers of All Ages*. New York: McKay, 1962.

This is an extremely comprehensive book, offering step-by-step instructions for making every conceivable kind of hand puppet, from the simplest to the most elaborate. It includes scripts and has more than 60 diagrams and illustrations. It is recommended for older and more experienced classes.

Dean, Audrey Vincent. *Puppets That Are Different*. New York: Taplinger, 1973.

This book was specially designed to teach beginners how to bring the hand puppet to life and how to develop the skills needed to mount a successful show. Every detail is included in a clear, attractive, step-by-step primer.

Engler, Larry, and Carol Fijan. *Making Puppets Come Alive*. New York: Taplinger, 1973.

This is a charming and practical text for the beginner of any age. To be used by the teacher, it offers help in making and handling puppets, including exercises to develop the skills needed to produce a show.

Freericks, Mary, and Joyce Segal. *Creative Puppets in the Classroom*. Rowayton, Conn.: New Plays, 1979.

As the title states, this book gives instruction for using puppets in the curriculum. Its suggestions of inexpensive materials and simple techniques add to its value for the teacher.

Hanford, Robert Ten Eyck. *The Complete Book of Puppets and Puppeteering*. New York and London: Drake, 1976.

This 157-page paperback concentrates on an overview of puppetry—past, present, and future; the tools of the trade; the production; and techniques and tips from the pros. It is an excellent book, written in a clear, definitive style with simple yet complete instructions on all aspects of puppets and puppet productions.

Hunt, Tamara, and Nancy Renfro. *Puppetry in Early Childhood Education*. Austin, Tex.: Nancy Renfro Studios, 1982.

This is one of the most comprehensive books on the subject. Teachers, librarians, and recreation leaders will find it enormously helpful. It is highly recommended.

Jagendorf, Moritz. *Puppets for Beginners*. Boston: Plays, 1952.

This simple, comprehensive book with attractive illustrations is recommended for school and community use.

Krinsky, Norman, and Bill Berry. *Paper Construction for Children*. New York: Reinhold, 1966.

Masks and puppets are among the many projects described in this book. This delightful text has drawings and photographs to illustrate the brief but adequate explanations.

Luskin, Joyce. *Easy to Make Puppets*. Boston: Plays, 1975.

Instructions, patterns, and photographs show how to create 24 puppets: hand, glove, and marionette. It has a simple, attractive format.

Nobleman, Roberta. *Mime and Masks*. Rowayton, Conn.: New Plays, 1979.

A gifted teacher brings two areas together in this book: mime, which is an actor's tool; and the mask, which is used for dramatic projection. In this text, the performing and visual arts meet.

Peyton, Jeffrey, and Barbara Koenig. *Puppetry: A Tool for Teaching*. New Haven, Conn.: P.O. Box 270, 1973.

Simplicity and economy characterize this 100-page guide to puppetry for the curriculum. Prepared for the New Haven public schools, it is adaptable to other systems and a variety of subject areas.

Renfro, Nancy. *Puppetry and the Art of Story Creation*. Austin, Tex.: Nancy Renfro Studios, 1979.

This guide to story creating with simple puppet ideas has a special section on puppetry for the disabled.

Storytelling

Bauer, Caroline. *Handbook for Storytellers*. Chicago: American Library Association, 1977.

All facets of storytelling are covered: planning, promotion, story sources, multimedia storytelling, and programs. It is a must for all storytellers.

Champlin, Connie. *Puppetry and Creative Drama in Storytelling*. Illustrated by Nancy Renfro. Austin, Tex.: Nancy Renfro Studios, 1980.

This excellent resource for teachers is by one of our best-known puppeteers, who combines her art with education and practical help for the nonspecialist.

Maclay, Joanna Hawkins. *Readers Theatre: Toward a Grammar of Practice*. New York: Random House, 1971.

This is an excellent text on the subject. It covers a definition of readers theatre, gives a selection of material, and describes performance techniques. It is most useful to teachers of upper grades.

Ross, Ramon R. *Storyteller*. Westerville, Ohio: Merrill, 1975.

This superb book is on the development of skills in storytelling. Imaginatively and simply presented, it includes ideas on utilizing songs, puppetry, flannelboard, and game exercises to enrich storytelling.

Sawyer, Ruth. *The Way of the Storyteller*. New York: Viking Press, 1962.

This landmark book covers all aspects of the subject. It is practical and readable.

Schimmel, Nancy. *Just Enough to Make a Story*. Berkeley, Calif.: Sisters' Choice Press, 1978.

This small book is filled with good advice for storytellers and is written in a refreshing, personal style. Samples include a finger play, a cante fable (story with a song in it), and a story accompanied by paperfolding.

THEATRE FOR CHILDREN

Broadman, Muriel. *Understanding Your Child's Entertainment*. New York: Harper & Row, 1977.

This is the only book that discusses entertainment designed for the child audience in critical terms. The author, a critic, takes each of the performing arts in turn, pointing out common faults and offering guidelines to sponsors and parents. It is an invaluable aid for the adult who is responsible for selecting quality entertainment for young spectators.

Corey, Orlin. *Theatre for Children—Kids' Stuff or Theatre?* New Orleans: Anchorage Press, 1974.

This small collection of articles was written by a publisher and producer of plays for children and young people. A man of taste and judgment, Corey makes his points in a warm and lively style.

Davis, Jed, and Mary Jane Evans. *Theatre, Children and Youth*. New Orleans: Anchorage Press, 1982.

This is a college textbook on the subject, but it is included here for the use of some teachers of older children. Although the focus is on literature and production techniques, the text offers a wealth of information on the art, goals, and values of children's theatre.

Healy, Daty. *Dress the Show*. Rowayton, Conn.: New Plays, 1976.

This superb book on costume is for the teacher, community costumer, or parent faced with having to make and/or make over costumes. Written in a simple, readable style, it shows as well as describes the basic steps involved in this aspect of production. It probably is the best book available for the inexperienced costumer.

PART TWO: STORIES AND POEMS

ANTHOLOGIES OF CHILDREN'S LITERATURE

Arbuthnot, May Hill, ed. *The Arbuthnot Anthology of Children's Literature*. Rev. ed. Glenview, Ill.: Scott, Foresman, 1961.

This anthology contains the three classic Arbuthnot texts for children's literature: *Time for Fairy Tales, Time for Poetry*, and *Time for True Tales and Almost True*. Not all the stories and poems lend themselves to dramatization, but many of the poems can be used for choral speaking.

————— et al., eds. *Children's Books Too Good to Miss*. 7th ed. Cleveland: The Press of Case Western Reserve University, 1980.

Here is a treasury of materials for the elementary-school classroom. Poetry, stories, biography, as well as study guides and explanations of literary and other items, make this a useful and authoritative source.

Butler, Francelia, ed. *Sharing Literature with Children*. New York: Longman, 1977.

This well-known anthology is divided in a unique way: "Toys and Games," "Fools," "Masks and Shadows," "Sex Roles," and "Circles." The editor has included material for all age levels and provided a rich resource for the teacher to tell, read aloud, and use in creative playing.

Ciardi, John. *I Met a Man*. Boston: Houghton Mifflin, 1961.

These amusing verses for children, written by a well-known American poet, are useful for both creative drama and choral speaking.

—————. *The Man Who Sang the Sillies*. Philadelphia: Lippincott, 1961.

Here is another collection of amusing verse for both younger and older children.

Cole, William, ed. *Poem Stew*. New York: Harper & Row, 1981.

Fun for children, this collection has over 50 poems for reading and dramatic enactment.

Cummings, E. E. *Poems for Children*. New York: Liveright, 1983.

These 20 poems offer an introduction to the poet's work and provide an avenue to other modern experimental forms.

de la Mare, Walter, ed. *Come Hither: A Collection of Rhymes and Poems for the Young of All Ages*. New York: Knopf, 1957.

This collection of over 500 traditional poems with notes is interesting to children of all ages.

Fargeon, Eleanor. *Eleanor Fargeon's Poems for Children*. Philadelphia: Lippincott, 1951.

Some of these favorite poems by a well-known poet are good for dramatization, and many are suitable for choral speaking.

Fisher, Aileen. *Out in the Dark and Daylight*. New York: Harper & Row, 1980.

Selections from Aileen Fisher's books are compiled in a collection that is varied and representative of her work.

Fitzgerald, Burdette, ed. *World Tales for Creative Dramatics and Storytelling*. Englewood Cliffs, N.J.: Prentice-Hall, 1962.

This is a splendid collection of folk tales from around the world, many of which are little known.

Georgiou, Constantine. *Children and Their Literature*. Englewood Cliffs, N.J.: Prentice-Hall, 1969.

An excellent resource for teachers of all grades, this book treats the history and criticism of children's literature; divisions, genres, and analyses of old and new books. It includes extensive lists of stories for primary, intermediate, and upper grades.

Gruenberg, Sidoni M., ed. *More Favorite Stories*. Garden City, N.Y.: Doubleday, 1948.

This old but still good collection for primary and intermediate grades usually is available in public libraries.

Jennings, Coleman A., and Aurand Harris, eds. *Plays Children Love*. Garden City, N.Y.: Doubleday, 1981.

This is an excellent collection of plays edited by two of our best-qualified practitioners: a child-drama specialist and a leading children's playwright. In the first part are plays for children to enjoy as spectators; in the second part are plays for older children to perform. The latter are shorter, making them suitable for children to memorize and produce.

Johnson, Edna, Carrie E. Scott, and Evelyn R. Sickles, eds. *Anthology of Children's Literature*. Boston: Houghton Mifflin, 1948.

This classic text, still available, is filled with selections arranged according to subject matter and age level. Sections include fables, folk tales, myths, nature stories, travel, biography, literary fairy tales, and poetry.

Kase, Robert, ed. *Stories for Creative Acting*. New York: French, 1961.

Although compiled in 1961, this selection is well worth having in the library, for it includes stories used and recommended by leading creative-drama teachers. Many of them would be included today, if another such book were being assembled. The editor was a leading figure in the field and still devotes much time to drama/theatre, but with senior adults.

Lear, Edward. *A Book of Nonsense*. New York: Viking Press, 1980.

This collection of the poet's amusing limericks is always fun and good for all ages.

McCord, David. *One at a Time*. Boston: Little, Brown, 1977.

A collection of the poet's most popular work, this book is most useful to teachers of intermediate grades.

Mayer, Mercer. *A Poison Tree and Other Poems*. New York: Scribner, 1977.

For intermediate grades, these verses express children's feelings: anger, sadness, wishes, as well as less serious themes.

Merriam, Eve. *Rainbow Writing*. New York: Atheneum, 1976.

Light, descriptive verses covering a wide range of subjects, they are most useful on the intermediate level.

Moore, Lillian. *See My Lovely Poison Ivy*. New York: Atheneum, 1975.

These short verses with appeal for children in grades 3 to 6 are light and amusing.

Morton, Miriam, ed. *A Harvest of Russian Children's Literature*. Berkeley: University of California Press, 1967.

In this comprehensive collection of prose and poetry, the editor has included material for ages 5 to 7, 8 to 11, 12 to 15, and young adults. She has translated some material from the Russian, told some of the folk tales in her own words, and written introductions to each section. A wealth of material is presented for the classroom teacher as well as for the specialist.

Opie, Iona, and Peter Opie, eds. *The Oxford Book of Children's Verse*. New York: Oxford University Press, 1973.

In this classic text, teachers will find a wealth of material, some of which is suitable for choral speaking and creative drama.

Prelutsky, Jack. *The New Kid on the Block*. New York: Greenwillow Books, 1984.

These modern, childlike verses with a sense of humor can be enjoyed by children in lower and middle grades. The book is good for both creative-drama classes and choral speaking.

————, ed. *The Random House Book of Poetry for Children*. New York: Random House, 1984.

A collection of over 500 poems with more than 400 illustrations, this is a valuable addition to the library of books for creative playing. Amusing verse, witty rhymes, and serious poetry are all included in a source book for teachers and creative-drama leaders of children of all ages.

Sawyer, Ruth, ed. *The Way of the Storyteller*. Rev. ed. New York: Penguin Books, 1977.

This well-known book contains ways of telling and choosing stories, stories to tell, and a reading list.

Shedlock, Marie, ed. *The Art of the Story Teller*. 3d ed. rev. New York: Dover, 1977.

This is well-known and still one of the best books on the art of storytelling. In addition to chapters dealing with how to tell stories, it includes 18 selections and a list of others.

Siks, Geraldine Brain, ed. *Children's Literature for Dramatization: An Anthology*. New York: Harper & Row, 1964.

An anthology of poems and stories suitable for dramatization, it was assembled by a leader in the field. The stories are arranged for younger and older children. The poetry is categorized as "inviting action," "suggesting characterization," and "motivating conflict."

Stevenson, Robert Louis. *A Child's Garden of Verses*. New York: Random House, 1978.

These familiar verses are still interesting to children and good to use for both creative drama and choral speaking.

Viorst, Judith. *If I Were in Charge of the World and Other Worries*. New York: Atheneum, 1981.

The poet gives a variety of children's most secret thoughts, worries, and wishes in this collection. It is perceptive and humorous.

Ward, Winifred, ed. *Stories to Dramatize*. New Orleans: Anchorage Press, 1952.

In this volume, the author includes a rich collection of stories and poems from her own years of experience as a creative-drama teacher. It is arranged for players of various ages and contains material both classical and contemporary.

ANNOTATED BIBLIOGRAPHIES OF CHILDREN'S LITERATURE

Kimmel, Margaret Mary, and Elizabeth Segel. *For Reading Out Loud!* New York: Dell (Delacorte Press), 1983.

This book shows adults how to enrich children's lives and stimulate their interest by reading aloud to them. The authors explain why it is important to start early and how to do it successfully. The most valuable part of the book is a bibliography in which almost 150 books are described in detail. A long list of titles aids the teacher (or parent) in finding material for all age levels and interests.

Trelease, Jim. *The Read-Aloud Handbook*. New York: Penguin Books, 1982.

The author tells how reading aloud awakens the listener's imagination, improves language arts, and opens doors to a new world of entertainment. An important inclusion is an annotated list of more than 300 fairy tales, short stories, poems, and novels that the author describes in detail, with suggested age and grade levels.

TRADITIONAL TALES AND WELL-KNOWN STORIES FOR CHILDREN IN THE INTERMEDIATE GRADES

Aesop's Fables
"Beauty and the Beast" (French tale)
"Cinderella"
"The Firebird" (Russian tale)
"The Grey Palfrey" (French tale)

"The Lady Who Put Salt in Her Coffee"
"March and the Shepherd" (Italian tale)
"The Master Cat" (French tale)
"Midas and the Golden Touch"
"The Nightingale"
"The Pied Piper"
"Prometheus"
"The Sleeping Beauty"
"Snow White and the Seven Dwarfs"
"The Stone in the Road"
"Stone Soup"
"The Swineherd"
"The Tiger, the Brahman, and the Jackal" (East Indian tale)
"Urashima Taro and the Princess of the Sea" (Japanese tale)
"The Water of Life" (German folk tale)
"Whitewashing the Fence" (from *Tom Sawyer*)

STORIES FOR CHILDREN IN THE INTERMEDIATE GRADES

Angelo, Valenti. *Big Little Island*. New York: Viking Press, 1949.
Ardemia, Verna, ed. *Tales from the Straw Hat*. New York: Coward, 1960. (African)
Armer, Laura Adams. *In Navaho Land*. New York: McKay, 1962.
Arora, Shirley L. *"What Then, Ramon?"* Chicago: Follett, 1960.
Beim, Jerrold. *The Smallest Boy in the Class*. New York: Morrow, 1949.
Bernstein, Margery. *How the Sun Made a Promise and Kept It*. New York: Scribner, 1974.
Bond, Michael. *A Bear Called Paddington*. Boston: Houghton Mifflin, 1960.
Boston, Lucy. *The Children of Green Knowe*. New York: Harcourt Brace Jovanovich, 1967.
Brodsky, Mimi. *The House at 12 Rose Street*. London: Abelard-Schuman, 1966.
Cameron, Eleanor. *The Court of Stone Children*. New York: Dutton, 1973.
Carlson, Natalie Savage. *The Family Under the Bridge*. New York: Harper & Row, 1958.
Carroll, Lewis. *Alice's Adventures in Wonderland* and *Through the Looking-Glass*. Many editions.
Chambers, Aidan. *The Present Takers*. New York: Harper & Row, 1984.
Childhood of Famous Americans (series). Indianapolis: Bobbs-Merrill.
Cleaver, Bill, and Vera Cleaver. *Where the Lilies Bloom*. New York: Harper & Row, 1969.
Dagliesh, Alice. *The Courage of Sarah Noble*. New York: Scribner, 1954.
Dahl, Roald. *Charlie and the Chocolate Factory*. New York: Knopf, 1964.
de Angeli, Marguerite. *Bright April*. New York: Doubleday, 1946.
Dickens, Charles. *A Christmas Carol*. New York: Macmillan, 1950.
Estes, Eleanor. *The Hundred Dresses*. New York: Harcourt Brace Jovanovich, 1944.

Grahame, Kenneth. *The Reluctant Dragon*. New York: Holiday House, 1953.

———. *The Wind in the Willows*. New York: Scribner, 1935.

Haley, Gail E. *A Story—A Story*. New York: Atheneum, 1970.

Hamilton, Virginia. *How Jahdu Took Care of Trouble*. New York: Macmillan, 1969.

———. *The People Could Fly: American Black Folktales*. New York: Knopf, 1985.

———. *The Time-Ago Tales of Jahdu*. New York: Macmillan, 1969.

Juster, Norman. *The Phantom Tollbooth*. New York: Random House, 1961.

Kouzel, Daisy, and Earl Thollander. *The Cuckoo's Reward*. New York: Doubleday, 1977.

Krumgold, Joseph. . . . *And Now Miguel*. New York: Crowell, 1953.

Le Gallienne, Eva. *The Nightingale*. New York: Harper & Row, 1965.

L'Engle, Madeleine. *A Wrinkle in Time*. New York: Farrar, Straus & Giroux, 1962.

Lenski, Lois. *Strawberry Girl*. Philadelphia: Lippincott, 1945.

Lewis, C. S. *The Lion, the Witch and the Wardrobe*. New York: Macmillan, 1951.

Lindgren, Astrid. *Pippi Longstocking*. New York: Viking Press, 1950.

Lowry, Lois. *Us and Uncle Fraud*. Boston: Houghton Mifflin, 1984.

Lundbergh, Holger. *Great Swedish Fairy Tales*. New York: Dell (Delacorte Press), 1973.

McCloskey, Robert. *Homer Price*. New York: Viking Press, 1943.

———. *Lentil*. New York: Viking Press, 1940.

McKee, David. *The Magician Who Lost His Magic*. New York: Abelard-Schuman, 1970.

Meigs, Cornelia. *Mystery at the Red House*. New York: Macmillan, 1961.

Norton, Mary. *The Borrowers*. New York: Harcourt Brace Jovanovich, 1953.

Peare, Catherine Owens. *The Helen Keller Story*. New York: Crowell, 1955.

Petry, Ann. *Harriet Tubman: Conductor on the Underground Railway*. New York: Crowell, 1955.

Phelps, E. J. *"Tatterhood" and Other Tales*. New York: Feminist Press, 1978.

Selden, George. *The Cricket in Times Square*. New York: Farrar, Straus & Giroux, 1960.

Sheldon, Aure. *Of Cobblers and Kings*. New York: Parents Magazine Press, 1978.

Shotwell, Louisa R. *Roosevelt Grady*. New York: Grosset & Dunlap, 1963.

Speare, Elizabeth G. *The Witch of Blackbird Pond*. Boston: Houghton Mifflin, 1958.

Stevenson, Robert Louis. *Treasure Island*. New York: Scribner, 1924.

Thurber, James. *Many Moons*. New York: Viking Press, 1940.

Titus, Eve. *Anatole and the Cat*. New York: McGraw-Hill, 1957.

Tolkien, J. R. R. *The Hobbit*. Boston: Houghton Mifflin, 1938.

Travers, P. L. *Mary Poppins*. New York: Harcourt Brace Jovanovich, 1962.

Uchida, Yoshiko. *Sumi's Prize*. New York: Scribner, 1964.

Wagner, Jane. *J. T.* New York: Dell, 1969.

White, E. B. *Charlotte's Web*. New York: Harper & Row, 1952.

Wilde, Oscar. *Fairy Tales*. New York: Hart, 1975.

PART THREE: FILMS

FILMS AND VIDEOTAPES

British Broadcasting Corporation (producer). *Three Looms Waiting*, 1972. 52 min., color

Three Looms Waiting shows Dorothy Heathcote, one of the leading British teachers of drama, working with a group of children. An excellent demonstration of her method, this film shows drama as a tool for learning rather than as an end in itself.

Distributed by Time-Life Films, 43 W. 16 Street, New York, NY 10016

Creative Dramatics: The First Steps, 1960. 29 min., color, sound

Creative Dramatics: The First Steps is a vintage film that demonstrates the teaching of creative drama to a group of fourth-grade children. Guided by an experienced teacher, the group moves from the faltering first steps to the creation of a drama.

Distributed by Northwestern University Film Library, 614 Davis Street, Evanston, IL 60201

Everyman in the Streets, 1969. 30 min., color

This film shows creative work in drama by neighborhood children in Brooklyn, New York. It is nontraditional in its approach. The greatest value of the film lies in the encouragement it gives to leaders of after-school and Saturday activity groups working in churches, museums, community centers, and alternative spaces.

Distributed by WNET, 304 W. 58 Street, New York, NY 10019

Feil, Edward (producer). *Aurand Harris Demonstrating Playwriting with Children*, 1983. 24 min., color (¾'' U-MATIC; ½'' VHS; ½'' BETA)

The most-produced children's playwright in the United States demonstrates teaching playwriting to a class of fifth and sixth graders. The lesson is interspersed with Harris's discussion of what he is doing and how playwriting strengthens writing.

Distributed by Edward Feil Productions, 4614 Prospect Avenue, Cleveland, OH 44103

Ideas and Me, 1964. 17 min., color

In *Ideas and Me*, children participate in the various aspects of creative drama at a well-known community theatre.

Distributed by Dallas Theatre Center, 3636 Turtle Creek Blvd., Dallas, TX 75200

Irwin, Eleanor C. *Playing: Spontaneous Drama with Children*, 1973. 20 min., black and white

Playing: Spontaneous Drama with Children describes a number of forms of spontaneous drama with primary- and intermediate-grade children. Activities showing creative movement, puppetry, role playing, and improvisation are demonstrated. The nature of creativity, the developmental roots of drama, the importance of impulse control and of impulse expression, the individuality of children and their fantasies, and the value of dramatic play in both cognitive and affective learning are discussed.

Distributed by Eleanor Irwin, Park Plaza, 128 North Craig Street, Pittsburgh, PA 15213

One of a Kind, 1978. 58 min., color, sound

Intended for audiences of all ages, *One of a Kind* deals with the relationship between a child and her troubled mother. Through participation in a traveling puppet show, the child is enabled to express her anguish and needs. This powerful film can be used effectively with teachers of special education, creative drama, and language arts.

Distributed by Phoenix Films, 468 Park Avenue South, New York, NY 10017

Theatre for Children: Designing the Setting, 1975. 27 min., color

This is an attractive, informative, and interesting film that shows different kinds of scenery and the criteria used in designing backgrounds for children's plays.

Distributed by University of Southern California, Department of Cinema, Film Distribution Center, University Park, Los Angeles, CA 90007

Why Man Creates, 1970. 25 min., color

Why Man Creates is a popular film that seeks to learn about the human need to create. It bears showing more than once.

Distributed by Pyramid Films, P.O. Box 1048, Santa Monica, CA 90406

PUPPET FILMS

Manipulation of the Puppets
Blue Like an Orange, 1966. 25 min., color

Blue Like an Orange is a survey of puppetry as practiced around the world. It is considered to be one of the best of its kind.

Distributed by UNESCO, 345 E. 46 Street, New York, NY 10017

Chinese Shadow Play, 1947. 10 min., black and white

Chinese Shadow Play shows a production of a Chinese shadow theatre in New York City.

Distributed by the Donnell Library, 20 W. 53 Street, New York, NY 10019

Stop-Action Films
Reiniger, Lotte. *Caliph Stork, Carmen, The Frog Prince, Gallant Little Tailor, The Grasshopper and the Ant, Hansel and Gretel, Jack and the Beanstalk, Puss in Boots, Sleeping Beauty, Snow White and the Seven Dwarfs, The Three Wishes, Thumbeline.* 10 min. each, black and white (*Jack and the Beanstalk* in color)

These films of charming silhouette puppetry are the work of a pioneer Berlin filmmaker of the 1920s. They are outstanding.

Distributed by Contemporary Films/McGraw-Hill, McGraw-Hill Training System, P.O. Box 641, Delmar, CA 92014

Trnka, Jiri. *The Hand*, 1966. 19 min., color; *Archangel Gabriel and Mother Goose*, 1965. 28 min., color; *Passion*, 1970. 10 min., color

These films by a Czech filmmaker are outstanding and treat serious modern themes in a sophisticated and compelling manner.

Distributed by Contemporary Films/McGraw-Hill, McGraw-Hill Training System, P.O. Box 641, Delmar, CA 92014

PART FOUR: MOOD MUSIC

The following mood music is suggested for creative drama. It is listed in categories, implying different moods and conditions. Many leaders find music a great asset in freeing children and inducing creative movement. All the selections are well known and available. This is by no means an exhaustive list, and many teachers will have ideas of their own.

It is suggested that children first listen to the music, and then either move to it or talk about the feelings it suggests. It often is a good idea to play it a second or even a third time before attempting to do anything with it.

MUSIC SUGGESTING ACTIVITY

Beethoven, Ludwig Van.	Sonata op. 10, no. 2 [fourth movement]
Bizet, Georges.	March and Impromptu from *Jeux d'Enfants*
Chopin, Frédéric.	Mazurka in B-flat
Gershwin, George.	*An American in Paris*
Grainger, Percy.	"Country Garden"
Mendelssohn, Felix.	Tarantella from *Songs Without Words* op. 102, no. 3
Paganini, Niccolò.	"Perpetual Motion"
Prokofiev, Sergei.	Symphony no. 1 in D [fourth movement]
Rimsky-Korsakov, Nicolai.	"Flight of the Bumble Bee"
Strauss, Johann, Jr.	"Thunder and Lightning, Galop"
Wagner, Richard.	"Spinning Song" from *The Flying Dutchman*

Music Suggesting Animals, Birds, and Insects

Dvořák, Antonin.	"Legent No. 7"
Grieg, Edvard.	"Little Bird"
———.	"Papillon [Butterfly]"
Respighi, Ottorino.	*The Birds*
Rimsky-Korsakov, Nicolai.	"Flight of the Bumble Bee"
Saint-Saëns, Camille.	*Carnival of the Animals*
Schumann, Robert.	*Papillons*
Stravinsky, Igor.	Suite from *The Firebird*

Ballads and Folk Songs

Many well-known ballads and folk songs are appropriate for creative drama.

Environmental Music

Britten, Benjamin.	"4 Sea Interludes" from *Peter Grimes*
Debussy, Claude.	*La Mer* [*The Sea*]
Delius, Frederick.	"Summer Night on the River"
Mendelssohn, Felix.	*Fingal's Cave* Overture
Respighi, Ottorino.	*The Fountains of Rome*
Smetana, Bedřich.	"The Moldau" from *My Fatherland*
Strauss, Johann, Jr.	"Blue Danube" Waltz

Happy Music

Dvořák, Antonin.	Slavonic Dances
Mozart, Wolfgang Amadeus.	Serenade in G (*Eine Kleine Nachtmusik*)
———.	Symphony no. 40 in G Minor [first movement]
Nicolai, Otto.	Overture to *Merry Wives of Windsor*
Offenbach, Jacques.	*Gaité Parisienne*
Rossini, Gioacchino.	*La Boutique Fantastique*
Scarlatti, Domenico.	Harpsichord sonatas
Schumann, Robert.	*Carnaval*
Telemann, Georg Philipp.	*Don Quixote*

LULLABIES

Brahms, Johannes.	"Lullaby"
Godard, Benjamin Louis Paul.	"Berceuse" from *Jocelyn*
Grieg, Edvard.	"Cradle Song" from *Peer Gynt*
Khatchaturian, Aram.	"Lullaby" from *Gayne*

MILITARY MUSIC

Elgar, Edward.	*Pomp and Circumstance* marches
Sousa, John Philip.	Any marches
Suppé, Franz von.	*Light Cavalry* Overture
Tchaikovsky, Peter Ilyich.	*1812* Overture

MUSIC SUGGESTING MYSTERY

Dukas, Paul.	*The Sorcerer's Apprentice*
Grieg, Edvard.	"Abduction of the Bride" from *Peer Gynt*
———.	"March of the Dwarfs" from *Huldigungmarsch*
———.	"The Hall of the Mountain King" from *Peer Gynt*
Mussorgsky, Modest.	*Night on Bald Mountain*
———.	*Songs and Dances of Death*
Saint-Saëns, Camille.	"Danse Macabre"
Schubert, Franz.	"The Erlking"
Sibelius, Jean.	*The Swan of Tuonela*
Strauss, Richard.	*Death and Transfiguration*

ROMANTIC MUSIC

Beethoven, Ludwig van.	Sonata no. 23 for Piano (*Appassionata*)
Brahms, Johannes.	"Valse"
Liszt, Franz.	"Liebestraum [Love Dream]"
Mendelssohn, Felix.	*Songs Without Words* op. 38, no. 2
———.	*Songs Without Words* op. 102, no. 1
Paderewski, Ignace.	"Love Song"
Rubinstein, Anton.	"Melody"
Tchaikovsky, Peter Ilyich.	Overture to *Romeo and Juliet*
———.	Symphony no. 5 [selections]
Wagner, Richard.	Prelude to *Tristan and Isolde*

Music Suggesting the Seasons

Beethoven, Ludwig van.	Sonata op. 24, no. 5 for Violin and Piano (*Spring*)
———.	Sonata op. 27, no. 2 (*Moonlight*)
———.	Symphony no. 6 (*Pastoral*)
Debussy, Claude.	"Clair de Lune"
Delius, Frederick.	"Summer Night on the River"
Grieg, Edvard.	"Morning Mood"
———.	"To the Spring" from *Lyric Pieces*
Grofe, Ferde.	*Grand Canyon* Suite
Mendelssohn, Felix.	Melody in F ("Spring Song")
Prokofiev, Sergei.	"In Autumn"
———.	*Summer Day* Suite
Ravel, Maurice.	*Daphnis and Chloe*
Rossini, Gioacchino.	"The Storm" from the Overture to *William Tell*
Sibelius, Jean.	"Night Ride and Sunrise"
Vivaldi, Antonio.	"Spring" from *The Four Seasons*

Serene Music

Bach, Johann Sebastian.	Cantata no. 147 ("Sheep May Safely Graze")
Barber, Samuel.	"Adagio for Strings" from Quartet for Strings, op. 11
Bizet, Georges.	*L'Arlésienne* [third movement]
Debussy, Claude.	*Afternoon of a Faun*
———.	*Songs Without Words* op. 102, no. 6
Mendelssohn, Felix.	*A Midsummer Night's Dream*
Schubert, Franz.	Quintet in A Major for Piano and Strings (*Trout*)
Schumann, Robert.	*Traumerei*

Music Suggesting Strong Movement

Beethoven, Ludwig van.	Sonata op. 27, no. 2 (*Moonlight* [third movement])
Falla, Manuel de.	"Ritual Fire Dance" from *El Amor Brujo*
Holst, Gustav.	"Mars" from *The Planets*
Khatchaturian, Aram.	"Saber Dance" from *Gayne*
Prokofiev, Sergei.	*Scythian* Suite [selections]

Shostakovich, Dimitri.	Symphony no. 5 [fourth movement]
Tchaikovsky, Peter Ilyich.	"Marche Slav"
———.	Symphony no. 4

MUSIC SUGGESTING TOYS AND PUPPETS

Bratton, John.	"Teddy Bears' Picnic"
Coates, Eric.	*Cinderella*
———.	*The Three Bears*
Debussy, Claude.	*Children's Corner*
Delibes, Léo.	*Coppelia*
Elgar, Edward.	*Nursery* Suite
———.	*The Wand of Youth* Suites nos. 1 and 2
Herbert, Victor.	"March of the Toys" from *Babes in Toyland*
Humperdinck, Engelbert.	*Hansel and Gretel*
Jessel, Leon.	"Parade of the Tin Soldiers"
———.	"Tubby the Tuba"
Kleinsinger, George.	"Peewee the Piccolo"
Mozart, Leopold.	"Toy Symphony" from Cassation for Orchestra and Toys in G
Pierne, Gabriel.	"March of the Little Lead Soldiers"
Prokofiev, Sergei.	*Cinderella*
———.	*The Love for Three Oranges*
———.	*Peter and the Wolf*
Ravel, Maurice.	*Mother Goose*
Rossini, Gioacchino.	*La Cenerentola*
Tchaikovsky, Peter Ilyich.	*The Nutcracker*
———.	*The Sleeping Beauty*
———.	*Swan Lake*

WHIMSICAL MUSIC

Grieg, Edvard.	*Humoresque*
Mozart, Leopold.	"Toy Symphony" from Cassation for Orchestra and Toys in G
Ponchielli, Amilcare.	"Dance of the Hours" from *La Gioconda*
Strauss, Richard.	*Till Eulenspiegel*
Tchaikovsky, Peter Ilyich.	*Humoresque*

APPENDIX

STUDY GUIDE

to be used in conjunction with the production

KOJO AND THE LEOPARD

This Study Guide was designed for use in classrooms in conjunction with the presentation of the Howard University Children's Theatre production of *Kojo and the Leopard*. "Kojo is a mythical manchild in an imaginary African tribe. The customs, folkways, even the names encountered are an amalgamation of those traditional mores throughout Black Africa." The play was written by Ihunanya and directed by Kelsey E. Collie, Professor of Drama. This Study Guide was prepared by the students enrolled in Children's Theatre Workshop under the supervision of Professor Kelsey Collie.

I. Aims
   A. To foster an appreciation of a theatrical presentation.
   B. To afford students the opportunity to witness a ritualistic production.
   C. To deepen the appreciation of students who have had previous theatrical experiences for such presentation.
   D. To assist students in gaining insights into who they are, where they have come from, and where they are going.
   E. To introduce theatre to those students who may not have seen a live theatrical performance.

329

   F. To deepen the sense of awareness of the students in relationship to African mores, culture, and traditions.

  II. Resource

    A production of *Kojo and the Leopard*.

 III. Materials

    Depends entirely upon the type(s) of activity class engages in.

 IV. Motivation

    To stimulate pupil responses to African customs and legends.

  V. Procedure

   A. Oral discussion.

   B. Art projects.

   C. Written projects.

 VI. Class Activities

    Apart from any awakening of curiosity, Kojo is intended to give the Black child an identifiable "storybook character" and to give those of other races the awareness of a cultural tradition for all people.

    The following activities may be used prior to and/or after viewing the production. Any number of activities may be used. The more, the better. Please inform us as to how you used these suggested activities, and the response to each.

   A. Build an African Village

    Construct a model of an African village out of Popsicle sticks and grass and soil (and whatever else you think you need).

   B. Make a Family Tree

    Each of us was born in some place: Washington, D.C.; New York City; Silver Spring, Md.; Arlington, Va.; etc. And each of us has a family: Father, Mother, Sisters, Brothers, Uncles, Aunts, Cousins, Grandparents, etc. When we talk about a "family tree," we are referring to the people from whom we have come. The roots of a family tree are the ancestors in one family group. From these roots spring a tree with branches. When two people marry each other, then two trees are joined. Beginning with your grandparents, draw your family tree, indicating your parents and brothers and sisters. Some of you may be able to trace your ancestors back to your great-grandparents. You may start from wherever you choose.

   C. Find Out Who You Are

    Look in a mirror for five minutes (less if you prefer). Think about what you see. Try to describe that person staring back. Write down or tell orally the things you like.

    1. Think of a friend. In what ways are you like one another? In what ways are you different?

2. What things can you do better than your friend? What things can your friend do better than you?
3. In what ways are you different from someone in your class? (This can be described along racial and/or sexual lines.)
4. Everyone is important, not only the manchild, but the womanchild too. If you are the first born in your family, express to the class how it makes you feel. If you are not the first born in your family, express to the class how you feel in relation to your older sister(s) and brother(s). This expression can be oral, written, drawn, danced, or sung.

D. What Do You Want to Be?
1. What do you look forward to becoming? What are some things you can do in order to become how you would like to be? How can you use your special qualities to better your community? school? home?
2. Make a list of 20 possibilities of things that interest you. Place this list in order of your choice.

E. What Do These Pictures Say to You?
1. In a paragraph or two, write a brief story about one of several pictures your teacher has selected from a magazine, a newspaper, or another source. (Note: These pictures all have to do with Black people in some way. The pictures should be provocative and stimulating. They should lend themselves easily to discussion or writing.)
   a. What do you see in each picture?
   b. What do you think is happening?
   c. Is the situation happy or sad?
   d. What do you feel about the picture?
   e. Compare what you imagine and describe is happening in each picture with the ideas of other members of your class.

F. Write a Play with a Protagonist (central character) and an Antagonist (one who attempts to keep the protagonist from obtaining his/her goal)
1. Think of the story you want to tell.
   a. What message does it have?
   b. What is the story about?
   c. Who are the people in the story?
   d. How do you feel?
   e. How do they show their feelings?
   f. What decision does the protagonist make?
   g. What antagonist or what obstacles are in his or her way?

h. How does the protagonist solve his or her problem? (conflict)
   2. Begin to divide the story into sections.
      a. How does it begin?
      b. How can the conversation make the play seem more interesting? Remember to keep the sentences and the conversation short.
G. Ensemble Work
   1. Plan to work together as an ensemble on one or more of the following:
      a. Make a mural of different animals. (A mural is one large illustration.) It may also be a group of pictures telling about a single idea on one large sheet of paper.
      b. Create various situations whereby you must make a decision. This is your problem (conflict). How did you solve it? How did it make you feel? Did it help you grow? (Any decision-making process involves a conflict which must be solved and leads to a change in character. Each student must understand the decision-making process.)
      c. Cut out from magazines, pictures of Blacks and/or Africans in all walks of life. When you mount them on a sheet of paper (any size you like), they will make a montage. It is possible to create various designs and arrangements by the way one chooses to mount the pictures.
H. Naming Day
   Give each student in the class a new name. Have students look up their new names and the name they already have and tell the class and their parents what they mean.
I. Role Playing
   After the show, do improvisations on characters portrayed in the show. What would you have done to change the ending of the tale if you were one of the characters?
J. Characters Made Out of Sticks
   Draw a series of pictures in comic-strip form. Use stick figures in each square of pictures. Stick figures can be made by using circles for the head and straight lines for the arms, body, legs. Dots or different kinds of marks in the face can be used to give stick figures character and tell their needs.
K. Discuss the Production
   Answer the following questions and complete the phrases.
   1. I found out that I am . . .
   2. I felt that . . .

3. I discovered that . . .
4. I liked the presentation because . . .
5. I didn't like the presentation because . . .
6. Having seen the production, my attitude about Africans has (has not) changed because . . .
7. What new things did you learn about Africans?
8. What did you like most about the production?
9. What did you like least about the presentation?

L. Choral Reading

Find a poem by an Afro-American writer or an African writer that the class likes. Divide the poem into parts for boys and girls (or light and dark [heavy] voices). Read the poem aloud.

M. Radio Play

A radio play encourages the listeners to use their imagination, for the players are not seen. Only the voices of the players from behind the scenes can set the mood for the play and tell what the characters are like. Using one of the incidents from *Kojo and the Leopard*, write a script that would be suitable as a radio play.

N. Pantomime

Select a character (human, animal, or spirit) from the production and tell his/her story through pantomime. A pantomime is a story with characters acting out a situation but not using words.

O. African Music

Listen attentively to some African music. What instruments do you hear. Does the rhythm make you want to snap your fingers, pat your foot, etc.? Does the music say anything to you?

P. Word List—Define These Words

1. kinsmen	14. spirit
2. naming day	15. seed
3. manchild	16. warrior
4. Headman of the Village	17. feast
5. ceremony	18. nectar
6. gift	19. link
7. bull calf	20. spear
8. adulthood	21. moral
9. African	22. tribe
10. heritage	23. pet
11. generations	24. ritual
12. ancestors	25. trophy
13. birth	26. customs

Q. We are always happy to receive letters. Won't you write to us and tell us what you liked about the performance?

HOWARD UNIVERSITY CHILDREN'S THEATRE
Dept. of Drama/ College of Fine Arts
HOWARD UNIVERSITY
WASH., D.C.   20059

SELECTED LIST OF RESOURCES

1. Museums

Museum of African Art
318 A Street, N.E.   547-7424
11 A.M. to 5 P.M., Monday thru Friday; 12 to 5 P.M., weekends.
Public tours 3:30 P.M. Wednesday and Saturday. Group lecture tours by appointment.

2. Records

Boulton. *African Music*. Folkways.
(Library of Congress Catalogue Card number F B764 68-06051 579)
Letta. *Free Soul*. Capitol.
Olatunji, Michael. *Olatunji, Drums of Passion*. Columbia.
Verwilghen. *Songs of the Watutsi*. Ethnic Folkways Library.
(Library of Congress Catalogue Card number MUS AL 3228 C.3)

3. Literature

Biebriyck, Daniel, and Kahombo C. Mateene, eds. and trans. *The Mwindo Epic from the Banyanga*. (Congo Republic)
Cesaire, Aime. *Return to My Native Land*.
Hughes, Langston, ed. *An African Treasury*. (Collection of stories, poems, articles, and essays)
Knappert, Jan, ed. and trans. *An Anthology of Swahili Love Poetry*.
Moore, Gerald, and Ulli Beier, eds. *Modern Poetry from Africa*. (Drawn from the work of poets from 16 African countries)
Paulone, Denise, ed. *Women of Tropical Africa*.
Scheub, Harold. *African Images*.
Swahili Name Book, Jihad Productions
Wilson, Ellen Gibson. *A West African Cookbook*. (An introduction to food from Ghana, Liberia, Nigeria, and Sierra Leone adapted for American kitchens)

The University of Texas at Austin   The Department of Drama

STUDY GUIDE for the Theatre for Youth Production of

STEAL AWAY HOME
by
Aurand Harris

Based on the novel *Steal Away Home*, by Jane Kristof

Directed by Coleman A. Jennings

Music by the Gospel Choir of the Ebenezer Baptist Church,

Allyne Lewis, Director

Hogg Auditorium   November 14–24, 1975

People attending their first children's-theatre production often expect to see child actors taking all the parts. This seldom happens. Most productions are acted by adults or high-school students. It is the play *for* children and the audience *of* children, rather than the actors, that make a children's-theatre production.

In our production of *Steal Away Home*, all the roles will be played by college students.

PLOT SUMMARY

Scene: Stations on the underground railroad from South Carolina to Pennsylvania, 1853–1854.

Steal Away Home opens with a young slave named Amos singing a chorus from the song "Didn't My Lord Deliver Daniel?" which he explains is his favorite song and the one he sang on the Sunday when Preacher Prentice, also a traveling tinker, came to the plantation "That Sunday when it all began" . . .

On that Sunday, Preacher Prentice brought to Amos, Obadiah, his brother, and their Mama a secret letter from their Papa. After being sold, he had been taken to Lemhorn, near Philadelphia, and then freed after his Master's death. In the letter, he says he hopes to earn enough money to buy back Mama and Little Sally from Master Bricker. He also says, "I wish Amos and Obadiah were here to help me."

Amos and Obadiah, at the suggestion of Preacher Prentice, decide to travel the underground railroad north to Philadelphia to help their Pa earn money.

Early the next morning, the boys go to the new bridge over the Pee Dee River to meet Preacher Prentice, who hides them in his wagon for the first leg of their 500-mile journey.

Preacher Prentice takes the boys to a pharmacy in Raleigh, North Carolina, where Mrs. Strauss hides the boys their first night. Mrs. Strauss shows them the map for the underground railroad. Their next stop is a two-day walk to Dr. Culpepper's house in Henderson. The boys cannot read or ask directions, so Mrs. Strauss devises a plan whereby she writes a pass saying the boys are Dr. Culpepper's slaves and picking up medicine from Mrs. Strauss.

They are up before daylight and walk to Henderson, where they meet Melissa, Dr. Culpepper's daughter. Her fiancé, Edgar, is going to Philadelphia, and Melissa asks Edgar if he will take the boys in his carriage. He refuses, lectures her on the wrong of hiding runaway slaves, and goes off to report them.

Deciding to take them herself that night on the pretense of visiting her Aunt Emily, Melissa takes Amos and Obie to South Hill, Virginia, their next stop. The boys are to hide in a large woodbox, but when they reach the tannery, Joe, another runaway, is already in the box. As Joe tries to get rid of the two boys, two men hear them arguing and begin to search for them. One man notifies the sheriff; the next morning, Mr. McNaul moves the boys to a loft, where they will hide during the day, but later that day, Mr. McNaul hurriedly returns to the loft with the dreaded news: the slave catchers are on the way, it's no longer safe, and they must run. Through the back of the river, to Miss Holkums's house in Petersburg, the boys run from the tannery, and looking back, they see it go up in flames.

They arrive in Petersburg to find Miss Holkums sick with an infectious disease and unable to hide the boys. She directs them to Richmond, where they spend one night with Reverend Pringle. The next night, they start out for Hanover, the next station.

In the dark, they come upon some farmhouses. The farmer is alarmed when his dogs begin to bark. He fires at the boys and chases them. In doing so, he accidentally shoots himself in the leg. Refusing to leave the man to die, Amos goes to a neighboring farmhouse for help. There he is tied up by the other farmers and left in a shed. Obie, who has followed Amos, sees what happens and releases him. The two boys hide until they can continue their journey in the morning. The next day, they again see Joe, who has been captured. He is shot trying to escape. Amos and Obie keep running, and they reach Mrs. Johnson's place in Bowling Green. Because the sheriff is looking for the boys, the freed woman disguises them as her son and daughter. She takes Obie with her to gather wood, and Amos brings their lunch. The sheriff does not recognize them when they meet him.

The boys' next stop is Will Webber's farmhouse, where they stay a few days. The final leg of their journey to Philadelphia is by train, but the boys must travel in a trunk as part of Will's luggage. The Webbers notify the boys' father that they are coming. After a harrowing time, when someone almost opens the trunk, the boys arrive in Philadelphia, safely united with their father at last.

GENERAL PREPARATION FOR SEEING THE PLAY

Discuss with the children: slavery in the United States before the Civil War; the underground railroad; the Quakers' position on freedom vs. slavery and their customs of speech and dress.

Illustrate on the map the route of the 500-mile journey from North Carolina to Philadelphia. Compare distance between Austin and El Paso.

DETAILED PREPARATION FOR COMBINING THE PLAY
AND A HISTORICAL STUDY UNIT

(Afro-American History Study Unit—4th century A.D. to Emancipation, 1863)

I. Culture in Africa
   A. Ghana
      1. first power—4th century A.D.
      2. regulated supply of gold leaving the country
      3. sold salt and slaves in world-trade market
   B. Mandingo
      1. 1235 A.D. Sunangura took over Ghana
      2. extended territory to all gold-bearing areas of country
   C. Mali
      1. 1300s—most powerful
      2. Mansa Musa
         a. created a cultural center in Africa
         b. created the university
         c. son his successor and lost the land
   D. Sanghai
      1. 17th century
      2. developed states with governors
      3. good economy
         a. taxes
         b. roads
      4. rebuilds university and empire

  E. Moroccans
     1. took over the kingdom after son of Sanghai took rule
     2. wiped out Sanghai Empire
  F. Rulers
     1. Islamic and Muslim
     2. kings were divine (from god)
  G. Family
     1. more than one wife
     2. emphasis on number of children
  H. Religion
     1. more than one god
     2. prayer and sacrifice—animals
     3. rituals important
II. Slave trade
  A. 40 to 80 million involved in Atlantic slave trade
  B. Breakdown in family and customs
  C. Depopulation of Africa, creating a great loss to the empires in Africa
  D. Lasted 400 years
  E. Africans set price for slaves
  F. Process
     1. village attacked, people captured
     2. long march to the sea, tied by the neck
     3. sold to white person
     4. put in prison and branded
     5. placed in rowboats and taken to ship
     6. "The Middle Passage"
        a. 1 out of 4 died
        b. loose pack vs. tight pack
  G. Slave in South, U.S.
     1. living conditions
        a. house
           (1) dirt floors
           (2) place to sleep
           (3) shelter from inclement weather
           (4) not center of family life
        b. clothes and food
           (1) given by master
           (2) diet of pork and corn
     2. jobs of slaves
        a. shipyard workers
        b. blacksmiths
        c. cooks

      d. carriage drivers

      e. "waiting man" and "waiting woman"

    3. knowledge slaves brought with them

      a. grazing of cattle

      b. forestry and rice cultivation

      c. fur trade

      d. fishing

      e. plant knowledge (medicine and poison)

      f. guides

      g. dugout canoes

      h. frontier warfare

III. Different ways slaves were freed

  A. Bought their own freedom

  B. Master died and freed slaves in his will

  C. Runaway

    1. aided by former slaves who had run away

    2. "underground railroad"

      a. Harriet Tubman

      b. William Still

  D. Court decision

  E. Gradual emancipation—free after a certain date

  F. Petition to Congress

IV. Slave patrols—who were they?

  A. Owners of plantations

  B. People hired by slaveowners to take their place on patrols

V. Slave rebelling

  A. Personally

    1. stealing

    2. running away

    3. poisoning master and/or family

    4. arson

    5. conspiracy

    6. maim themselves

    7. attack overseers

    8. carelessness with tools and fire

  B. Stono Rebellion, 1739, South Carolina

  C. Nat Turner revolt, 1831, Virginia

VI. Acts and laws aiding slavery

  A. *Dred Scott* decision—slavery could not be excluded from any territory of the U.S.

  B. Missouri Compromise—free state entering the Union but Black is a noncitizen

    C. Compromise of 1850—Black men had to be sent back to state
       if accused of being a slave
    D. Fugitive Slave Law

VII. Quaker position on slavery
    A. Viewed Negro beyond emancipation
       1. condition after emancipation
       2. education of Blacks
    B. Men
       1. Antony Benezet
       2. Woolman

VIII. People to study
    A. Black men
       1. William L. Garrison
       2. Frederick Douglass
       3. James Forten
       4. Benjamin Banaker
       5. Paul Cuffe
       6. John Hope Franklin
       7. Benjamin Quarles
    B. White men
       1. John Brown
       2. Andrew Jackson
       3. Abraham Lincoln
       4. David Ruggles
       5. William Still
    C. Black women
       1. Sarah Forten
       2. Sojourner Truth
       3. Harriet Tubman
       4. Sarah Douglass
       5. Phillis Wheatly

IX. Emancipation Proclamation
    A. January 1, 1863
    B. Not a full-throated cry for human freedom

Map Study   United States map—color code and label

    1. Confederate states
    2. Union states
    3. Border states

Union States

Minnesota	New York
Wisconsin	New Jersey

Iowa	Delaware
Illinois	Connecticut
Kansas	Rhode Island
Indiana	Massachusetts
Michigan	Vermont
Ohio	New Hampshire
Pennsylvania	Maine

Border States

Missouri
Kentucky
West Virginia
Maryland

Confederate States and Dates of Secession from Union

Virginia	April 17, 1861
North Carolina	May 20, 1861
Tennessee	May 7, 1861
South Carolina	December 20, 1860
Georgia	January 19, 1861
Alabama	January 11, 1861
Mississippi	January 9, 1861
Arkansas	May 6, 1861
Louisiana	January 26, 1861
Texas	February 1, 1861
Florida	January 10, 1861

Selected Bibliography

Winthrop D. Jordan, *The White Man's Burden*. New York: Oxford University Press, 1974.

Leon F. Litwack, *North of Slavery*. Chicago and London: University of Chicago Press, 1961.

Daniel P. Mannix, *Black Cargoes*. Harmondsworth: Penguin, 1962.

Benjamin Quarles, *Black Abolitionists*. New York: Oxford University Press, 1969.

————. *Frederick Douglass*. New York: Atheneum, 1976.

Kenneth M. Stampp, *The Peculiar Institution*. New York: Random House (Vintage Books), 1956.

Peter H. Wood, *Black Majority*. New York: Norton, 1974.

CREATIVE DRAMA DURING THE HISTORY STUDY UNIT
AND BEFORE SEEING THE PLAY

1. Establish the characters and create an improvisation for:
   a. An African village.
   b. Slave traders invading the village.

    c. Loading the big ship.

    d. On the ship to America.

    e. Arrival in America; the first weeks; after two years.

2. Other improvisations

    a. Southern slaveowner talking to a Quaker.

    b. Slave wanting to be freed talking to his master, who does not plan to let him go.

    c. Free Black wanting to purchase family from slaveowner, who is willing to release them if he is paid a large sum of money. The wife is ill, but the slaveowner does not reveal this fact.

    d. Slave patrol of two or three approach a Black man who is hiding several runaways.

    e. The reunion in New York of freed family.

3. Research and dramatization

    a. In small groups, select an appropriate person for study. Dramatize a major experience from his or her life.

    b. Organize the Confederate state leaders and present a declaration of war to President Abraham Lincoln.

4. Creative drama the day before seeing the play

    a. Recall the plot summary and discuss the most exciting moment.

    b. Imagine a time when you left home on a trip without your parents.

    c. Recall a time you were alarmed, scared, afraid.

    d. Compare the students' experiences with those of the characters in the play.

    e. Dramatize a few of the experiences from the students' lives.

    f. With only the plot summary as a guide, dramatize the two most exciting moments in the story.

5. Visualizing the production of the play

    a. Discuss the various locations needed for the play.

    b. Discuss the type of costumes the characters would have worn.

    c. If possible, share the scenery and costume designs.

    d. Discuss the gospel music to be used in the play and its importance in Black culture.

DISCUSSION QUESTIONS, ASSIGNMENTS,
AND CREATIVE DRAMA AFTER SEEING THE PLAY

1. Questions

    a. Why didn't Pa write directly to Amos and Obie's Mama instead of sending a letter to Preacher Prentice?

    b. Why couldn't Amos and Obie read?

    c. Discuss Melissa's meaning when she asked, "What can you do if the law tells you to do what you're sure is wrong?"

    d. Why was Joe so bitter?

    e. Discuss Jud's treatment of Amos when the boy returned to help him after the man was shot.

    f. Why did Amos have to pretend to be a girl?

    g. Was Will brave or foolish to hide the boys in a trunk for the last part of their trip? Why?

    h. Discuss other instances when children have been brave or have undertaken a difficult task.

2. Map study

    a. On a United States map, locate the cities and rivers mentioned in the play.

Chesterfield	Richmond
Cheraw	Hanover
Pee Dee River	Bowling Green
Raleigh	Susquehanna River
Henderson	Fredericksburg
South Hill	Washington, D.C.
Petersburg	Philadelphia

    b. Determine distances between each station and calculate how many miles the boys walked.

3. About the production

    a. How did the designers of the scenery, costumes, props, and lights use their imaginations?

    b. In what ways were they asking us to use our imaginations?

    c. What does the director of a play do?

    d. When you think about the production you saw, which colors come to mind?

    e. What did all the costumes have in common?

    f. How did the wagon used in the play differ from one that might have really been used for traveling from town to town?

    g. Select three words to describe each of the characters in the play.

    h. Select a color which would help describe each character. (It need not be any of the actual colors that are used in the character's costume.)

4. Dramatization

    a. If we as a class were to play or act out one scene from the play, which would you select? Why?

    b. Show us how each of the six characters moved. What were the differences in their movements?

    c. Create the scene in which the boys leave their mother and join Preacher Prentice.

    d. Create the scene when the boys meet Joe.

    e. Create the hiding in the loft scene.

    f. Create the final scene when the boys meet their father.

    g. Think of other stories of courage, feeling afraid, being hungry and tired, and then finally reaching a goal.

    h. Create a meeting of the U.S. Senate when the senators are discussing the Fugitive Slave Bill and the Freeing of the Slaves Bill.

INDEX